The EVERYTHING®
Irish History & Heritage Book

Dear Reader:

As you might have guessed from our names, we are brother and sister, grown from our days of sibling rivalry to amicable collaboration. We come from New Orleans Catholic stock, Irish supplemented with Italian, French, and German. Our Irish ancestors came to United States fleeing the Great Famine, as did so many unfortunate souls—we wish they could see Ireland in its current, happier days.

We are both trained historians with specialties in European and American history. Amy used to be a lawyer and Ryan used to be an e-commerce guru, but now we both earn our bread by our pens (or computers). Ryan has written and edited travel guides to Ireland. Amy has written a book about world mythology and a law dictionary.

Though we have both kissed the Blarney Stone, we hope eloquence hasn't come at the cost of accuracy. We know this book can't cover "everything," but we hope it gives a fun introduction to the best parts of Ireland's history and heritage. We encourage you to read more about this fascinating island and its culture. *Sláinte!*

Amy Hackney Blackwell   Ryan Hackney

The EVERYTHING® Series

Editorial

Publishing Director	Gary M. Krebs
Managing Editor	Kate McBride
Copy Chief	Laura MacLaughlin
Acquisitions Editor	Eric M. Hall
Development Editor	Julie Gutin
Production Editor	Jamie Wielgus

Production

Production Director	Susan Beale
Production Manager	Michelle Roy Kelly
Series Designers	Daria Perreault
	Colleen Cunningham
Cover Design	Paul Beatrice
	Frank Rivera
Layout and Graphics	Colleen Cunningham
	Rachael Eiben
	Michelle Roy Kelly
	Daria Perreault
	Erin Ring
Series Cover Artist	Barry Littmann
Interior Illustrator	Michelle Dorenkamp

Visit the entire Everything® Series at everything.com

THE
EVERYTHING®
IRISH HISTORY & HERITAGE BOOK

From Brian Boru and St. Patrick to
Sinn Féin and the Troubles, all you
need to know about the Emerald Isle

Amy Hackney Blackwell & Ryan Hackney

Adams Media
Avon, Massachusetts

Dedicated to Lucille Eileen Wichser and her Irish forebears.

An Everything® Series Book.
Everything® and everything.com® are registered trademarks of F+W Publications, Inc.

Published by Adams Media, an F+W Publications Company
57 Littlefield Street, Avon, MA 02322 U.S.A.
www.adamsmedia.com

ISBN: 1-58062-980-6
Printed in the United States of America.

J I H G F E D C B A

Library of Congress Cataloging-in-Publication Data
Hackney Blackwell, Amy.
The everything Irish history & heritage book /
Amy Hackney Blackwell and Ryan Hackney.
p.   cm.
(An everything series book)
Includes bibliographical references.
ISBN 1-58062-980-6
1. Ireland–History–Handbooks, manuals, etc. 2. Ireland–Civilization–
Handbooks, manuals, etc. I. Hackney, Ryan. II. Title.
III. Title: Everything Irish history and heritage book.
IV. Series: Everything series.
DA911.H33   2003
941.5–dc22   2003014352

This book is available at quantity discounts for bulk purchases.
For information, call 1-800-872-5627.

Contents

Acknowledgments / ix
Top Ten Places to Visit in Ireland / x
Introduction / xi

Prehistory: Stones, Tombs, and Sundials / 1
The Earliest Inhabitants **2** • The First Irish Farmers **3** • Where Legend and Archaeology Meet **4** • Ireland's Stonehenge **6** • The Bronze Age **8** • Iron Comes to Ireland **9**

Celts and the Age of Kings / 11
Who Were the Celts? **12** • Gaelic and Indo-European Languages **13** • Celtic Ireland **15** • Brehon Laws **18** • Learned Men—the Druids **20** • Celtic Art and Poetry **20** • Celtic to the End **22**

Celtic Mythology / 25
Celtic Pantheon **26** • The Otherworld **28** • Celtic Festivals **29** • Creation Myths **30** • The Táin Bó Cuailnge **33** • Conchobar and Deirdre **38** • Finn MacCool **38** • Myths for All Time **41**

Arrival of Christianity in Ireland / 43
Christianity in Late Antiquity **44** • St. Patrick, the Patron Saint **44** • St. Brigid, the Generous **49** • St. Columcille, Felonious Monk **51** • St. Columbanus, Missionary to Europe **53** • Wild and Crazy Irish Saints **55**

The Monastic Tradition / 57
A Unique Irish Blend of Traditions **58** • Irish Asceticism **58** • Monasteries—Where It's At **59** • Latin, the Lingua Franca **61** • Schools and Universities **62** • A Life of Copying **63** • The End of a Golden Age **66**

6 The Viking Invasions and Brian Boru / 67

The Rise and Fall of Irish Dynasties 68 • Anglo-Saxons in Britain 69 • Bring on the Vikings 70 • On the Bright Side 73 • Brian Boru Unifies Ireland 75 • Scramble for the Top 78

7 The Fight Against the English / 79

The Normans Arrive 80 • The Irish Strike Back 82 • Tudor Colonization 83 • The Protestant Reformation 84 • The 1641 Rebellion and Its Aftermath 86 • The Williamite War 89

8 The Protestant Ascendancy / 93

Protestants Take Hold 94 • Catholic Life 96 • The Second City of the British Empire 97 • Protestant Irish Nationalism 98 • Grattan's Parliament 99 • Wolfe Tone's Rebellion 100 • Daniel O'Connell, the Liberator 103 • Catholic Emancipation 104 • Years of Peace and Resentment 107

9 Roman Catholic Church in Ireland / 109

Before the Reformation 110 • The English Become Protestant 112 • Ireland and the Counter-Reformation 113 • The Calamitous Seventeenth Century 113 • Religious Tensions in the North 115 • Catholic Revival and Nationalism 116 • Catholicism in Today's Ireland 117 • Declining Popularity 119

10 Preserving Irish Traditional Culture / 123

Traditional Life 124 • The Irish Language 124 • Irish Music 126 • Before There Was Riverdance 128 • Parties to Raise the Dead—Irish Wakes 130• Irish Beliefs of the Supernatural 131 • Irish Sports 133

11 Storytelling—An Irish Tradition / 135

Ireland's Rich Folklore Heritage 136 • Folkloric Revival 137 • Tales of the Supernatural 138 • Christian Stories 141 • Historical Figures 142 • Irish Wit and Humor 143

The Great Irish Potato Famine / 145

Potatoes, for Better or for Worse **146** • A Fungus Among Us **147** • Life During the Famine **148** • Help for Victims **151** • The Results of the Famine **156** • Looking Back at What Happened **158**

The Immigrant Experience / 159

Why They Left **160** • Where They Went **161** • The Hardships of Emigration **162** • The Immigrant Experience in the United States **164** • Irish Communities in Other Destinations **169** • The Impact of Emigration **171**

The Road to Independence / 173

The Rebirth of Nationalism **174** • The Home Rule Party **175** • Political Stalemate and Celtic Revival **179** • The Decision to Divide Ireland **180** • World War I Changes the Game **182** • The War of Independence **185** • The British Call for Peace **186** • The Irish Civil War **187**

The Path to Republic of Ireland / 189

The Irish Free State **190** • De Valera Rises to Power **192** • The Fianna Fáil Path to Independence **193** • A New Constitution **194** • Ireland's Neutrality in World War II **195** • A Republic at Last **197** • Ireland under the Republic **198** • Trouble Brewing in the North **199**

The Troubles / 201

The Roots of the Troubles **202** • A Civil Rights Movement Gone Bad **204** • Bloody Sunday **206** • A Failed Hope for Peace **208** • Dark Days in Northern Ireland **209** • The Peace Process **212** • Good News on Good Friday **213** • A Fragile Peace **214**

Ireland's Contribution to Literature / 217

Irish Literary Tradition **218** • Irish Writers in England **219** • The Celtic Revival **221** • Transformation of the Modern Novel **223** • Brilliant Playwrights Abroad **226** • The Irish Struggle in Literature **228** • Seamus Heaney: Poet of the Troubles **229**

Emigrants and Exports / 231
Irish-Americans in Politics **232** • The Kennedys **233** • Irish-Canadian Prime Ministers **237** • Ned Kelly—Irish-Australian Outlaw **239** • St. Patrick's Day **241** • Irish Pubs Around the World **242**

Family and Food / 245
Irish Family Life **246** • Irish Food: Potatoes, Beef, and Potatoes **247** • A Cup of Irish Tea **248** • The Irish Pub **250** • The Irish Love for Beer **251** • Whiskey—a More Potent Beverage **253** • Understanding the Irish **256**

Geography and Climate / 257
Around the Island **258** • Ireland's Neighbors **260** • Pack Your Raincoat: Irish Climate **261** • Terrain: Lakes and Forests **262** • Bog, Burren, and the Giant's Causeway **263** • Animal Life **267** • Environmental Organizations and National Parks **269**

Ireland Today and Tomorrow / 271
The Celtic Tiger **272** • Ireland and the European Union **273** • Modern Politics **274** • The Liberalization of Ireland **277** • Women in Charge **280** • The Changing Face of Ireland **282**

Guide for Descendants of Irish Emigrants / 283
It's All in the Name **284** • O'Somebody **284** • MacSomeone **287** • Other Common Names **289** • How to Trace Your Roots **291** • Visiting the Relatives **293**

Appendix A • A Primer of the Irish Language / **296**
Appendix B • Irish Proverbs and Blessings / **298**
Appendix C • Books and Movies about Ireland / **299**

Index / 300

Acknowledgments

We thank the librarians at Furman University and the Houston Public Library for wisdom; Grace Freedson and Eric Hall for professional support; Chris and Casey for amiability; and Chauncy and Favignana for constancy.

Top Ten
Places to Visit in Ireland

1. **Dublin:** From pubs and architecture to the astounding Book of Kells, Dublin continues to be one of the most interesting cities in Europe.

2. **Cliffs of Moher:** It's a tough claim to make in a country as beautiful as Ireland, but these amazing 600-foot sea cliffs might just be the most picturesque spot on the island.

3. **Rock of Cashel:** This monastery, church, and fortress is the island's most visually stunning reminder of medieval Ireland.

4. **Belfast:** The recent peace agreement has allowed people to appreciate the city's impressive architecture and culture; there is no better place to get an understanding of the Troubles.

5. **Giant's Causeway:** This eerie conglomeration of honeycomb-shaped stones on the Antrim Coast never fails to impress.

6. **Ring of Kerry:** There's a reason it's packed with tourists—the mountains, lakes, and streams of this park are spectacularly beautiful.

7. **Galway:** This booming college town in the West is packed with pubs, art, and energy.

8. **Newgrange:** This fascinating collection of Stone Age tombs along the Boyne River Valley is known as Ireland's Stonehenge.

9. **Glendalough:** This monastery's striking setting near mountain lakes almost makes you want to become a monk.

10. **Aran Islands:** These craggy islands on the far-western coast give a salty taste of what Irish life was like 100 years ago.

Introduction

▶ERIN, ÉIRE, IRELAND—the Emerald Isle of the north Atlantic is a beautiful island with beautiful names. The ancient Irish called it Éire ("Ire"), which might have meant "fertile country." Put Éire together with the Old English word *land* and you get Ireland. Anglicize *Éire* and you get Erin, a romantic English synonym for Ireland.

Ireland is divided into thirty-two counties, grouped into four provinces: Leinster, Ulster, Connacht, and Munster. Twenty-six counties are in the Republic of Ireland, and six are in Northern Ireland. Northern Ireland is part of the United Kingdom, and the Republic of Ireland is an independent nation. (A map of Ireland and its environs has been provided on the inside back cover of this book for your reference.)

There's something unique about Ireland. It's a place where you can sit on an incredibly green field with a Neolithic tomb to your left and an ivy-covered monastery to your right. A farmer might drive a herd of sheep past you, then return to his thatch-roofed house to check his e-mail. Ireland is a place with a rich history, where the layers of different cultures have blended together into a beautiful mix found nowhere else. Its history has been filled with poetry, humor, and tragedy. It's a place worth getting to know.

Ireland has a long and colorful history, and to cover everything about the island would require an entire library. While this book can't contain every detail, it does provide the major elements of Irish history and heritage. It gives a solid overview of the Irish story and provides a starting point for learning more through reading or travel.

There were people in Ireland in prehistoric days, long before the dawn of Christianity. Ireland's earliest residents built enigmatic structures out of rock and made some intriguing pottery and jewelry, but their lives are still mostly a mystery. Historians know more about the Celts, whose culture overtook the island around the time the Romans were running most of Europe. They left behind a body of myths and culture that became a touchstone for later Irish people who wanted to define "Irishness."

Christianity arrived in Ireland in the fourth or fifth century, supposedly through the influence of St. Patrick. The Celtic people incorporated the new faith into their lives, and Ireland became a center for scholarship and missionary work—the island of saints and scholars. Both saints and scholars lost their momentum in the ninth century when Viking invaders arrived and began an era of pillaging and conquest. Eventually, the Vikings either left or became upstanding Irish citizens themselves. They introduced several cultural innovations and founded many major towns, including Dublin.

The Viking era later became a symbol of Irish resistance to occupation; the king Brian Boru became an icon of Irish nationalism and bravery. A more tenacious invader, however, was to arrive shortly after the Vikings. The British came in the 1100s and never really left. The years of British wars and occupation had their share of low points—Cromwell's depredations, the Ulster Plantation, the Great Famine—but Irish culture continued to develop. Irish writers from Swift to Yeats showed a genius for using the Irish language, while Irish cooks demonstrated a world-class facility with the potato.

Ireland eventually won its independence and has worked hard to regain its own identity. It has had difficulties—lingering economic problems, the Troubles of Northern Ireland—but the Irish people have continued to push forward. Today, with peace in the North and amazing economic developments in the Republic, Ireland is enjoying its best times ever.

In addition to its fascinating history, Ireland also has an extremely vibrant culture. One reason Irish culture is so well known is that Irish people have spread all over the world. Hard times at home forced many people to emigrate to other countries. These emigrants became important members of their new societies and continue to embrace their heritage today. Ⓔ

Chapter 1

Ⓔ Prehistory: Stones, Tombs, and Sundials

Ireland is an island with a past. People lived there millenniums before anyone started recording history, and they left their mark on the landscape—standing stones, odd-looking structures, great mounds of earth. The presence of so many prehistoric remains ties Ireland's past to its present.

8000 B.C.E.–7000 B.C.E.
Humans come to Ireland

7000 B.C.E.–5500 B.C.E.
Early Mesolithic Period

5500 B.C.E.–4000 B.C.E.
Later Mesolithic Period

4000 B.C.E.–2400 B.C.E.
Neolithic Period (New Stone Age)

2400 B.C.E.–800 B.C.E.
Bronze Age

800 B.C.E.–400 C.E. Iron Age

350 B.C.E.–100 B.C.E.
Celtic colonization of Ireland

The Earliest Inhabitants

Compared with the European mainland, Ireland hasn't been inhabited for very long. Africa, the Middle East, and central Europe have all housed humans for hundreds of thousands of years, and there is evidence of humans in England going back at least 250,000 years. But it was only about 9,000 years ago that anyone ventured to the Emerald Isle. Why was this? One word: ice.

Snow and Ice and Everything Nice

Ireland was covered with ice for a very long time. It had few plants, and the only animals who lived there were creatures that prefer snow and ice, such as reindeer, woolly mammoths, and the spectacular Irish giant deer. The temperature fluctuated, but mostly just in variations on the same theme of cold.

QUESTION?

Is it certain there were no humans in Ireland before 8000 B.C.E.? No. There were Neanderthal people in England for thousands of years before Ireland was definitely inhabited, and they might have ventured to Ireland. But so far no one has found traces of them, and they probably weren't there during the last ice age.

About 13,000 years ago, the ice finally started to recede and Ireland warmed up. This was bad for some of the larger mammals, which became extinct, but it was good for smaller creatures and plants. No one knows for sure how Ireland's wildlife got there; maybe it floated across the Irish Sea, or maybe there was a temporary bridge of land between Ireland and England. In any case, by about 5000 B.C.E. Ireland was covered with forests and full of wild beasts.

The Mesolithic Period

These conditions made Ireland even more attractive to humans. The early settlers did not leave behind much information about themselves. Mostly, archaeologists have found stone tools—things like axes, knives, and scrapers. People used these tools to chop plants or skin animals. Ireland is full of these stone tools, many of which have been picked up by amateur collectors.

Flint is one of the best stones for tool making, and the best flint in Ireland is in the northeastern corner. And that's where most of Ireland's stone tools have been found—in Antrim, Down, and the Strangford Lough area. One of the best Mesolithic sites is Mount Sandel in County Derry, where archaeologists have found the remains of several little dome-shaped huts, built there between 7010 and 6490 B.C.E. Here people lived, huddled around their fires, eating nuts, berries, pigs, birds, and fish.

FACT

Modern people use the term *Stone Age* to describe anything hopelessly primitive and benighted. But Stone Age hunter-gatherers seem to have lived quite well. Plants and animals for food were plentiful and provided them with a balanced diet and ample leisure time. The archaeological record suggests that people only turn to the more "advanced" agricultural way of life when local free supplies run low.

The Mesolithic Period, also known as the Middle Stone Age, lasted for several thousand years. Stone technology did not change much during this time. People lived a fairly migratory existence, moving around in pursuit of plants and animals.

The First Irish Farmers

Around 4000 B.C.E., things changed. People began to grow food and make pottery. They cleared forests for their fields and built more permanent settlements. Archaeologists call this new period the Neolithic Period, or New Stone Age.

It's possible that the Mesolithic Irish developed this new technology on their own, but it's more likely that these changes came over the ocean with new immigrants. The newcomers either conquered the people already living there, or, more likely, they just assimilated them, intermarrying and sharing techniques for making tools and growing food.

Neolithic people built their houses out of wood. These houses have mostly decayed, but their foundations are still visible. Archaeologists have also found lots of new tools for grinding wheat and a huge number of polished stone axes made from a stone called porcellanite.

Where Legend and Archaeology Meet

Stone Age people built a lot of tombs or tomblike structures out of gigantic rocks covered with mounds of earth; this building technique makes the tombs look like big, grassy mushrooms from the outside. These ancient tombs continue to intrigue people today; there are so many of them all over the landscape, they're hard to miss.

The megalithic tombs were probably constructed shortly before the arrival of the Celts, who called them *fairy mounds* and believed that the spirits of ancient people—bold heroes and brave maidens—lived there. The Celtic creator gods, the Tuatha Dé Danann, were known to be fabulously good at building things, and perhaps it was they who constructed the tombs dotting the countryside.

Eventually the spirits inhabiting the fairy mounds transformed into the *little people* of later Irish legends—leprechauns and fairies and brownies, whose spirits are said to haunt the land.

Passage Tombs

Many of these tombs are called passage tombs because they contain passages leading to burial chambers underneath the mound. The walls of the passage and chamber are made of rock, often elaborately carved.

FACT

There are passage tombs all over the northern part of Ireland. Many of these have legends attached to them. For example, the complex of tombs at Carrowmore, near Sligo Town, supposedly contains the grave of the legendary queen Mebd; it has never been opened to verify this claim.

Court Tombs

Court tombs, or cairns, have an open, roofless courtyard in front leading into two, three, or four chambers at back. Archaeologists have found human remains in them, but think that they might originally have been built as temples. They tend to be evenly distributed about 3 miles apart instead of clustered like graves; generally structures that are spaced like that are places of worship, but there's no way to tell for sure how people used them.

Wedge Tombs

Wedge tombs also occur primarily in the northern part of Ireland. These tombs have stone walls and roofs; the roof gets lower and the passage narrower as one goes into the tomb, hence the name *wedge*. Most of them face west or southwest, toward the setting sun.

Wedge tombs are numerous; there are about 500 of them all over the northern part of the country. The ones that have been excavated contain human remains, and some contain pottery, which suggests that they were made toward the end of the Neolithic period. Labbacallee ("Hag's Bed"), in County Cork, is an excellent wedge tomb. It got its strange name because it contained the skeleton of a headless woman when it was first opened.

Portal Tombs

Portal tombs, also called dolmens, consist of several large upright stones topped by a giant capstone. Putting these rocks in place must have been a stupendous effort—some capstones weigh as much as 100 tons. These dolmens were originally surrounded by a mound of earth, and people were buried inside them. A giant dolmen at Poulnabrone, County Clare, had more than twenty people buried in it over a 600-year period; this might mean that only royalty was buried there.

There are dolmens all over Ireland, as well as in Wales and Cornwall. The Kilclooney More dolmen in County Donegal is particularly cool—its capstone is almost 14 feet long.

Ireland's Stonehenge

Some of the most spectacular archaeological sites from the Neolithic period are in the Boyne Valley in County Meath. These sites are called Brú na Bóinne, which means "Boyne Palace." They consist of large stone tombs built around 3200 B.C.E., several centuries before the great pyramids of Egypt. The three main components of this site are Newgrange, Knowth, and Dowth.

People have known about these tombs for centuries; Vikings plundered them and Victorians hunted treasures there and carved their initials on the walls. The sites gradually deteriorated and were even quarried at one point. The Republic of Ireland has become very interested in its history, however, and consequently, the tombs have been extensively restored.

Newgrange, Knowth, and Dowth were built around the same time that Stonehenge was erected in the south of England. They have generated nearly as much speculation as to their purpose as their English cousins. The most convincing theory about their use is the suggestion that they functioned as an ancient form of a solar calendar.

At Newgrange

The tombs at Newgrange are built inside a huge, grassy mound of earth. The stones at the entrance and some of the stones holding the tomb together are elaborately carved with spirals.

These stones are not local; some of them came from Wicklow, 50 miles away, and others from Northern Ireland. This indicates that whoever built them was very organized—it's not easy to assemble the manpower to transport big rocks over that many miles. The tomb might have been surrounded by a ring of giant stones, though only twelve of these now remain.

Inside the mound is a long passageway leading to a subterranean burial chamber. Inside this chamber are three recesses for holding

◀ The front door of Newgrange, solar observatory extraordinaire.

bodies; when the tomb was first excavated by experts, archaeologists found the remains of at least three cremated bodies and some human bones. Offerings of jewelry were probably once there as well, but these were stolen long ago.

Solar Miracle Sites

No one knows exactly why these mounds were built. They might have been a burial place for kings; ancient legends certainly suggest that as a possibility. Or they might have served as calendars. Many megalithic sites are constructed to catch the sun at particular times of the year, and they are astonishingly accurate.

Newgrange is the best-known example of this. Every year during the winter solstice (December 19–23), the rising sun shines through a slit over the entrance and lights up the burial chamber for seventeen minutes. At the time the tomb was built, the sunlight would have shone directly onto a spiral design carved into the wall.

Similar solar phenomena happen at other megalithic sites. The light of the setting sun at winter solstice illuminates one of the chambers inside Dowth. At Knowth, the eastern passage seems to have been designed to catch the rising sun of the spring and autumn equinoxes, while the western passage might have caught the setting sun on those same days.

Mystical Site on the River Boyne

The tombs at Brú na Bóinne are an extremely popular tourist destination. The tour of Newgrange features a fake winter solstice sunrise, so that visitors can see how the sun illuminates the chamber. But don't get your hopes up about seeing the real thing; Newgrange at sunrise in December is booked solid for the next fifteen years, and the waiting list has been closed.

The River Boyne, which flows past these mound tombs, has long been very important spiritually to the Irish people. Legend says that the first occupant of Newgrange was named Elcmar. His wife was Boann, the spirit of the river.

FACT

The Boyne was said to be both magical and earthly, and that it flowed from the well of Segais in the otherworld. Segais is the source of all wisdom. It is surrounded by seven hazel trees, and hazels periodically drop from their branches and flow down the Boyne.

The Bronze Age

Around 2400 B.C.E., life in Ireland began to change again. People started making tools out of metal instead of stone. These metalworkers might have been a new wave of immigrants bringing their craft with them, or they might have been the folks already in Ireland. Whoever they were, their metal tools were much better than stone ones.

This period is called the Bronze Age because most of these tools were made of bronze, an alloy made of copper and tin mixed together. Ireland has tons of copper, and archaeologists have found traces of many copper mines. Tin is harder to get; people might have imported it from England or possibly from Brittany in France.

Smiths shaped bronze into all kinds of objects, including axes, spearheads, and jewelry. They decorated some of these with triangles and zigzags, which gives the impression that these objects might have been more for show than for use.

Ireland also had a fair amount of gold hidden in its hills, and Bronze Age smiths used it to make some spectacular jewelry—thick bracelets and necklaces called torques, fancy hairpins, and half-moon-shaped trinkets that they probably hung around their necks. They also made disks of thin sheets of gold with hammered decoration; these are called *sun-discs*, and people might have worn them as jewelry, too.

E-SITE

If you've got a hankering to check out Ireland's prehistory in person, visit the Irish National Heritage Park in beautiful County Wexford. The park's full-size replicas of dolmens, ogham stones, and Irish houses through the ages will give you a feel for what life was like before Ireland got all fancy and civilized.

Iron Comes to Ireland

The Bronze Age in Ireland ended around 800 B.C.E. Bronze tools disappeared and iron ones took their place. This must have been the result of increased contact with Britain, which was in closer contact with the rest of Europe, where iron was all the rage.

Ugly but Cheap

Early iron wasn't superior to bronze—in the day before steel was invented, iron was ugly and of poor quality. But iron ore was readily available almost everywhere, and supplies of tin, necessary for making bronze, were not. And so blacksmiths stuck with it and gradually got better at using it.

The Iron Age didn't start all at once. People gradually started using more iron and less bronze. In the late eighth century B.C.E., iron was prevalent on the Continent, and a century later it was widespread in Britain. Irish smiths at this time were working with both metals, producing distinctive swords and other artifacts.

The iron-using people also had horses. Archaeologists have found many bits for bridles and other tidbits of equestrian gear. They have also unearthed miles and miles of wooden tracks beneath the bogs, paths made of giant oak planks laid side by side; these would have made transporting goods by horse and cart much easier than dragging them through Ireland's soft soil.

FACT

Ironically, some of the best-preserved artifacts from the Iron Age are made not of iron but of bronze—such as 5-foot-long bronze trumpets. Iron corrodes badly in Ireland's climate, but bronze doesn't.

The Dawning of the Age of the Celts

The advent of iron is often associated with the arrival of the people called the Celts. By 300 B.C.E., the Celtic artistic style was thoroughly established in the northern part of Ireland. The Celts spread their culture and language throughout Ireland over the next several centuries, mixing their beliefs with Christianity and resisting foreign assailants as long as they could.

Chapter 2

Celts and the Age of Kings

Celtic culture is everywhere in Ireland, from the stone crosses in the country-side to patterns knit into wool sweaters. Modern Irish people still look back to their pre-English ancestors to get a feel for what their country should be today. The influence of the Celts is remarkable, considering how little is actually known about them.

c.800 B.C.E. Celts in Alps and Mediterranean

c.500 B.C.E. Celts in France and Czech Republic

387 B.C.E. Celts attack Rome

c.350 B.C.E. Celts in Ireland

55 B.C.E. Julius Caesar lands in Britain

c.122 C.E. Hadrian's Wall built in Britain

Who Were the Celts?

It's hard to say anything conclusive about the Celts, because they didn't record their history themselves. They couldn't write (with one minor exception, which we discuss later in this chapter). Most everything we know about them today comes from either the archaeological evidence or the accounts of Roman visitors that were transcribed by medieval Christians. This means that all of our written records on the Celts were filtered through two sets of biases: the Romans, who looked on them as an alien culture that needed to be conquered, and the Christians, who thought the Celts were pagans who hadn't seen the truth of Christ. And modern observers have all kinds of opinions that color their views.

The word *Celt* is properly pronounced *kelt,* with a hard initial consonant. The name of the former world-champion basketball team in Boston, however, is pronounced *seltiks.* If you encounter Celtics fans, don't try to correct their pronunciation.

Geographic Origins

According to classical writers, most of the people who lived in northwestern and central Europe were Celts—*keltoi* in Greek. Ancient writers knew of Celtic people in Spain, France, Germany, Switzerland, and modern Austria. Celts were hard to miss, because they were violent; various Celtic peoples started attacking Greek and Roman settlements around 400 B.C.E. and kept attacking as long as there was loot to be had.

The ancients thought the Celts had originated in Switzerland and spread out from there. They envisioned the Celts as a warrior people who marched from country to country, attacking civilized people and settling wherever they conquered. Modern scholars think it more likely that the Celtic language and culture spread from group to group through trade, though there was certainly some fighting involved, too. This Celtic culture moved over the Continent and into the British Isles until, by the fourth century B.C.E., most of the people in northwestern Europe and Britain were members of this cultural group.

FACT

The biblical Galatians were a Celtic people who wound up settling in Asia Minor (modern-day Turkey) sometime in the third century B.C.E. Like the Celts in Ireland, they weren't literate, so we don't know much about their history. By the time St. Paul wrote them letters in the first century C.E., they'd begun reading and writing Greek.

Cultural Spread Is Not Conquest

Historians have long imagined ancient history as a series of peoples taking over land from one another. When they envisioned the Celts, they saw warriors who came marauding over the countryside, laying waste and taking over local wealth. While there is some truth to this picture, it seems that cultural spread was actually a much gentler process most of the time.

The people who became known as the Irish were probably a mix of indigenous peoples—remember the folks who built those mounds and tombs?—and immigrants who brought new language and technology with them. The newcomers entered Irish society by marrying the natives, although there was probably some violence as well. Irish legend gives the impression that a bunch of warriors arrived several centuries before Christ and established chiefdoms for themselves all over the country. The Celtic languages became predominant either through military domination or because they were more prestigious for other reasons. However it happened, by the time the Romans arrived, the Irish people were speaking Celtic languages.

Gaelic and Indo-European Languages

Although Celtic languages and cultures were similar to one another, they were by no means identical; there were a vast number of physical types and cultural traditions that fell under the heading *Celtic*. The Celts who settled in France became known as Gauls. The ones in Britain became the Bretons and the Welsh.

Many people think of the Irish people as having red hair, green eyes, and freckles. This is something of a stereotype—only a small percentage of the Irish actually look like this—but it does match ancient descriptions of some Celts. The Romans and Greeks also described many of them as blond-haired and blue-eyed.

The Celts who arrived in Ireland sometime around 350 B.C.E. didn't belong to the same group as the Celts in Britain. Most of the ancestors of the Irish Celts came from Spain. Language is the clue to their origin.

The Indo-European Group

Linguists classify languages into *families* of related tongues. Almost all European languages—including French, German, English, and Irish—are grouped into a giant family called Indo-European, which also includes such ancient languages as Latin, Sanskrit, and Hittite. (Finnish, Hungarian, Basque, and Estonian are exceptions—they are European but do not belong in the Indo-European group.) All Indo-European languages show basic similarities in vocabulary and grammar that suggest they might have come from a single language—proto-Indo-European.

It is believed that proto-Indo-European may have been spoken many thousands of years ago somewhere north of the Black Sea. The people who spoke this language apparently traveled extensively in Central Asia and Europe, and forms of their language took root throughout these regions. One of the major language groups to develop this way was the Celtic family.

What about Irish Celtic?

There were many Celtic languages, and the Irish language is just one of them. Irish comes from the Celtic branch called Goidelic, which also includes Scots Gaelic. The term *Goidelic* comes from the Irish Celts' name for themselves, Goídil, which gives us the modern word *Gaelic*. Irish is not very closely related to the languages spoken nearby, particularly Welsh and Breton (spoken in Brittany, France), but instead had its roots in Spain; hence, scholars think the ancestors of the Irish came from Spain.

FACT

The Latin word for the Irish was *Scotti*. In the early centuries of the Common Era, many "Scots" from Ireland migrated to the Hebrides and Argyll, just a short boat ride from Antrim. That territory became known as Scotia, which later turned into *Scotland*.

Celtic Ireland

People studying Ireland actually have an advantage over those scrutinizing Celts from other lands, because a number of ancient Irish stories and other writings survive. The Celts didn't write these things down themselves; they transmitted their culture orally. But centuries later, medieval monks, in their zeal to preserve stories of the oral tradition in written form, wrote down a bunch of ancient Celtic legends and books of laws, and these offer the modern reader a unique glimpse into ancient Irish life. (See Chapter 3 for more on Celtic mythology.) This life seems to have included heroes, feasts, cattle raids, and love affairs.

The land was divided into five areas:

1. Leinster—the southeast
2. Meath—the middle
3. Connacht—the west
4. Ulster—the north
5. Munster—the southwest

Each of these provinces was divided into 100 or so smaller sections called *tuatha*, or tribes, each governed by its own chieftain, called a *rí*. People were divided into clans, and several clans made up a tribe. Ordinary people swore allegiance to their local king. Sometimes one man would rise above all the others and become high king of all Ireland.

Wild and Crazy Heroes

The Irish were obsessed with war, weapons, and heroics. If their poetry is any indication, they spent most of their time at war with one another, stealing cattle, and feasting on pork.

The Celts scared the Romans and other "civilized" contemporary observers. When they went into battle, they would strip naked and dash at their enemies dressed in nothing but sandals and their fancy necklaces. They howled as if possessed by demons, their shrieks augmented by loud bagpipes.

Some warriors would be so overcome by battle-frenzy that their very appearance changed. They called this transformation the warp-spasm. The Táin Bó Cuailnge has an excellent description of the hero Cuchulain (or Cú Chulainn) undergoing this phenomenon, which involved most of his body turning itself inside out and fire and blood shooting out of his head, after which he killed hundreds of enemy warriors and walked away unscathed.

E-SITE

One of the most spectacular archaeological sites in Ireland is the Iron Age fort Dún Aengus in the Aran Islands. It's on a cliff, surrounded by a ring of sharp stone spikes, and further protected by fierce waves pounding the stones below. Some hapless tourists have been blown off the site by the strong winds and fallen to their deaths on the rocks.

Cattle Raids

Cattle and metal treasure were the main forms of wealth in ancient Ireland—metal because it was rare, and cattle because they were useful. Cattle provided milk to drink and to make into cheese, and hide and meat after they were dead. If a king demanded tribute from his subjects, it would probably be in the form of cattle—in fact, a wealthy farmer was called a *bóiare,* or "lord of cows." In the famous poem Táin Bó Cuailnge, a major war starts because Queen Mebd discovers that her husband has one more bull than she does.

Celtic chieftains spent quite a bit of their energy stealing cattle from one another. They even had a special word for this activity, *táin*. (Cattle raiding wasn't just an amusement for the ancient Irish; modern Irish people were stealing one another's cattle well into the twentieth century.) Anyone whose cattle got stolen had to try to retrieve them, which occasioned many heroic expeditions and battles.

The Seat of Ancient Kings

Tara is a hill in County Meath that was the seat of ancient Irish kings. It was considered the center of Ireland. People buried their ancestors in mounds surrounding it and periodically gathered there for festivals and rituals. Kings and their armies would gather there before marching to war.

Tara was special because it was the home of the Lia Fáil, or "Stone of Destiny." It was used to identify rightful kings—it shrieked if the feet of the rightful king rested on it.

FACT

The O'Hara plantation in the novel *Gone with the Wind* is named Tara. The plantation was named by Scarlett O'Hara's father, Gerald, an Irishman who had long suffered the hunger for land that came from living as a tenant on what had been his people's own lands. Fittingly, when he finally acquired a big piece of property in Georgia, he named it after the seat of the high king of Ireland.

Fortifications

Ireland has tons of forts scattered all over the countryside, many of them built during the Bronze or Iron Ages and used for many centuries thereafter. The number and ingenuity of these forts suggest that the ancient Irish considered defense a high priority, though some experts think they were more likely built to impress. The most common form is the ring fort. These forts were built on top of circular mounds of earth with a wooden fence running around the circumference of the mound at the top and a moat surrounding the bottom.

Some forts were built entirely of stone or on the edges of cliffs, which provide a natural barrier to attack. Others, called *crannogs*, were built on artificial islands in the middle of lakes or bogs. They were used as late as the seventeenth century.

Brehon Laws

The best picture we have today of ancient Irish social organization comes from the Brehon laws, which were written down in the seventh and eighth centuries C.E. These laws describe a very structured society, with several classes of people and clearly defined punishments for infractions.

ESSENTIAL

The ancient and early medieval Irish were governed by a group of judges, lawyers, and professional poets; these either came from the druidic educational system or the Christian church, depending on the period. They were called *breitheamh,* or brehons. Brehons developed laws, interpreted them, and applied them to individual situations.

Uncertain Origins

For many years, historians believed that the Brehon laws came from the pre-Christian pagan past—possibly from the druids—and that they summarized centuries of laws and beliefs transmitted orally long before they were written. More recent scholars suggest that the Brehon laws were written by later Christians, who combined ancient Irish practice with foreign information and the Bible to create laws for the Irish people.

This would mean the Brehon laws as described might not have entirely reflected the reality of Celtic society, but instead the Irish society of some centuries later. Still, many of the principles would have applied to the Celts, especially the emphasis on social status, honor, and recompense for offenses.

The Class System

There were five classes of Irish people. At the top were the nobles, who belonged to the dominant families and owned property. Below them were ordinary freemen, who rented the land and farmed it, and then base clients who had fewer rights; the lords would give their clients cattle, and in return receive rents and other services. At the bottom were slaves. The fifth class of people was the group of learned men, including doctors, judges, poets, and craftsmen. Members of this group enjoyed special privileges and could move most freely outside their own clans.

Brehon laws applied to civil, criminal, and military matters. They delineated five major classes of people and their rights and duties. All relationships, such as between landlords and tenants, parents and children, and masters and servants, were carefully regulated. Professionals were required to charge only the fees set by law, and they were ranked according to the status of their profession.

A person who injured another was required to compensate his victim for the loss or to have the person nursed back to health at his expense. Brehon law generally did not otherwise punish wrongdoers. People could kill outlaws who had committed serious crimes, but kings could ransom these outlaws and get them freed of obligation—if, for example, a king's ally had committed some atrocious crime and another noble wanted to kill him, the king could ransom the ally and get him off the hook.

FACT

Brehon law also regulated marriage. Husbands and wives were free to divorce. A husband could take a second or subsequent wife, but the first wife would have higher status than the second. The first wife received the second wife's bride price for her own and was allowed to do anything she wanted to the second wife (short of killing her) during the new wife's first three nights at home.

Learned Men—the Druids

The druids were an ancient caste of learned men. What they learned and what they did has long been a matter of much discussion and debate. Herodotus claimed that they were descended from Noah, originated in the western Danube region, and espoused Pythagorean philosophy. Pliny and Tacitus noted their fondness for the oak and their refusal to worship the gods under roofs. Julius Caesar described their schools, where they memorized vast amounts of information, and their sacrificial practices, which involved placing humans or animals in wicker cages and burning them alive.

The Romans distrusted the druids and did their best to put them down. In 61 C.E. the Roman Suetonius rounded up a number of druids and killed them, and that ended druidism in Roman territory (which didn't include Ireland). But the druids were too fascinating for people to forget them; many still think of the megalithic dolmens as druid altars, where the ancient priest-magicians sacrificed their victims.

The Stuff of Legend

In Irish legends, druids can predict the future by interpreting the actions of birds; they use this information to tell their leaders when to march into battle. They wear white robes and sport long beards.

One of the most famous is the druid Cathbad in the Táin Bó Cuailnge. In some versions of the story, he was the father of King Conchobar of Ulster (or Conor mac Nessa). Cathbad ran a school of druidry with eight students. After the hero Cuchulain accidentally killed his own son in battle, the soldiers of Ulster (on Cuchulain's side) feared he might kill them in his frenzied grief; Cathbad saved the army by casting a spell on Cuchulain to make him think the waves in the ocean were warriors, so he would fight them and expend his anger there.

Celtic Art and Poetry

The Celts produced some spectacularly beautiful art. Much of their best work was done in metal. They applied the same attention to intricate detail to their poetry. Poets, like great craftsmen, were honored members of society, welcome in any noble home.

Metalwork

Celtic metalwork is intricately decorated. Celtic smiths worked in gold, iron, and bronze. The Celtic aristocrats liked to have nice things on hand to give as gifts to honored guests, which would bring great honor to the giver, and they especially liked finely wrought metal.

◀ A traditional Celtic design

Celtic men and women wore heavy necklaces of twisted gold, called torques. These became status symbols, and the gods were also represented as wearing them. Celtic burial sites are full of decorative pins called fibulae, which are similar in design to the modern safety pin. Archaeologists have also discovered mirrors, combs, and a beautiful little model boat with oars. Many of these artifacts are elaborately decorated with the distinctive spirals and interweaving designs that the Celts are famous for.

Celtic smiths must have been very skilled to produce their works. They used the lost-wax casting technique—molding an object out of wax, surrounding it with clay, baking the whole thing so the clay hardened and the wax ran out, and then pouring in metal to form the object. They also formed objects out of sheets of metal, hammered thin and then cut and formed into the desired shape.

Celts held their craftsmen in high regard. Craftsmen belonged to a special privileged class of learned men, and the ordinary rules of serfdom and allegiance to a lord did not apply to them. They traveled from patron to patron plying their trade, and their status protected them from assault.

The Celts couldn't write, with one exception—the druids. They used ogham (oh-yam), a rather cumbersome system of parallel lines carved on either side of a vertical centerline, based on the Roman alphabet. Ogham usually appears on stone pillars. Many people believe it was used for magical and occult inscriptions.

Celtic Poetry

Poetry was extremely important to the ancient Irish. Poets, like craftsmen and judges, belonged to the privileged class of learned people. Poets preserved the history of the clan and of Ireland, including lore of the gods and the genealogy of the ruler. The ancient myths and legends were preserved by countless generations of poets, who memorized them and recited them to their listeners.

Poets came in several grades; a poet of the highest status was equal to any chieftain. Training to become a poet took years and involved memorizing thousands of lines of verse. Poets also had a reputation for knowing something about magic and prophecy. A patron would expect a poet to sing his praises, but he had to be careful; poets demanded large rewards, and an unsatisfied poet could create burning satire that could ruin a chieftain's reputation.

Celtic to the End

The Romans never saw a land they didn't want to conquer, but they never conquered Ireland. Julius Caesar initiated contact with Britain in 55 B.C.E., and for over a century the Romans planned to conquer the whole island. Though some Britons became Romanized, many locals didn't appreciate being colonized and fought their conquerors tooth and nail. The Romans couldn't keep enough troops on the island to hold them at bay. They had other frontiers to guard, after all. By 122 C.E., Hadrian had decided it would be wise to wall off Scotland to keep the barbarians separate from Romanized territory. Over the next two centuries, Rome gradually lost control over Britain.

The Romans knew Ireland existed; Ireland's Latin name is Hibernia, which might mean "Land of Winter." (Another theory holds that it comes from Iberia, or Spain.) Julius Caesar mentioned Ireland in his *Commentaries*, but just to note that it was less than half the size of Britain. The Greek geographer Strabo claimed that Ireland was on the edge of habitable earth and that the inhabitants of the island were complete savages living a miserable existence due to the cold climate. The Roman Tacitus, writing around 100 C.E., thought Ireland was very much like Britain. In the late first century C.E., Agricola, a Roman governor of Britain, considered conquering Ireland and even did reconnaissance; he decided that the Romans could take the island with just one legion of soldiers, but it probably wouldn't be worth the effort.

But the Romans never tried to conquer Ireland. The distance from Rome was too great and the potential payoff too uncertain, and they already had their hands full with Britain. And so the Irish remained Celtic.

FACT

Some "experts" thought Ireland must be some sort of El Dorado, a land of fabulous wealth. Solinus, writing in the third century C.E., claimed that Ireland's grass was so rich that Irish cows regularly exploded from eating too much of it. He also noted that there were no snakes in Ireland, which probably made St. Patrick's job a lot easier when he arrived in the next century.

Chapter 3
Celtic Mythology

The Celts had a bunch of myths and legends. Celtic myths tell the stories of gods and goddesses and of ancient heroes—just like ancient Greek myths, but with a unique Celtic spin on things. These stories explain the origin of the Irish people, the relationship they had with their deities, and why certain people and places were more important than others.

Celtic Pantheon

Most of what modern people know about Celtic mythology didn't come straight from the Celts themselves, because they didn't write down any of their stories. Scholars over the past two millenniums have cobbled together a picture of Celtic beliefs by combining archaeological evidence, details from Irish legends, and the writings of contemporary observers. Julius Caesar and other classical authors recorded a great deal of information on Celtic mythology, which is still useful today.

The Celts believed that there were a bunch of gods and goddesses, and that these deities had relationships with one another and with humans. There were gods of love, writing, light, death, and, of course, war.

Celtic Gods

The Celts had a number of gods; here are a few of them:

- The Daghdha, or "Good God," was the chief god of the Irish pantheon. He carried a club that could both kill and bring people back to life, and he had a giant magic cauldron that was always full of food.
- Donn was the god of the dead. The druids claimed that all people were descended from him.
- Oenghus was the son of the Daghdha. He was a handsome young man and functioned something like a god of love.
- Oghma invented the ogham alphabet, a system of writing used by druids.
- Lug was the sun god, god of genius and light. He was the hero Cuchulain's father. Julius Caesar thought that Lug was the most important Celtic god.
- Nuadhu Airgedlámh is an ancestor god-king. He lost an arm in battle and replaced it with one made of silver.
- Dian Cécht was the "Divine Physician." Mortally wounded people could be cast into a well, and he would sing over it, whereupon they would come out again healed.

- Boibhniu was the leader of three craftsman gods. He was also the host of the Otherworld Feast, where he served a drink that made people immortal.
- Manannán was a sea god. He oversaw the journey over the sea to the otherworld.

These were not the only Celtic gods. Many others existed, though not all of their names have been recorded. There are still strange statues in Ireland that depict fearful beings, many with two or three faces; who they were or what they did, no one knows.

Celtic gods and goddesses embodied different aspects of life. Many of them, like Brigid, proved to have great staying power and became incorporated into Christian religious beliefs.

Celtic Goddesses

The Celtic pantheon included a number of female deities. Many of them traveled in groups of three, such as the Macha-Mórrígan-Babd trio of war/fertility goddesses.

- Anu, or Danu, was the mother goddess and mother of the gods. She was connected with fertility and nurture.
- Brigid was the daughter of the Daghdha. She was goddess of fertility and patron of poets. She had two sisters, also named Brigid, who were associated with craftsmanship and healing; the three of them were often treated as one entity. Brigid's symbol was fire, and there was a fire kept alight for her in County Kildare from pre-Christian times until 1151. She later transformed into the Christian St. Bride, or St. Brigid.
- A trio of sisters—Macha (MA-ha), Mórrígan, and Babd (bahv)—were known as the Mórrígna. They were war and fertility goddesses; they played an important part in the war between the Tuatha Dé Danaan and the Fomorians.

- Mórrígan embodied war fury. There are a number of sites in Ireland that bear her name.
- Babd was both sinister and sexual; she sometimes appeared as a crow, sometimes as a hag, and sometimes as a beautiful young woman. She urged the hero Cuchulain to go fight his last battle that led to his death.
- Scáthach was the "Shadowy One." She taught the young Cuchulain all his magic.
- Boann was a water goddess who embodied the spirit of the Boyne River. She and the Daghdha had a child together—Oenghus, who functioned something like the god of love.

The Otherworld

The world of Celtic gods and spirits was known as the otherworld, Mag Mell ("Plain of Honey"), Tír Tairngire ("Land of Promise"), and Tír na nÓg ("Land of Perpetual Youth"). It was a place of simple and sensuous pleasures. Everyone living there could eat as much as they wanted, and many heroes found loving women there. The cauldron of the Daghdha was there, and it was always full of food.

◀ The Gundestrup Cauldron, found in Denmark, depicts Celtic deities

Heroes would occasionally make special trips to the otherworld; these voyages were called *imrama* (or *immrama*). A famous legend about an *imram* is the Immram Brain Maic Febail, the story of the Irish king Bran's journey to the otherworld (in other versions, the journey is to the Land of Women).

Celtic Festivals

The Celts divided the year into two halves, the bright, warm half known as *samh,* or summer, and the dark, cold half called *gamh,* or winter. They punctuated the year with four festivals marking the different seasons:

- **Imbolc** (IM-bulk) took place on February 1. It was the feast of the goddess Brigid, associated with the birth of lambs and the lactation of ewes.
- **Beltane** (bal-thu-na) was celebrated on May 1. People lit bonfires, danced around maypoles, and made merry. This feast marked the start of summer.
- **Lughnasa** (LOO-na-sa) was a harvest festival held in late summer in honor of the god Lug. Festivities included games, drinking, dancing, matchmaking, and racing horses naked.
- **Samhain** (SOW-in) corresponds to modern Halloween and marked the end of summer. This is the day that tombs opened and ghosts walked about with gods and goddesses.

All four of these festivals correspond very closely to the solar equinoxes and solstices, all of which were easy to identify using the solar devices incorporated into various megalithic mounds. The Celts were masterful astronomers, given that they didn't have telescopes. They knew about the planets Mercury, Venus, Mars, Jupiter, and Saturn, and their year lasted 365 days.

E-SITE

The fairy cave at Cruachain in County Roscommon was an important center for celebrating Samhain; legend said that lots of ghosts came out of this cave, led by the Mórrígan, or "Great Queen."

Creation Myths

According to legend, the island of Ireland was invaded six different times in its prehistory. The story of these invasions is told in a body of myth called the Mythological Cycle, much of which was recorded in the twelfth century in the Book of Invasions. The ultimate consequence of all these invasions was a final battle between two groups of supernatural people, the Tuatha Dé Danaan and the Fomorians, and the establishment of civilization and social order.

Invasions by Descendants of Noah

The first invasion was led by one of the granddaughters of Noah (the Biblical Noah who built the Ark), but her timing was bad; all of her people drowned in the great flood. Three hundred years later, another descendant of Noah, Parthalón, settled Ireland, building houses and clearing fields for farming. Parthalón's sworn enemies were the Fomorians, one-armed, one-legged monsters descended from Noah's cursed son, Ham.

Parthalón and his people all died of plague. Thirty years later, the third invasion arrived, led by a man named Nemhedh. They attacked the Fomorians, but most of them died in the effort. A few survivors fled to Greece, where they became slaves; they were called the Fir Bolg.

The Fir Bolg came back to Ireland, which they divided into the five provinces of the Celts. They established a kingship and ruled the land for thirty-seven years. Their last king, Eochaidh mac Eirc, was a perfect, just ruler; during his reign no rain fell, only dew; there was no year without a harvest; and nobody told any falsehoods.

The First Battle of Magh Tuiredh

The Fir Bolg had a nice arrangement, but it was too good to last. Yet another group of people decided to invade Ireland: the Tuatha Dé Danaan.

The Tuatha Dé Danaan were the people of the mother goddess Anu. According to Irish legend, they arrived around 350 B.C.E. They came from four cities in ancient Greece, which is where they learned about prophecy and magic, the secrets of the druids. They brought with them four treasures:

- The cauldron of the Daghdha—this vessel was always full of food.
- The spear of Lug—this weapon ensured victory to its holder.
- The sword of Nuadhu Airgedlámh—no enemy could escape from it once it was drawn from its sheath.
- The Lia Fáil—known as the "Stone of Destiny," it shrieked when the feet of a lawful king rested on it; this ended up on Tara Hill, seat of Irish kings.

The Tuatha Dé Danaan were skilled in magic and fighting. Their leader, Nuadhu Airgedlámh, brought them into battle. But a Fir Bolg warrior named Sreng cut his arm off at the shoulder. Sreng made peace with the Tuatha Dé Danaan and agreed to leave them all of Ireland except for Connacht (or Connaught), where he led his own people.

Poor Nuadhu Airgedlámh couldn't be king anymore, because no one with a physical defect (such as a missing arm) could be king. A man named Bres got to be king instead. Bres was the son of the Fomorian king Delbáeth; he had been adopted and raised by the Tuatha Dé Danaan, and they obviously thought they could trust him. But there they were mistaken.

FACT

Fostering was a common practice in ancient warlike states. Kings and chieftains would send their children to be raised at the courts of other rulers. This broadened the educations and connections of their children. It also provided the rulers with ready-made hostages should their allies consider becoming their enemies.

The Second Battle of Magh Tuiredh

Bres, the Fomorian, ruled the Tuatha Dé Danaan for seven years. This was a lousy time for the Tuatha Dé Danaan. The Fomorians demanded a tribute of cattle, and the gods were reduced to menial labor; even the Daghdha himself was forced to dig ditches and build a fortress for Bres.

Meanwhile, the Tuatha Dé Danaan were planning their recovery. Dian Cécht, the "Divine Physician," made a new arm for Nuadhu out of silver, which would allow him to be king again. After a poet named Cairbre mac Étain (son of Étain) sang a verse mocking Bres, he gave up the kingship and went off to gather an army of his Fomorians. Nuadhu was reinstated as king; he and the Daghdha and Lug got together to decide how to get back at the Fomorians. (Lug had recently appeared at the court, and he had impressed everyone so much with his skill in all arts, creative and warlike, that they let him be one of their leaders.)

The Daghdha went to see Mórrígan at the festival of Samhain. She was standing astride the River Unius washing herself. They made love standing over the water, which gave that spot the name "Bed of the Couple." She told the Daghdha that the Fomorians were coming to attack the Tuatha Dé Danaan and that he should bring his soldiers to her. She killed the son of the Fomorian king and gave two handfuls of the blood to the Tuatha Dé Danaan before they went into battle. She and her sisters Babd and Macha went to the Mound of the Hostages at Tara and made the sky rain blood down onto the battle.

E-SITE

Magh Tuiredh is a real place in County Sligo. Its name means "Plain of Reckoning" or "Plain of Weeping." Some historians believe that at least one of the battles there was a real historical fight between the men of Ulster (the Tuatha Dé Danaan) and the men of Connacht (the Fir Bolg).

Lug led the Tuatha Dé Danaan in the second battle of Magh Tuiredh. The Mórrígan entered the fray, cheering on the Tuatha Dé Danaan and pursuing any Fomorians who tried to run away. Blood ran freely over the white-skinned warriors and the River Unius was clogged with corpses. Lug and his armies finally defeated the Fomorians and drove them to the sea.

After the fighting was over, Lug spared Bres in return for some information about agricultural techniques. The Mórrígan finished off the story by declaring victory for the Tuatha Dé Danaan and predicting the end of the world.

Invasion by the Milesians

The conquests of Ireland didn't stop with the Tuatha Dé Danaan. They were themselves invaded by the Milesians, the sons of Míl, also known as the Gaels.

Míl came from Galicia in northwest Spain. His full name was Miles Hispaniae (Latin for "soldier of Spain"). His wife was named Scota ("Irishwoman"). A druid named Caichér had predicted that Míl's descendants would rule Ireland, and they did.

Míl himself didn't go to Ireland, but his sons did. The Milesians arrived in Ireland sometime after the Tuatha Dé Danaan had established themselves, perhaps between 350 and 250 B.C.E. They landed in southwest Ireland during the Feast of Beltane and fought a huge battle with the Tuatha Dé Danaan. They proceeded to Tara and clinched their hold on the country.

After the battle, a poet named Amhairghin divided Ireland between the two parties. The Milesians got the part that was aboveground, and the Tuatha Dé Danaan got the underground. The defeated Tuatha Dé Danaan retreated to the hills and mounds to become the fairy people.

FACT

Some scholars think that in the original myths, the Tuatha Dé Danaan were divine, not the supernatural beings they appear to be. According to this theory, medieval monks who recorded the stories demoted the Tuatha Dé Danaan to their current stature, not wanting to suggest that any other gods could rival the Christian one.

The Táin Bó Cuailnge

The Táin Bó Cuailnge (toyn boe cooley), or the Cattle Raid of Cooley, is one of the most fabulous epic stories to come out of ancient Ireland. It is set around the first century B.C.E. The oldest manuscript that records it is the Book of Leinster, written in the twelfth century. The Táin is part of the body of stories known as the Ulster Cycle. The story concerns the conflict between Ulster and Connacht, and the question of whether men can accept a female ruler.

Mebd and Ailill

One night, Ailill (ahl-il), the king of Connacht, and his wife, Queen Medb (mayv), lay in bed arguing over which one of them was richer. Ailill suggested that Mebd had improved her lot by marrying him and that it was proper for a man to rule the kingdom instead of her, but Mebd insisted that she was as rich and tough as any king. They couldn't agree, so that very night they did an inventory. They laid out their garments and jewelry and lined up the livestock. And for every possession Ailill put up, Mebd put up one just as good, except for one thing: a beautiful, white-horned bull.

This bull had been born to one of Mebd's cows, but it had left her herd because it didn't want to belong to a woman. Mebd was devastated, and she decided then and there that she would get a bull to equal the white-horned one. The only bull as good as this one was the brown bull of Cuailnge, the property of Daire mac Fiachna, king of Ulster.

Mebd sent messengers to Ulster requesting the loan of the brown bull for one year. She offered generous terms: fifty yearling heifers, a large piece of land, a fabulous chariot, and her own "friendly thighs." Daire agreed readily, but that evening Mebd's messengers boasted that if he had not accepted her terms, they would have taken the bull by force. After that, the deal was off.

Mebd wasn't particularly perturbed by this; she had sort of expected this to happen and quickly assembled a vast army. It marched off to Ulster to capture the brown bull.

Heroic Deeds of Cuchulain

The Ulster army started marching to meet its attackers, but on the way the soldiers were all struck by strange, debilitating pains, the result of an old curse by the goddess Macha. So instead of encountering an army, Mebd's warriors met a single hero: Cuchulain (koo-hool-n).

FACT

Macha's curse has its own story. Years before, Macha had taken human form and married a man. He was so proud of her legs that he forced her to run a race with the king's chariot—nine months pregnant! She tied with the chariot but delivered twins at the finish line. Then she announced that all the descendants of the men who heard her scream would feel the pain of childbirth in their most desperate moments.

Cuchulain was like the Celtic Achilles. He was seventeen years old, handsome, and utterly fearless. He had grown up as a foster son of King Conchobar (konn-r) of Ulster. Cuchulain's name means "Culann's hound." He got this name because when the hound of Culann the smith attacked him, he killed it with his bare hands. Culann was upset because his watchdog was dead, and Cuchulain offered to do the job himself until he found a replacement canine.

When Cuchulain met the army from Connacht, he killed 100 soldiers single-handedly. Next, he fought a series of Mebd's warriors in single combat. Mebd persuaded soldiers to fight for her by bribing them with anything from land, to her own daughter in marriage, to her own thighs, which she had previously offered in exchange for the brown bull. Her warriors found these rewards enticing enough, but Cuchulain defeated all of them.

Turning back toward Ulster, Cuchulain discovered Mebd's forces leading away the brown bull. He killed the leader, but the rest escaped with the bull, much to Cuchulain's distress. He took to his bed and slept for three days and nights, while the god Lug healed his wounds.

The Warp-Spasm

While Cuchulain slept, the army of Ulster fought Mebd's forces. The Ulster side was winning, but in the process lost 150 soldiers. When Cuchulain woke up and heard about this, he was furious and was transfigured by the warp-spasm, a battle-rage that turned him into the most fearsome sight anyone had ever seen. Possessed by this rage, he slaughtered hundreds of warriors, women, children, horses, and dogs.

No man from Connacht escaped uninjured, but Cuchulain came away without a scratch on himself.

Cuchulain was a fearsome opponent, but Mebd finally came up with a way to get the best of him. She forced him to fight his foster brother, Fer Diad, whom Cuchulain loved more than any other man. She persuaded Fer Diad to fight on her behalf by promising him her daughter as a wife. The men fought for three days without either one gaining an advantage, and each one sent assistance to the other at night. On the fourth day, though, Cuchulain killed Fer Diad with the *gae bolga,* a frightful weapon that would expand into twenty-four barbs within a wound, like an exploding shell. Then Cuchulain sang a lament over his fallen friend.

The Ulster forces pursued Mebd's army all the way to the border of Connacht. There, Cuchulain met Mebd face-to-face and chose to spare her because she was a woman. But the conflict wasn't over.

E-SITE

Although of course no one knows what the real Cuchulain looked like, there is a bronze statue of him in the Dublin General Post Office. Appropriately enough, later Irish heroes made their headquarters for the Easter Rebellion (also known as the Easter Rising) of 1916 in the General Post Office. Modern tourists can see both the ancient Cuchulain and modern battle scars in the same spot.

A Massive Bull Fight

Mebd had sent the brown bull straight to Connacht to keep it safe. As soon as it arrived, it bellowed three times. The white-horned bull heard it and came racing to defend his territory. All the warriors watched this mighty duel, which lasted into the night and ranged over the entire island of Ireland.

In the morning, the brown bull reappeared, carrying the dead white-horned bull on his horns. He galloped back to Ulster, scattering bits of his enemy's flesh as he went. When he arrived at the border of Cuailnge, his heart broke and he died. Mebd and Ailill made peace with Cuchulain and the men of Ulster, and there was no fighting between them for the next seven years.

The Death of Cuchulain

Truce or no, Mebd spent the years of peace scheming to get revenge on Cuchulain. During the cattle-raid wars, he had killed a man named Cailidín, who had six children. Mebd sent off Cailidín's children to study sorcery. When they returned, she got them to make Cuchulain think that all of Ulster was overrun by invading armies. Deceived, Cuchulain prepared to go to battle.

Conchobar feared some trickery and sent Cuchulain to the Valley of the Deaf, where he wouldn't be able to hear the fake battle cries. The children of Cailidín redoubled their efforts to convince Cuchulain that battle was nigh, and Babd, one of the girls (and also a goddess of war), went to the hero in the shape of his mistress and asked him to fight the men of Ireland. Cathbad the druid and Cuchulain's real mistress tried to tell him that he had been bewitched, but he went off to fight anyway.

◀ A statue of the hero Cuchulain in the Dublin General Post Office

The sons of Cailidín hit Cuchulain with a magical javelin. The hero knew that he was about to die, so he tied himself to a pillar so that he could die upright and facing his enemies. No one dared approach him for three days. Finally, they saw a bird land on his shoulder and peck at his eyes. His enemies went and cut off his head and right hand.

Conchobar and Deirdre

Conchobar, king of Ulster, was not a pleasant character, especially not with his wife Deirdre, whom he met back in the days before the big cattle raid. Before Deirdre was born, Cathbad the druid predicted that she would be very beautiful but would bring ruin on the kingdom of Ulster. Conchobar liked the sound of the beautiful part, so he hid her away, intending to marry her when she was grown.

Deirdre grew up alone, away from the court. One day she saw her foster mother skinning a calf in the snow and a black raven drinking its blood. She said that she would like a husband with hair as black as raven, cheeks red as blood, and a body white as snow. As it happened, just such a man lived nearby: Naoise, son of Uisneach.

Deirdre and Naoise got together and ran away to Scotland. They lived at the Scottish court for a while, but the Scottish king began to want Deirdre for himself, so they returned to Ireland. There, Naoise was killed by Conchobar's ally Eoghan mac Durthacht, and Deirdre went to Conchobar's court.

She spent a year there, never smiling or lifting her head from her knee. One day Conchobar asked her what she hated most, and she replied "you and Eoghan." Conchobar decided to give her to Eoghan. As she was riding in a chariot with both men, she leaped out of the chariot and smashed her head to pieces on a giant rock.

Finn MacCool

Fionn mac Cumhaill, or Finn MacCool, was a great warrior and a major hero of ancient Ireland. His stories come from the Duanaire Finn (the

"Lays of Finn"), part of the Fenian Cycle. Scholars have long debated whether Finn was a real historical figure from the third century C.E., but the current consensus is that he was completely mythical.

Don't Mess with a Druid's Daughter

Finn was the son of Cumhaill, king of Leinster; he served the high king Conn, who reigned at Tara. Cumhaill was head of the Fianna, an elite band of warriors. Men seeking admission to this band had to pass a test of skill, such as fending off six men with spears, armed only with a shield and a stick. All members had to swear an oath of allegiance to the high king. If one of the Fianna was killed, the dead man's relatives were supposed to let the Fianna avenge him.

FACT

The idea of the Fianna—brave warriors defending Ireland—was very popular with the Irish Nationalists of the nineteenth and twentieth centuries. The Fenian independence movement of the 1860s took its name from the Fianna, and when Éamon de Valera needed a name for his bold new political party in the Irish Free State, he called them Fianna Fáil—"Soldiers of Destiny."

After Cumhaill refused an order to attend a meeting at Tara, Conn declared war on him. While he was getting ready to fight, Cumhaill met Muirne, the daughter of a druid, and got her pregnant. Her outraged father vowed that Cumhaill would die in battle.

Cumhaill told Muirne to run away and hide someplace where she could raise the baby in safety. Another druid had foretold that this child, Finn, would be a great leader of the Fianna, and Cumhaill wanted to make sure that this came to pass. Then he died, slain by the king's ally Goll mac Morna.

Kind of Old to Be Sucking His Thumb

Muirne fled to a cave and gave birth to Finn, who grew up vowing revenge on Goll mac Morna and all his clan. Finn went to study with a druid named Fionn. Fionn was perpetually searching for the salmon of knowledge, a fish that would bring boundless knowledge to whoever ate it. One day, Finn caught the fish and went to cook it for Fionn. A blister rose up on its skin, and he pressed it down with his thumb. He then put his thumb in his mouth to soothe the burn, and he realized that he now knew everything. From then on, whenever Finn didn't know something, he would suck his thumb, and all would be revealed to him.

Hunters in the Wilderness

Finn became leader of the Fianna. The Fianna loved the woods and wild animals. They cooked their meals in *ovens of the Fianna*, small, circular holes lined with stones and surrounded by low stone walls. (You can still find these all over Ireland.) Finn had two hounds that were actually his own nephews. His wife was a deer-woman from the otherworld. She raised their son Ossian in the wilderness; he grew up to be the poet of the Fianna and was a famous bard. (The stories about Finn are sometimes called the Ossianic Cycle because Ossian supposedly composed them.)

E-SITE

There is no lack of place names associated with Finn, such as Loch Finn in County Donegal and the Blackwater River in County Meath, which used to be called the River Finn. James Joyce refers to Finn throughout the book *Finnegan's Wake*.

Finn and the Fianna had many magical adventures. They encountered ghosts and witches but always escaped with their lives. They got magical weapons from a giant with three arms, one foot, and an eye in the middle of his forehead; he was a fabulous blacksmith who could make blades fiercer than any made by humans.

A Jealous Lover

When Finn was an old man, he got engaged to a beautiful young woman named Gráinne. She didn't want to marry him, so she cast a spell on Diarmait, the handsomest of the Fianna. Diarmait and Gráinne ran away together and lived happily for a while.

One day, all the Fianna went to hunt the magic boar of Beann Ghulban. This boar had been Diarmait's foster brother, and there was a prophecy that it would cause his death. Sure enough, the boar gored Diarmait and ripped open his belly. The only way to save his life was for Finn to bring him a drink of water in his hands. Finn went and got the water, but then he remembered how Diarmait had stolen Gráinne away from him, and he let it trickle out through his fingers. Diarmait died, and the god Oenghus took his body away to Brú na Bóinne, where he was buried in Newgrange tomb.

FACT

Finn himself died an old man. He had retired to the side of the Boyne River, where he could finish his life in peace, when a fisherman murdered him with his gaff; evidently, he was hoping for everlasting notoriety and thought this deed would secure it. One of Finn's faithful followers then cut off the fisherman's head.

Myths for All Time

These Celtic myths have been around for a long time. Christians of the medieval period read and wrote down stories about Celtic heroes, adding their own Christian twists. Irish storytellers have always loved these legends and embellished them, creating scenarios in which pagan heroes from ancient days encountered Christian saints from a later time. Irish patriots of a more modern day took mythical characters as models for heroism. All of these myths have helped the Irish create a sense of their own unique Irishness. (E)

Chapter 4

Arrival of Christianity in Ireland

It's impossible to understand the spread of Christianity in Ireland without examining the lives of the men and women who made it their life's work to teach others about their new faith—the lives of the Irish saints. We don't know what actually happened and what was added by imaginative storytellers. But that's no reason to dismiss the stories of saints as pure fancy.

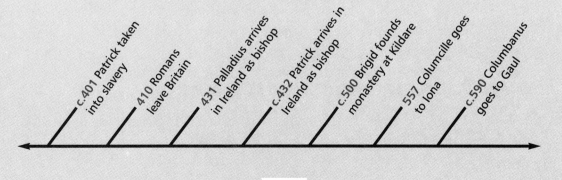

c.401 Patrick taken into slavery

410 Romans leave Britain

431 Palladius arrives in Ireland as bishop

c.432 Patrick arrives in Ireland as bishop

c.500 Brigid founds monastery at Kildare

557 Columcille goes to Iona

c.590 Columbanus goes to Gaul

Christianity in Late Antiquity

The Roman Empire formally accepted Christianity when the emperor Constantine converted in 312 C.E. (Although there had been Roman Christians during the previous three centuries, they were persecuted and Christian practices were illegal.) As Christianity spread gradually throughout the empire, it percolated up through Gaul and into Britain. It arrived in Ireland sometime in the early 400s.

QUESTION?

What is a saint?
According to the Catholic Church, a saint is a person who lived a holy life, performing miracles before or after death. Often, there's a popular cult associated with the person, and many saints died as martyrs. The process of making someone a saint is known as canonization.

The Unknown Palladius

Although everyone knows that St. Patrick brought Christianity to Ireland, it's possible that someone beat him to it. In 431—the first reliable date in Irish history, as recorded by Prosper of Aquitaine—a Christian missionary named Palladius was ordained by the pope to go to Ireland as the island's first bishop. But St. Patrick also supposedly arrived in Ireland as bishop around this time—432 is the traditional date for his arrival. So who was this Palladius person?

No one knows. There is nothing else written about Palladius. Patrick, on the other hand, left behind a written record of his accomplishments. The medieval Irish all credit St. Patrick with bringing Christianity to Ireland. Some people think Palladius and St. Patrick were the same man, or that Palladius's deeds have been subsumed into the St. Patrick legend. Some people even suggest that St. Patrick never existed.

St. Patrick, the Patron Saint

Irish tradition credits St. Patrick with bringing Christianity to the Irish and transforming the island from a wild warrior society to a peaceful, scholarly kingdom. Not much is known about his life, or whether he existed at all. Most of what modern scholars know about the historical Patrick comes from his *Confession*, an autobiographical sketch he (supposedly) wrote toward the end of his life. It's very short, and actually pretty readable, though some parts of it are incomprehensible—Patrick wasn't very good at writing Latin. Patrick never mentions dates, so any dates that scholars claim for his deeds are just guesses.

◀ St. Patrick

Early Life

Patrick's family was of British Celt (Briton) ancestry, who had lived in Britain for several centuries. His father was a well-to-do landowner, and Patrick probably grew up as a privileged young man, waited on by servants and educated in the classical tradition as it survived in Britain at the end of the Roman Empire. His family was Christian; his father was a deacon and his grandfather a priest. Young Patrick was not a pious youth. By his own account, he had turned his back on the Christian god, and he committed some serious, unknown crime in his midteens (more on that later).

When Patrick was almost sixteen, he was captured by a group of Irish slave traders and was sold into slavery in Ireland. Patrick spent the next six years herding sheep alone in the hills, hunger and cold his constant companions. In his desolation, he turned to God and prayed constantly.

E-SITE

Tradition says that Patrick established his own church in Armagh, Northern Ireland; the cathedral of the Church of Ireland is still there. Armagh was an important ancient and medieval town. The legendary queen or goddess Macha supposedly lived there before Christianity, and Brian Boru was buried there in 1014.

Patrick's Great Escape

One day God spoke to Patrick, telling him that his ship was ready to take him away from Ireland. It was not nearby, but in fact 200 miles away (which is unlikely, since very few places in Ireland are 200 miles from any body of water). Patrick set off on foot over the countryside, taking a great risk by running away from his master; he had no idea what he was headed for, but Patrick had no fear.

He reached the coast and found a ship ready to set sail. He asked the captain if he could sail with them, and the captain brusquely refused. So Patrick returned to the hut where he was staying and started to pray. Before he had finished his prayer, the sailors called him back and said that he could sail with them.

The ship sailed for three days and then landed. It's not clear where; Patrick reports that he and the sailors wandered "in a desert" for twenty-eight days, and there's no place three days' sail from Ireland that matches that description. Some scholars have suggested that they landed in Gaul (modern France) after it was ravaged by barbarians in 407; others think it more likely that they were making circles around Britain.

In any case, they had nothing to eat. The captain turned to Patrick and asked him what his Christian god could do for them. Patrick admonished him to put his faith in God and ask Him to send them food that very day. Sure enough, a whole herd of pigs came running across their path. The sailors killed and cooked a few, and their problems were solved.

A Divine Calling

Eventually, Patrick got back to his parents, who were overjoyed to see him after so many years and begged him never to leave them again. But Patrick discovered that home wasn't home anymore; he had changed too much in the last few years to feel comfortable resuming his life as a British landowner.

One night, he dreamed about a man named Victoricus, whom he had known in Ireland. Victoricus gave him a letter entitled "The Voice of the Irish." At the same time, Patrick heard the voices of Irish people calling him back to them. He knew that Ireland would be his destiny.

He left home again and studied for the priesthood. Some scholars think he went to Gaul, while others are sure he stayed in Britain, but it doesn't really matter. Patrick struggled with his coursework. His education had been interrupted by his abrupt enslavement back when he was a teenager, and he never did make up the ground he had lost; in his later writings, he often laments that his Latin is not very good and that he is uneducated. But he managed to learn the required material and was ordained a priest.

FACT

The night before his ordination, Patrick confessed some old sin to a close friend. He never reveals in his *Confession* what this sin was, but it did come back to haunt him in later life when some bishops tried to use it to ruin his career. Although Patrick's confession obviously didn't stay private, it was the origin of the Catholic ritual of private, confidential confession.

Spreading the Word to the Irish

Now a priest, Patrick went back to Ireland as its bishop, one of the first Christian missionaries in history; the traditional date for this journey is 432. There was a lot for him to do in Ireland. The Irish were still barbarians, worshipping Celtic gods, raiding one another's cattle, and abducting slaves. Patrick was genuinely concerned about these problems; he found slavery to be particularly bad for women (his respect and concern for women made him very unusual among early medieval leaders).

Patrick was incredibly successful. He converted thousands of Irish to Christianity, established monasteries, and ordained priests all over the island. He placed bishops next to local kings, both to improve the Church's position with the Irish and to have someone to keep an eye on the worst raiders and warriors. By the end of his life, the Irish had stopped their endless tribal warfare and the slave trade had ended.

Converting the Irish wasn't always easy. As the Romans left Britain, local British kings grabbed the abandoned territory and took over the piracy trade. One British king named Coroticus attacked in northern Ireland and killed or carried off thousands of recent converts. Patrick sent some priests to Coroticus to ask for the return of his people, but the king only laughed at them. Patrick responded with his "Letter to Coroticus," one of the two pieces of writing he left behind, in which he took the king to task for visiting this horror on his people. He also excommunicated him from the Christian faith, the worst punishment a priest could inflict on a believer. Patrick knew firsthand what it meant to be a slave, and his genuine love of his flock and grief at their suffering comes through in his prose quite clearly.

QUESTION?

Were there any snakes in Ireland before Saint Patrick?
Alas, for believers who would love to credit him with removing serpents from the Emerald Isle, it appears that there were not. This story was concocted about 300 years after his death. It is possible, though, that *snakes* was a metaphor for *pagans*.

Myths about St. Patrick

Over time, Patrick developed into a legendary figure. As the patron saint of Ireland and founder of Irish Christianity, he has been credited with numerous deeds that may not have a basis in historical fact. Here are a few of them:

- He banished snakes from Ireland—standing on top of Croagh Patrick, a hill in County Mayo, he rang a bell, and all the snakes in Ireland fled.
- He used the Irish shamrock, a three-leafed clover, to teach his converts about the Trinity, the one-in-three union of God, Jesus, and the Holy Spirit.

- He argued with High King Laoghaire at Tara and won for the side of Christianity.
- He was on speaking terms with both God and an angel, and once climbed Croagh Patrick to speak with God.
- He wrote the lovely prayer known as "Saint Patrick's Breastplate."

None of these myths can be verified, at least not as they are described today. The shamrock story appeared centuries after Patrick's death, and the "Breastplate" was probably written in the seventh or eighth century. It is possible that Patrick did face down a king over some issue of Christianity, but probably not as it is told in the famous story about Laoghaire.

E-SITE

Croagh Patrick is a hill in County Mayo; according to legend, this is where Patrick blasted venomous snakes out of Ireland. On Reek Sunday, the last Sunday in July, thousands of people climb to the top of the hill as an act of penance.

St. Brigid, the Generous

Brigid of Kildare was one of Patrick's converts to Christianity. She became abbess of a huge monastery that admitted both men and women. Some historians say she was actually a bishop. Most of what we know about St. Brigid is not historical fact, but it is fairly certain that Brigid was an immensely powerful woman who did a lot to advance Christianity in Ireland.

A Noble Daughter

Brigid's father was an Irish nobleman. She converted to Christianity while still living at home. The first thing she did was to start handing out her father's food and goods to beggars. Her father was furious; he tossed her into his chariot and drove off to see the king of Leinster, to offer him Brigid as a wife.

When they got to the king of Leinster's palace, Brigid's father went in alone to see him. Out of respect, he first took off his sword and left it in the chariot with Brigid. While her dad was in the castle negotiating her marriage, a leper came up to Brigid and asked her for help. The only thing available was her father's sword, so she gave him that.

Her father and the king of Leinster then came back out. Of course, her father immediately noticed that his sword was gone and wanted to know what Brigid had done with it. When he found out, he flew into a rage and beat her.

The king of Leinster, intrigued by this unusual young woman, stopped her father from hitting her and asked her why she gave away his things. She replied that if she could, she would steal all of the king's wealth and give it away to the poor. Not surprisingly, the king decided not to marry her after all.

Brigid Founds a Monastery

Brigid's monastery was huge; it contained a school of art and a scriptorium that produced gorgeous religious manuscripts. Brigid never abandoned her desire to help the poor, and her monastery was famous for its hospitality. After her death it turned into a center of pilgrimage, almost as big as a city. It became a place of refuge for anyone in Ireland, where people fleeing invaders could find safety and where kings could store their treasures.

Brigid was radical in more ways than one. She admitted both men and women to her monastery, and she seems to have performed all the duties of a priest. This was an outrage for the Catholic Church, which has never approved of female leadership, though it's possible that people broke many rules in far-flung Ireland in the early medieval days.

Legend says that Brigid had some connections to the druids. She supposedly took her vows on the Hill of Uisneach, a place important to ancient Celts, and started her monastery under an oak tree, the sacred tree of the druids. Its name, Kildare, means "church of the oak."

A Beloved Irish Saint

Brigid is sometimes called the Mary of the Gael. In one legend, she shaped a cross out of reeds to teach people about Christianity, much like St. Patrick used the shamrock to explain the Trinity; today, Irish people still keep St. Brigid's crosses. Brigid's feast day is celebrated on February 1.

February 1 is also the Celtic feast of Imbolc, dedicated to the Irish fertility goddess Brigid. Coincidence? Certainly not—the Irish incorporated many aspects of their pagan Celtic religion into their version of Christianity. Another pagan-Christian combo associated with Brigid was St. Brigid's fire, which was started in ancient times and burned into the Middle Ages.

E-SITE

In County Louth there is a hill designated as a shrine to St. Brigid, who supposedly was born near it in 453. Visitors walk past a stream where Brigid performed miracles, climb a path marked with the Stations of the Cross, and then walk down to a grotto containing a statue of Mary visiting Brigid. A field across the road from the shrine contains healing stones in the shapes of body parts—head, eye, hoof—that have magical curative powers.

St. Columcille, Felonious Monk

Columcille, usually called Columba by non-Irish writers, converted thousands of Celts to Christianity and founded a plethora of monasteries. But he didn't do this simply out of love of God; he committed some serious sins and then threw himself into God's work as a form of atonement. Part of his penance was permanent exile from Ireland, which turned out to be the key to his impressive missionary accomplishments.

From Noble to Monk

Columcille's real name was Crimthann, which means "fox" in Irish. He was the son of a nobleman of the Conaill clan, and was well educated in his youth. When he had finished his secular education, he went to study with Bishop Finian in Clonard, Gaul.

Finian owned a beautifully decorated Psalter, and Crimthann fell in love with it. He wanted to copy it, but Finian wouldn't let him. So Crimthann stole into the darkened church at night and copied it in secret. He had no candle, but the fingers of his left hand shone with lights to illuminate his work. Sadly for Crimthann, he got caught, and King Diarmait (or Dermot) made him give the copy back to Finian.

Crimthann became a monk and took the name Columcille ("Dove of the Church"). He made a pilgrimage to the grave of St. Martin of Tours, a legendary founder of monasteries. Inspired by Martin's work, he returned to Ireland and began founding monasteries right and left. By the time he was forty-one, he had founded forty-one monasteries.

The Causes of Exile

But Columcille wasn't a good, peace-loving Christian. King Diarmait had one of Columcille's followers killed, and Columcille got angry; he persuaded all his warrior relatives to go fight the king. They defeated Diarmait, and Columcille took this opportunity to reclaim the Psalter he had copied from Finian years ago. It was thereafter called the Cathach ("warrior").

But a monk is not supposed to go to war. Columcille was excommunicated and told that he must leave Ireland forever. Three thousand enemy soldiers had died in the conflict, and Columcille set himself a penance of converting 3,000 pagans to Christianity. With this daunting task ahead of him, Columcille enlisted twelve followers and sailed away to the island of Iona, off the coast of Scotland.

Much of what we know about medieval saints comes from a kind of writing called "hagiography." Hagiography tells the stories of saints' lives, but not in a strictly historical manner. Usually, the writer is more interested in glorifying the subject and impressing the reader than providing just the facts.

The White Martyrdom

Columcille and his followers had embraced the White Martyrdom, the sacrifice of leaving behind the land they loved best and moving to an unknown territory, there to fast and do penance in a monastery they built. Soon, they found themselves unaccountably popular. People from all over Ireland, Scotland, and Britain heard about this new monastery with the famous abbot, and they came to visit. Many of them decided to become monks themselves.

Columcille decided that Iona could only hold 150 monks. When there got to be too many men on the island, he would send off groups of thirteen monks to found new monasteries elsewhere in Scotland. Would-be monks kept coming, so Columcille kept sending off new groups of monastery founders. By the time he died, more than sixty monastic communities had been founded by his men all over Scotland, and he had met his goal of 3,000 conversions many times over.

E-SITE

Columcille was supposedly born in County Donegal near the village of Church Hill, where St. Columba's Stone has long been a destination of pilgrims seeking cures for loneliness, homesickness, and the pain of childbirth. Nearby are some fish-shaped rocks. They got that way after the saint asked some local fishermen for some of their catch; when they refused, he turned their fish to stone.

St. Columbanus, Missionary to Europe

Columcille had spread Christianity through Scotland; Columbanus (or Columban) took it even further. He took his mission to Gaul, through Switzerland, and into northern Italy, converting barbarians everywhere he went.

Columbanus was born in Leinster around 540. As a young man, he traveled to Ulster to study and then entered a monastery in Bangor, County Down. He worked and prayed there for twenty-five years.

On a Mission to Gaul

Around 590, Columbanus and twelve companions went to Gaul to found a monastery there. He was so successful that he actually founded three: Annegray, Fontaines, and the important Luxeuil. He worked with the uncivilized barbarians living in the forest, trying to convert them to Christianity.

This went against the practice of the local bishops, who preferred to stay in larger towns and cities and preach to their local believers. The bishops disapproved of Columbanus and summoned him, but he refused to go; instead, he sent them a letter in which he basically told them that they weren't doing their jobs. In Columbanus's opinion, a bishop ought to be out in the countryside trying to reach the pagans.

Further Travels

The bishops conspired with the evil queen Brunhild of Burgundy to have Columbanus deported. He and his followers went to Nantes to catch a ship back to Ireland, but it sank. Columbanus and four companions survived and headed for northern Italy. In the Alps, his German translator, Gall, got sick and refused to go on. Columbanus had a big fight with him, and then left him behind.

FACT

Gall stayed where he was and worked on converting the local people, the Alemanni. He became quite famous, and after his death a monastery called St. Gall of the Alps was erected in his honor. Before Columbanus died, he sent a message to Gall apologizing for fighting with him and praising his work.

By 612, Columbanus and his companions were in Bobbio (in Lombardy, Italy). There they built the first-ever Irish-Italian monastery. Columbanus spent the rest of his years writing outrageous letters to his fellow churchmen. He is best known to us through his extraordinary correspondence, written in impeccable Latin and thoroughly grounded in Scripture. He never stopped criticizing his colleagues, and he seemed to have had no sense of humility or respect for rank. He even sent letters of scathing criticism to two popes. Columbanus died in Bobbio in 615.

Wild and Crazy Irish Saints

You can't swing a cat in Ireland without hitting a saint. Most towns and professions have their own patron saints who take a special interest in their affairs. For example, St. Mac Dara is patron saint of fishermen in the Aran Islands. Other saints became famous by founding monasteries or teaching other saints. St. Enda from the Aran Islands taught many holy men, including St. Ciaran. Others became famous for their miraculous deeds, great wisdom, and courage, or their unbelievable love of discomfort.

Kevin of Glendalough, the Tree-Hugger

Kevin was a member of the royal house of Leinster. He was born around 498. As a boy, he was taught by three holy men, and when he grew up, he moved to Glendalough, a spectacular site in a valley surrounded by sheer cliff faces and between two lakes.

Kevin is said to have taken up residence in a tree. He was very close to the animals—once a bird even laid an egg in his hand. He later moved into a tiny cave called St. Kevin's Bed. He spent his days either standing naked in one of the frigid lakes or hurling himself naked into a patch of nettles.

Kevin's fame spread, and he soon had a number of followers who persuaded him to let them build a monastic community on the shore of one of the lakes. They got him to move out of his cave into a little stone hut that they built for him.

E-SITE

The original site of St. Kevin's Monastery (Teampall na Skellig) is still visible in Glendalough, in the Wicklow Mountains. The cave that Kevin supposedly lived in is visible in a rock face about 30 feet above the surface of a lake. His living conditions may have been rough, but don't feel too bad for him—the site is stunningly beautiful.

St. Declan

Declan brought Christianity to southeast Ireland in the fifth century. It's said that he was adrift at sea, praying, when a stone floated by with his bell and vestments. He vowed that he would land wherever the rock landed and would there find his resurrection. He and his stone washed ashore at Ardmore, County Waterford, and there his stone still sits on the beach today. It would cure the rheumatism of any believer (except a sinner) who could manage to crawl under it, a feat that would be difficult for anyone afflicted with that ailment.

St. Ciaran

Ciaran (or Kieran) was born in Connacht in 512 and became famous for founding the great monastery of Clonmacnoise in County Clare. Clonmacnoise was exceedingly isolated—it was surrounded by bog and could only be reached by river or by walking along a ridge called the Pilgrim's Road. (Bogs notwithstanding, this is another beautiful site.) This monastery flourished for 600 years as an international center of learning. It produced many illuminated manuscripts, including the Book of the Dun Cow, the earliest known manuscript in the Irish language; it was named after Ciaran's cow, which might have supplied the hide that bound it.

St. Brendan the Navigator

Brendan was a very popular saint in medieval Europe. According to legend, he set out with twelve disciples in search of the land promised to the saints. At Clonfert, County Galway, he founded a monastery around 512. His adventures along the way, which included an encounter with a crystal column on the ocean and a passage through a curdled sea, thrilled generations of people in Ireland and Europe. (E)

Chapter 5
The Monastic Tradition

The early Middle Ages in Europe are often called the Dark Ages. But in Ireland, this period was a Golden Age, at least for Christian monks. The Irish Christians lived a peaceful existence, devoted to scholarship and prayer. A group of Irish monasteries became a destination for scholars from all over the Continent; they produced a body of astonishingly beautiful works of art and preserved classical learning for posterity.

A Unique Irish Blend of Traditions

Ireland is a long way from Rome. As a result, the Irish developed a form of Christianity that didn't follow Rome's rules to the letter. The Irish were much more open to different beliefs and accepting of nonbelievers. They didn't set as much store in the infallible authority of the church fathers, and they were more willing to allow women a say in how things would be run.

Early Irish Christians built their religion on top of a pre-existing culture and set of religious beliefs. The Celtic gods and the druidic traditions were still present, and everywhere people looked they saw the prehistoric mounds that were supposedly inhabited by the old deities. People still celebrated the old festivals, but put a new Christian veneer on them. For example, Samhain turned into All Hallows' Eve, better known as Halloween; All Hallows' Eve and All Saints' Day are still celebrated by the modern Catholic Church.

Some of the most beautiful reminders of Ireland's early Christians are the high crosses they left all over the country. These tall stone crosses are distinguished by a ring surrounding the intersection of the cross. The ring is thought to represent the sun, in an attempt to reconcile Christian beliefs with earlier sun worship. Many crosses are carved with Celtic designs.

Irish Asceticism

After St. Patrick introduced Christianity to Ireland, many new Christians in the fifth and sixth centuries wanted to show how dedicated they were to their new religion. Patrick had told them stories of early Christian martyrs, men and women who were thrown to lions or murdered for their faith in other glorious, horrible ways. But Ireland was now peaceful, and no one was persecuting Christians there. So how could an Irish person match that level of commitment? Ever resourceful, they found a solution: leaving society and its comforts to commune with God alone.

The Irish came up with an intriguing theory of the kinds of martyrdom available to them, now called the "threefold martyrdom":

- **Red Martyrdom:** Red because the martyr sheds blood for faith's sake—this is the conventional martyrdom by torture and death.
- **Green Martyrdom:** Leaving the comforts of home to live in some isolated spot in the wilderness, studying Scriptures and communing with God.
- **White Martyrdom:** Leaving Ireland to lead a monastic life in some foreign land, the most extreme form of sacrifice.

The Green Martyrdom

For most serious Irish Christians, the Green Martyrdom was the most likely plan of action. They had read stories about Egyptian and Middle-Eastern hermits who had lived alone in the wilderness, fasting and doing penance, and they decided to adopt this model for themselves. They gave up material pleasures; in return, they hoped for grace in the next life. But they didn't count on becoming the most popular phenomenon to hit Ireland in the early Middle Ages.

FACT

Both men and women went to live in monasteries. Men became monks and women became nuns; female monasteries are sometimes called nunneries or convents. The head of a monastery is called an abbott or abbess. Some monasteries took both men and women, but the majority were single-sex.

Monasteries—Where It's At

One of the most notable features of medieval Ireland was its absence of cities. The Irish lived in the countryside, farming little plots of land and grazing their cattle, and they never settled down in large groups. On the Continent, cities served as gathering places for educated people and as nuclei for cultural exchange; bishops had their headquarters in cities and spent their time preaching to their local, relatively wealthy, urban flocks. In Ireland, monasteries began to serve this purpose, with predictably different results.

Emerging Communities

The earliest Irish monks went off to live by themselves as solitary hermits. But they didn't stay alone for very long. Word got out about their wonderful isolation and asceticism, and people with their own aspirations toward monasticism would come and ask to become their students.

Before long, a solitary ascetic would become the head of a small community. These groups built themselves little enclosures containing huts for the monks, a church for believers to hear Mass, and often a library. Many monasteries also included a guesthouse, where visitors could stay to learn about Christianity and pray with the monks or nuns. The hospitality of Irish monasteries was famous; visitors were always welcome, and monks and abbotts were always willing to baptize new believers.

Monasteries actually looked like small towns. Many of them contained a number of small buildings surrounded by a wall. The most distinctive type of architecture from this period was a kind of hut shaped a little like a beehive, constructed of stones held together without mortar. The skill involved in building one of these was extraordinary, because the technique required balancing all the rocks perfectly; the monks grew so good at this job that some of their beehive huts remain standing today.

◀ A beehive hut

The Daily Services

Medieval monastics' primary purpose was to worship, and worship they did—several times a day! The following is an outline of the traditional monastic services, or "offices":

- Matins, sung before daybreak (in the middle of the night)
- Lauds, sung at sunrise
- Prime, sung at about 6 A.M.
- Terce, sung at 9 A.M.
- Sext, sung at noon
- Nones, sung at 3 P.M.
- Vespers, sung at sunset
- Compline, sung right after Vespers

E-SITE

Skellig Michael, or Great Skellig, is a tiny island in the Atlantic off the tip of the Kerry Peninsula. A particularly ascetic group of monks lived there from the sixth through the twelfth centuries. The island still contains the remnants of the monastery; their sturdy beehive huts provide a haunting memory of solitude. Many seabirds live there now.

Monks had to get up twice in the night to walk over to the chapel and sing their offices. They complained about it, but that was the point—monastic life was supposed to include some suffering and misery. But there would have been some reward even for people dragged out of their beds at midnight in midwinter—their prayer services were often done musically. The monastic offices are the origin of the famous Gregorian chants, beautiful a capella musical arrangements of psalms and other pieces of Scripture.

Latin, the Lingua Franca

Latin, the language of the former Roman Empire, became the language of the Christian church. All religious documents and correspondence, including the Bible, were written in Latin, and the Mass was performed in Latin. The Irish monks who entered the Church in the sixth century spoke the Irish language, but all of them had to learn Latin in order to write.

The Irish had to start from scratch in learning their new language. New Christians in other parts of Europe had been in contact with the Romans and their traditions and often knew the basics of Latin; French and Spanish are largely derived from it. But the Irish language is not closely related to Latin. The Irish needed a book that described Latin from the very beginning.

Studying Latin Grammar

This was apparently the first time this problem had ever come up— there weren't any basic Latin grammars. So the Irish took on the task of producing one (generations of students of Latin have them to thank for their suffering). An obscure scholar named Asper took a grammar by the Latin grammarian Donatus and adapted it for the Irish market. This grammar, called the *Ars Asporii*, used a question-and-answer format to convey Latin sentence structure and vocabulary, but with an Irish monastic twist. The author removed all pagan terms and substituted the language of monastic life. The book was a huge success (for a Latin textbook); it was established as a key authority by the seventh century.

FACT

The Irish have always loved language, which can be seen today in the huge body of Irish literature. Irish monks not only learned Latin, but also quickly added Greek and Hebrew. They even invented their own private language based on Latin that is used in a text called *Hisperica famina*, probably composed in the sixth century.

Schools and Universities

One of the most important functions of monasteries was as schools. Monastic schools were well attended (mostly by boys). Some of the students were treated as foster children by the monks, living in the care of another family until they were ready to return to their homes and adult responsibilities. Many noble warrior fathers seem to have thought that their sons would be safer in a monastery than at home. Students had to find and prepare food for the monks and help out with the business of running the monastery. But most of their time was spent studying and working.

By the sixth century, Irish schools had a firm curriculum. Students studied Latin grammar, biblical exegesis, and the ecclesiastical calendar. A monastery's library would contain several basic texts, including the Bible (the Latin Vulgate, translated by St. Jerome), various commentaries on Scripture, Jerome's book on early Church writers called *De uiris illustribus,* and a church history by Eusebius. The computation of the ecclesiastical calendar was of special interest to Irish monks and medieval religious scholars in general, and big monasteries would stock several works on the subject. The seventh-century scholar Columbanus mentioned calendrical problems in several of his letters.

E-SITE

There are still many monastic sites standing in Ireland today. Some of the best include Glendalough, Clonmacnoise, Skellig Michael, and the Rock of Cashel. Most of the buildings still standing were built after the Vikings had come and gone, between 800 and 1200; Vikings tended to be hard on buildings.

A Life of Copying

In the days before photocopiers and scanners, the only way people could copy a book was the hard way—by hand. Every book at a monastery, from the Bible to the textbooks used in the schools, had to be hand-copied. This took up much of the monks' time. Monasteries lent books to one another for the purpose of copying; often the borrowing monastery would make two copies, one for themselves and one for the lending monastery.

The early monks didn't write on paper, but on parchment, which is made of dried sheepskin. The most important texts sometimes got transcribed on vellum, which is made from dried calfskin.

How Irish Monks Saved the Classical Tradition

The Irish monks, copying away in their monasteries, didn't realize that their work would have lasting implications for all of European history. But they did, in fact, preserve classical learning for posterity.

After the Roman Empire fell, the state of education fell along with it. The Romans and the Greeks were consummate scholars and wrote learned treatises on all manner of topics—history, science, and literature. In the early medieval period, much of that literature was in danger of being lost forever. People on the Continent didn't know its importance, and many of them were too busy fighting barbarians. In Ireland, though, peace prevailed.

The Irish monks even transcribed their own local epics in Irish. These texts, including Irish epics such as the Táin Bó Cuailnge, are some of the earliest examples of vernacular literature.

FACT

Medieval monks, like modern people, sometimes didn't have pen and paper when they wanted them. Once a group of monks asked St. Molaissi of Daiminis if they could copy the beautiful book he carried, but no one had a pen. The saint raised his arms to heaven, and a feather fell from a passing bird into his hand.

Illumination in a Dark World

The Irish monks weren't content to simply copy texts. They had to embellish them, to make them into works of art. They were fascinated with the shapes of letters and experimented with ways of making them more beautiful. They invented a script called Irish miniscule that was easier to read and write than many other medieval scripts had been; it was so successful that monasteries across Europe adopted it.

Monks also used color and drawings to decorate their texts, in a technique called illumination. They took their inspiration from ancient Celtic art, the spirals and zigzags that decorated the tombs at Newgrange and myriad metal objects. Using paints made from various pigments, including insects, they applied brilliant colors to their complicated drawings to create books that would dazzle the eye of the reader. Letters themselves became fabulously embellished; sometimes an entire page would be filled with a fabulously decorated single letter. Sometimes artists even decorated their pages with gold leaf that would catch the light and literally "illuminate" the text.

Ireland is home to several famous illuminated books that survive today:

- The Book of Kells
- The Book of Durrow
- The Book of Armagh
- The Book of Dimma

Each of these is a masterpiece by the standards of any day, full of illustrations and text painstakingly planned and executed.

E-SITE

Visitors to Dublin can see the actual Book of Kells in the Trinity College library. Usually two volumes are on display at a time, one showing an illumination and one showing text. The caretakers open them to a new page every day. The Book of Durrow is there, too, and is also well worth seeing.

The Book of Kells

The Book of Kells is probably the most famous illuminated manuscript in the world. Its several volumes contain the four gospels and supplemental texts. The reason for its fame is the extraordinary art that graces almost every one of its pages.

The history of the Book of Kells is murky and full of legend, but the most common story is that it was written around 800 at St. Columcille's monastery on Iona, off the coast of Scotland. Vikings started hitting the monastery at about this time, and the monks fled with the book to Kells in Ireland. The first written reference to the book is a report from the year 1007, noting that the great "Gospel of Columkille" had been stolen and found soon after, buried in the ground. At some point, the metal shrine containing the book disappeared, perhaps stolen by Vikings. Along the way, the book lost about thirty of its folios.

In 1661, the Book of Kells ended up at Trinity College in Dublin. It wasn't always cared for properly and was occasionally mistreated; in the eighteenth century, a bookbinder actually trimmed its pages, which caused irreparable damage. It was rebound into four volumes in 1953. Its modern keepers have been much more diligent about protecting it from light and moisture and keep it in strictly controlled conditions. Astonishingly, given all the book has been through, it is still mostly intact, and the colors are still bright.

Today, the people of Kells want their book back. The librarians at Trinity College aren't sure that it would be cared for properly, but they have considered the possibility of returning the book to its medieval home. Meanwhile, it still resides in Dublin.

The End of a Golden Age

Medieval Ireland became known as the Island of Saints and Scholars. Irish monasteries such as Glendalough and Clonmacnoise were famous all over Europe, luring students from England and the Continent. Clonmacnoise was known as the University of the West. But it didn't last.

Beginning in 795, Viking raiders started coming to Ireland. They weren't interested in learning or art, but they knew where to find riches—in monasteries. Over the next 200 years, Vikings attacked and burned hundreds of monasteries and killed countless monks. Ireland's Golden Age was coming to an end.

ESSENTIAL

A charming aspect of Irish medieval texts is the way the personalities of the Irish scribes shine through. They felt free to add their own comments to the work of other authors. Occasionally they even inserted little poems about their own lives.

Still, the Irish remember their medieval Christian forebears and their glorious heyday. They have carefully preserved the relics of that day, the exuberant decorated texts and works in metal. People travel from all over the world to visit Irish shrines and holy sites. And the world still has access to classical texts, which would not have been possible if Ireland had not created a group of joyful, imaginative scholars and an age of peace.

Chapter 6

The Viking Invasions and Brian Boru

Early medieval Ireland was a site of battles, deadly rivalries, and relentless invaders. While monks led secluded lives in their monasteries, Irish lords were vying for rule of the island. When the Vikings arrived, some Irish lords fought against them, but others took the Vikings' side. It was in the midst of this complicated situation that the great hero Brian Boru emerged.

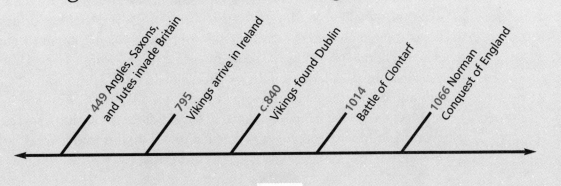

449 Angles, Saxons, and Jutes invade Britain

795 Vikings arrive in Ireland

c.840 Vikings found Dublin

1014 Battle of Clontarf

1066 Norman Conquest of England

The Rise and Fall of Irish Dynasties

Ireland in its early days of Christianity was still ruled by the same Celtic noble families as before; the difference was that now they were Christian. Their new religion, however, didn't stop the old traditions of tribal warfare and cattle stealing. Irish historians used to claim that the tribal societies of pre-Viking Ireland had strict rules for warfare that limited the damage of conflicts, and that the Vikings ruined this state of relative peace. Historical evidence, though, indicates that the Irish were at least as violent and prone to ravage the countryside as their invaders.

The abundance of observant monks in Ireland has given modern scholars a fairly good picture of Irish politics in the years from 400 to 800 C.E. Monks kept annals, genealogies, and lists of kings that record the lines of succession in territories all over the island.

The Centers of Power

The most powerful family during this period was the Eóghanacht, who had occupied the plain of Munster by the seventh century. Their home base was at the Rock of Cashel, in County Tipperary. "Cashel" is an Anglicized version of the Irish *caiseal,* which means "fortress"; it got this name because Cashel is a high hill covered with fortifications. (Cashel rivaled Tara as a seat of power during the medieval period.)

To the east of Munster lay Laigin, which became the modern province of Leinster. To the north lay the kingdom of Ulaid, which became Ulster. In the center was Meath, which was overtaken by members of the Uí Néill clan, the ancestors of the modern O'Neills. To the west was Connacht, named after a relative of the Uí Néills named Conn Cétchatchach; this province was dominated by the Uí Briúin clan. The Uí Néills were particularly prolific; they eventually laid claim to all of Ireland and called their king the "high king."

Irish genealogy was anything but simple and clear. Kings took several wives and had many sons, thereby splitting royal families into several branches. These branches fought with one another and with outside enemies. Families rose and fell in power and there was no clear sense of national unity, whatever the Uí Néills might try to claim; there was no "Ireland" as such, only small kingdoms fighting and stealing one another's cattle.

E-SITE

Legend says that St. Patrick converted Aengus, leader of the Eóghanacht, at the Rock of Cashel, so it's also known as St. Patrick's Rock. The Rock of Cashel is now a popular tourist site.

Anglo-Saxons in Britain

After the Celts spread across central and western Europe, another group of people came in their wake. These were the Germanic people, who spoke a completely different language. They spread into the Baltic region, through northern Germany, Denmark, the Netherlands, and north into Norway and Sweden.

The people who lived in the southern part of that area spoke the Germanic languages, which eventually evolved into modern German dialects; the ones who lived in Scandinavia spoke Norse tongues, ancestors of modern Norwegian, Danish, and Swedish.

Angles, Saxons, and Jutes

Around the time the Romans left Britain, the Germanic peoples started to cast longing gazes at the fertile island to their west. In 449 C.E., a whole passel of them got into their boats and sailed across the North Sea to Britain. Old English chronicles name them as the Angles, Saxons, and Jutes. They were fearsome people, eager for violence, and the native Britons (who were Celts) fled before their swords and fires. As they established themselves, people in Britain began to refer to them collectively as the Angles, or the English; this time in British history is known as the "Anglo-Saxon" period.

The Anglo-Saxon language, also called Old English, looks nothing like modern English. Old English works such as *Beowulf* (c.700 C.E.) are completely impenetrable to someone who hasn't studied the language.

The Celts retreated to Wales, Cornwall, and Scotland, which, along with Ireland, are the few places that Celtic languages are left today. The invaders took over everything else, the most fertile parts of Britain. The extent to which they overwhelmed the natives is evident in the scarcity of Celtic words in the English language.

Bring on the Vikings

Once the Anglo-Saxons had settled in England, they calmed down somewhat. They built towns, converted to Christianity, stopped raiding, and behaved like "civilized" people. But in the eighth century, they were attacked by another group of invaders: the Vikings.

The Vikings were Scandinavian people from Norway, Sweden, and Denmark, basically a northern version of the earlier Germanic invaders. Between 750 and 1050, Scandinavians spread all over northern Europe and into the Atlantic, establishing colonies in faraway Iceland, Greenland, and even Labrador. They were collectively called *Vikings*, which either comes from the Norse word *vik*, meaning "bay," or the Old English word *wic*, meaning "camp." Either is possible: Viking boats were often found in bays, and they set up camps across Western Europe.

The Vikings called themselves Ostmen, or "men from the east." They were excellent sailors, and they had a reputation for raiding, stealing, and burning whatever they found in their way.

The Assault on Ireland

The Vikings first hit Ireland in 795, landing their technologically advanced warships at Lambay Island near the site of modern Dublin. From there they launched attacks up and down the coast, first concentrating their raids on the northern and western seaboards. Between 820 and 840, they ventured down rivers into the interior of the island, attacking churches for booty and captives.

QUESTION?

Did Vikings really wear horned helmets?
Only in fiction. In the nineteenth century, northern Europeans developed a passion for their medieval ancestors, and they created all sorts of art and literature about the Vikings. The image of Vikings in picturesque horned helmets was invented during this period.

The Vikings developed a quick and efficient style of hit-and-run attack. Although the Irish fought back, the Vikings were at least as ferocious as the Celts and much better armed. Also, the Irish were never unified against the Vikings; the wealth of the monasteries attracted the attention of several Irish lords, and sometimes monks found themselves under attack by their own countrymen.

◀ A round tower dating from the Viking conquest

The monks responded by fortifying their monasteries, reinforcing wooden walls with stone and adding other defensive structures. The most famous of these fortifications were round towers, tapering stone cylinders 100 feet high that doubled as bell towers and watchtowers; a five-story staircase led up to the top.

The entrances to these towers were raised off the ground and could only be entered by climbing a ladder. When the monks were under attack, they could all climb into the tower and then pull up the ladder after themselves. Then they could climb up to the top and watch their monastery burn as they themselves slowly starved; the hope was always that the invaders would leave before that happened.

Dublin Is Founded

Eventually the Vikings stopped raiding and started settling down. They built settlements called *longphorts,* which were similar to naval camps. They used these encampments as bases for further attacks, but also as foundations for towns. The Vikings founded Dublin around 840, when they spent the winter moored there. The city's name comes from the words "Dubh Linn," which means "Black Pool." Dublin became the Vikings' chief base in Ireland, the place from which they launched raids on unconquered lands.

E-SITE

A number of round towers built as lookout posts still dot the Irish countryside today. Some of the more famous ones are at the monastic sites at Clonmacnoise, Kells, and Monasterboice.

The Problems of Disorganization

One of the things that prevented the Irish natives from defending themselves against the Vikings' earliest onslaughts was the endless state of mild to severe warfare that they maintained against one another. They couldn't stop arguing among themselves long enough to join forces against their common invaders, nor did they have any sense of a single Irish nation.

As the Vikings became more settled, though, they became more vulnerable to attack; people without property have nothing to defend, but someone with a house and farm has to keep watch over them. Norse Vikings and Danish Vikings fought over the same Irish territory. Starting in about 850, Irish kings began to launch their own raids on the Vikings with some success. A funny thing happened around that time; Irish kings and Vikings started to form alliances to fight other Irish kings, who had their own Viking allies.

By 900, the Vikings' Irish administration (such as it was) was in complete disarray, and the invaders had turned their attention to new raids in Iceland and northern Britain. This gave the Irish a window of opportunity, and they expelled the Vikings from Dublin in 902. Many Vikings left Ireland and bothered Britain instead for a few years.

Unfortunately, it was only a brief respite for the Irish. The Vikings came back in 914, took back Dublin, Munster, and Leinster, and spent another twenty years in power. After 950 they ceased to be much of a military threat, but they stayed on in the parts of Ireland that had become their home.

On the Bright Side

Despite the constant warfare, the reality is that most Irish people lived most of their lives just like they had before the Vikings arrived. In fact, some people lived better; the Vikings brought with them a number of valuable ideas from the mainland. They built the first Irish towns, they brought fancy boat-building techniques, and they could coin money. They used these things to help increase trade to and from Ireland, which brought in artistic influences from the outside.

In Dublin's Fair City

When the Vikings returned to Ireland in 914, they built a new stronghold at Dublin 2 miles closer to the sea than their earlier settlement; apparently, they wanted to be able to escape more quickly if necessary. They planned the city carefully, laying out streets and houses with great attention to detail. There was even a rudimentary drainage system, which suggests the presence of a strong leader in charge of urban development. By the late tenth century, the Kingdom of Dublin was one of the most important political units in western Europe.

E-SITE

The meeting place in Viking towns was a giant mound of earth called the "Thing"; the governing council that met there was called the "Thingmote." The huge Thing in Dublin, at Church Lane and Suffolk Street, was used for pageants and miracle plays until 1685, when it was destroyed. After that, the mayor of Dublin continued to review his troops at the old Thing site.

A Time of Trade

Thousands of people lived in Viking Dublin. There were merchants and craftsmen of all types—carpenters, shipwrights, blacksmiths, weavers, leather-workers, and others. Dublin's location put it right on the trade routes from Scandinavia down to England, and the Vikings traded vigorously with the people of England and continental Europe. They got wine, silver, and wool from England and Europe, which they sent on up to Scandinavia; from Scandinavia they received amber, ivory, furs, and slaves, which they moved on to European markets.

The Vikings also traded with the Irish people. This brought them into close contact with their new neighbors, and it appears that the two groups coexisted in relative harmony. (Some of those slaves traded by the Vikings did happen to be Irish, but the sad fates of a few individuals didn't necessarily hurt Viking–Irish relations on the whole; the Irish didn't all love one another.) The Irish taught the Vikings about Christianity. Members of the two groups married one another and sent their children to be fostered in one another's homes. Scandinavian artistic styles appear in Irish art around this time, and some of Ireland's most "characteristic" metalwork patterns of interlaced spirals with free-flowing tendrils, sometimes incorporating the shapes of animals, date from this period.

Brian Boru Unifies Ireland

The Vikings displaced some of the Irish chiefs who had held sway throughout the island. This allowed other Irish families to try to take their places. The most important of these families were the rulers of Dál Cais in the lower Shannon region, who took over the lands of the displaced Eóghanacht.

Lords of Munster

In the first half of the eighth century, the Irish lord Cennétig, son of Lorcán, became king of north Munster, a region called Thomond; he died in 951. Cennétig had two sons, Mathgamain and Brian. Mathgamain added east Munster to his kingdom, along with the Viking-controlled areas of Limerick and Waterford. He became known as king of Cashel.

Mathgamain died in 976. His brother Brian succeeded him and became known as Brian Boru, the greatest of Ireland's high kings.

Big Bad Brian

Brian was born around 941. His nickname, Boru, came from the old Irish word *bóruma,* which might have meant "of the cattle tribute." Or it might have come from the name of a fort in County Clare called Beal Boru.

Brian Boru was an excellent soldier. In 978 he led his warriors to victory in the Battle of Belach Lechta, in which the Dál Cais took the kingship of all of Munster from the Eóghanacht.

FACT

While Brian was in Armagh, he left an offering of gold coins at the altar of St. Patrick and took a look at the famous Book of Armagh. While the book was out, the monk on duty added a note to it, recording that he was in the presence of Brian, emperor of the Irish (Imperator Scotorum in Latin).

The rulers of other provinces took note of this; if Brian had all of Munster, he might want more territory. The high king of the Uí Néills,

Máel Sechnaill, brought an army down to Munster and cut down the tree of Magh Adhair, a sacred tree on the Dál Cais family's royal inauguration site. This was a way of saying that the Uí Néills didn't recognize Brian's claim to the throne.

However, Brian refused to back down and quickly took over most of the southern half of Ireland. In 997, Brian met with Máel Sechnaill and the two kings agreed formally to divide Ireland between themselves. Brian got the south and the Uí Néills got the north.

But Brian wasn't content to stop there. In 1001 he defeated Máel Sechnaill and went about northern Ireland reinforcing his claim to it. In 1005 he went to Armagh and stayed at Emain Macha, the ancient capital of Ulster.

The Battle of Clontarf

The problem with building an empire is that you can't watch your old territories while you're off conquering new ones. As Brian marched around, adding Ulster and other lands to his kingdom, Dublin and Leinster rebelled. He pushed them back in late 1013 and then fought a huge battle at Clontarf on April 23, 1014.

Soldiers came from the Isle of Man and other islands in the channel to help the rebel forces. Brian's army from Munster finally won, but Brian himself was killed. His followers took his body to Armagh, where they held a wake that lasted twelve days, and then buried him.

E-SITE

There are a number of sites associated with Brian Boru. He is said to have studied at the monastery of St. Finan Lobhar in the Killarney region. Killaloe in County Clare is the site of Brian's castle Kincora and Beal Boru, or Boru's Fort. You can see his grave at Armagh's Church of Ireland Cathedral. Nenagh, County Tipperary, boasts the site where his soldiers killed 1,000 Leinster men.

A National Hero

Many legends sprang up about the Battle of Clontarf. Later observers claimed that it was a battle between Irish and Viking invaders, with the king of the Irish winning a great victory for his nation and sacrificing his life in the process.

According to a popular version of the story written long after the event, Brian was too old to go to battle. While his soldiers fought, he knelt in his tent, praying with his Psalter. The Viking warrior Brodir ran into Brian's tent and hacked at the old king. An Irish boy named Tadhg raised up his arm to protect Brian, but the Viking sliced through his arm and cut off Brian's head in the same stroke. The boy's wound healed instantly when Brian's blood touched it. This episode portrays the Vikings as monsters and glorifies Brian's heroic, patriotic sacrifice as leader of the Irish resistance.

FACT

The Irish people still consider Brian Boru a great cultural hero. One of the images associated with him is the Brian Boru's Harp. It occupies a prominent place in everyday Irish culture—as the symbol of Guinness Stout. You can see the original harp in the Trinity College library, although it is unlikely that Brian actually owned it.

Modern scholars think it more likely that the battle was an internal conflict; Vikings no doubt were involved, but simply as soldiers for one side or the other. Brian himself was married to a Viking woman and might have given his daughter to a Viking in marriage. The men of Leinster were allied with the Vikings of Dublin. Certainly, the Vikings didn't leave Ireland after the conflict; they were too thoroughly integrated into Irish society by that point. Most historians now say that the Battle of Clontarf, though it made for some lovely literary interpretations, actually wasn't very important and held no real political significance.

Brian's own family was severely disadvantaged after the battle, mainly because most of them had died in it. His descendants, the O'Briens, managed to hang on to some power in Munster, but they were definitely not in a position to claim the high kingship.

Brian turned into a national hero. Later, Irish Nationalists would hold him up as an example of an Irish leader defeating foreign forces. They saw the period between Brian's death and the Norman invasion under Strongbow in 1170 as an age when there were no foreigners in Ireland.

Scramble for the Top

Brian's victory did have some real repercussions for Ireland. The Uí Néills had lost their stranglehold on the high kingship, and though they recovered it occasionally over the next 150 years, the title itself had lost most of its meaning. Without the Uí Néills in power, the leadership of Ireland was an open question, and many men were ready to take the job for themselves.

Economic changes in this period actually made warfare more dangerous. People were growing more food and producing more resources than they had in earlier centuries, and consequently the population was increasing. Lords required their growing populations to pay dues of livestock and money, a situation similar to the feudal system in effect in England and Scotland. With the added resources and manpower, chiefs had the wherewithal to march farther afield and sustain longer campaigns, with accompanying higher fatalities.

To defend themselves, Irish lords built larger castles and fortifications. The kings of the provinces struggled against one another, but no one came out on top. Every time it looked as if one man would prevail, one of his so-called allies would do something treacherous and it would all come tumbling down.

By 1170, however, the question of an Irish high king was irrelevant; the Anglo-Normans had arrived, and from that point on Ireland's destiny was inextricably linked with that of the larger island to the east—England. Ⓔ

Chapter 7

The Fight Against the English

Just as the Irish were beginning to see the emergence of truly powerful high kings, something happened that altered the course of their history forever—the Normans arrived. The Norman English, who had recently consolidated their rule over Britain, began a conquest that eventually led to English domination of Ireland.

1170 Strongbow arrives

1250 Peak of Norman power

1315 Edward Bruce invades

1536 "Silken" Thomas Rebellion

1536 Henry VIII becomes head of the Church of England

1603 James I initiates the Ulster Plantation

1641 Irish Rebellion

1649 Cromwell arrives

1691 Battle of Aughrim

The Normans Arrive

The ironic thing about the Norman arrival is that an Irishman invited them in. Dermot MacMurrough, king of Leinster, was unseated from power in 1166 by Rory O'Connor, king of Connacht. MacMurrough had heard that the Norman knights over in England were particularly tough, so he asked his English neighbor King Henry II if he could borrow some of them to get his throne back. Henry, alert to the possibilities of the situation, sent over Richard FitzGilbert de Clare—known to the world as Strongbow.

QUESTION?

Who were the Normans?
The Normans—originally Norse-men—were the descendants of Vikings who settled in northern France (Normandy). They quickly picked up the European traditions of feudalism. Their most lasting impact came with their conquest of England under William the Conqueror in 1066.

An Easy Victory for the Normans

MacMurrough had guessed right about one thing—the Norman knights were tough. In 1170 Strongbow and his team of heavily armored knights plowed through the relatively lightly armed forces of Irish lords. The Irish probably could have put up a good fight if they'd joined together. But Ireland at that time was divided up between 100 or more kings, who tended to wait in their home territories for the Normans to arrive. When they did, the result was invariably Norman victory.

What MacMurrough didn't expect, though, was that the Normans might like Ireland and want to stick around. MacMurrough allowed Strongbow to marry his daughter Aoife, and when MacMurrough died in 1171, Strongbow had himself declared lord of Leinster. No one in Ireland could afford to object.

But someone back in England wasn't so happy about all this—the English king. Henry II watched Strongbow's string of successes and began to worry that his knight was getting too many ideas about his own power. So Henry sailed to Ireland to oversee the campaign and assert his own rights.

Richard FitzGilbert de Clare wasn't the only English Strongbow to knock out the Irish. Strongbow cider, a tasty and potent brew, is the top-selling product for the English beverage company Bulmers. It's a consistent favorite in Irish pubs.

Norman Consolidation of Power

To consolidate the Norman victories, Henry declared Strongbow the king of Leinster but granted the province of Meath to Hugh de Lacy, a loyal knight. In 1175 Henry signed the Treaty of Windsor with Rory O'Connor, MacMurrough's old rival. The treaty declared O'Connor high king of Ireland, but it also said that he was a vassal of the king of England. Through these maneuvers, Henry established a system of competing lords in Ireland, who all ultimately owed their allegiance to the English Crown.

Over the next seventy years, Anglo-Norman knights extended English control over about three-fourths of Ireland. It wasn't so much an organized campaign as a series of advances by Norman adventurers who wanted their own fiefdoms. They only took property that they judged worth fighting for, so substantial portions of northwest Ulster and southwest Munster remained Irish.

Hugh de Lacy, Norman king of Meath, built Trim Castle in 1172 to provide a defensive stronghold and to impress his new subjects. Trim Castle still dominates the town of Trim, northwest of Dublin. It provides such a convincing display of Norman power that Mel Gibson chose to sack it in *Braveheart* (1995).

The Irish probably thought they'd be able to take back their lands as soon as the Normans let down their guard, but the Normans did something the locals didn't expect—they built castles. Irish nobles generally moved around with their cattle, so they rarely built substantial structures. But Normans immediately set their serfs to building motte castles—earthen mounds defended by ditches and wooden towers. The mounds from these motte castles still dot the Irish countryside. Once these were in place, they built more substantial castles out of stone.

The Irish Strike Back

Norman power in Ireland reached its peak around 1250 to 1275. After this, Irish lords began to reclaim their rights to the land. There were a number of reasons for this.

First, the definitions of Norman and Irish became vague. As Norman families spent a few generations in Ireland, they had less and less in common with their cousins in England. Distinctions of loyalty and family allegiance became blurred as the descendants of Norman settlers began to think of themselves as Irish.

Another reason was the impact of foreign politics. England was constantly fighting with Scotland and mainland Europe, and the king demanded that the Norman-Irish lords contribute men and money. This weakened the power of the Norman-Irish lords.

The English Lose Their Grip

In one instance, the English war with Scotland led to a direct attack by Scots on Normans in Ireland, when the Scot Edward Bruce invaded Ireland between 1315 and 1317. While he didn't achieve any lasting conquests, his army inflicted such damage that many Norman towns did not recover for decades. His invasion also revealed to the Gaelic lords that the Normans were not unified.

The Irish kings took advantage of this Norman weakness. Starting from their strongholds in Connacht and Munster, they pushed Norman lords off their estates one by one. To improve the strength and discipline of their armies, the Irish lords hired tough mercenaries from Scotland called "gallowglasses." By the late fourteenth century, the Irish had regained much of their land.

Richard II Fails to Reconquer

The English king Richard II wasn't too happy about this. He personally led two reconquest expeditions in 1394 to 1395 and 1399, and he took back much of his lost territory. But the rebellion of Henry Bolingbroke (recounted in Shakespeare's *Richard II*) forced Richard to return home to England, where he eventually lost his throne and his life. With the English leadership gone, the Irish grabbed their property right back again.

For the next few decades, the English monarchs were too tied up in the War of the Roses to worry about Ireland, so the Irish lords continued to extend their power. By the early 1500s the area under English control had shrunk down to the city of Dublin and a small area surrounding it. This area of English influence was known as "the Pale."

FACT

The Irish Pale has given us the term "beyond the pale," which refers to actions or situations that are outside of what is normally accepted. For the English, going beyond the pale meant venturing into the strange and barbaric lands of the Irish.

Tudor Colonization

When Henry VIII became king of England in 1509, he also inherited the title "Lord of Ireland." English kings had carried this title for years without it meaning much. But, as people throughout Europe were to learn, Henry VIII was the kind of guy who liked to get his way.

The Norman-Irish lords had essentially been ruling themselves as independent monarchs for years. The most significant of these lords were the earl of Kildare and the earl of Desmond, both from the FitzGerald family (called the "Geraldine earls"), and the earl of Ormond from the Butler family. Garrett Og FitzGerald, earl of Kildare, served as lord deputy of Ireland for many years and was effectively the most powerful man on the island.

Henry VIII had three problems with Garrett Og: he was too powerful; his father had supported the York family's claim to the English throne over the Tudors; and he wasn't taking Henry's side in his fight with the pope on whether he could divorce Anne Boleyn. So Henry had Garrett Og thrown into the Tower of London.

"Silken" Thomas Lord Offaly, Garrett Og FitzGerald's son, started a largely symbolic rebellion in 1534 to show that Henry needed the support of the FitzGeralds to govern Ireland. Henry took the symbolism literally and sent over an army to set them in line. Thomas's supporters backed off, and soon the FitzGeralds surrendered on the condition that they receive mercy. Henry agreed, and then promptly had most of them killed. The loss of Ireland's most powerful family left a power gap that Henry promptly filled with his own supporters.

The Protestant Reformation

Religion added a new twist to the conflict in 1536, when the English Parliament passed the Act of Supremacy. This made Henry the head of the Church of England and introduced the Protestant Reformation to the British Isles. England had been a Catholic country, but now it became officially Protestant. The Church of England was not especially different theologically from the Catholic Church, but it was different enough to provoke fights. Most importantly, Henry now refused to acknowledge the pope in Rome as the supreme leader on Earth; instead, Henry was now the head of his own church.

ESSENTIAL

Two types of Irish lords opposed Protestant rule: the Old English and the Irish. The Old English were the Norman families, such as the Butlers and FitzGeralds, who were loyal to the king but wanted to remain independent and Catholic. The Irish were the old Celtic families like the O'Neills, who wished that the Normans had never come.

The Irish were still Catholic and wanted to stay that way. Although an Irish Parliament officially recognized Henry as the head of their church in 1537, most Irish maintained allegiance to the pope—and considered this ample reason to take up arms. This was the start of religious violence that has plagued Ireland for nearly 500 years.

The Reign of Elizabeth I

This religious dispute became much more serious during the reign of Queen Elizabeth I. Elizabeth was an avowed Protestant. She spent much of her reign fighting with Catholic leaders in Rome and in Spain, who were constantly trying to topple her from the English throne. Under these conditions, she couldn't allow Catholics to attack her from her own back yard, so she gave tacit approval for Protestant adventurers to go claim land in Ireland from Catholic landowners.

E-SITE

The town of Kinsale, just south of Cork, has an interesting history. Elizabeth's army fought there, James II arrived there with his army from France, and the *Lusitania* sank just off its harbor in 1915, launching the United States into World War I. Today, Kinsale has a thriving harbor and some great restaurants.

The Irish were still resisting Protestant rule. In 1579, James Fitz Maurice Fitzgerald, cousin to the earl of Desmond, went to the Continent and brought back a small army to oppose Protestant rule in Ireland. Elizabeth responded by sending over a bigger army of English soldiers, who broke up the Irish rebellion. She confiscated the earl of Desmond's lands, had most of his family put to death, and resettled his old estates with loyal English subjects.

Elizabeth's greatest Irish challenge came with the revolt of Hugh O'Neill, earl of Tyrone. The O'Neills were an old Irish family originally from Ulster that once had claims to the high kingship of Ireland. O'Neill appealed for help in his rebellion to the king of Spain, who sent more than 4,000 soldiers to help fight England. Spain was Elizabeth's greatest enemy, so she raised a massive army of 20,000 soldiers to crush the rebellion. In 1601 her army defeated the Hiberno-Spanish force at Kinsale.

O'Neill and his fellow Catholic earls tried to mount another attack, but they couldn't gather sufficient forces to have any chance of victory. In 1607 they fled Ireland in the "Flight of the Earls."

James I Ascends to the Throne

James I became king of England, Scotland, and Ireland in 1603. He knew that O'Neill's strongest supporters had come from the north; Ulster at this time was the most Catholic and least Anglicized area of the island.

James I, therefore, decided to fix Ulster by settling it with loyal Protestants from England and Scotland, a plan that came to be known as the Ulster Plantation. The Protestant population that he settled there developed on very different lines from the Catholic Irish in the south. This led to considerable difficulties during the Irish struggle for independence, and more recently, during the Troubles in Northern Ireland.

The 1641 Rebellion and Its Aftermath

The Rebellion of 1641 began as a political rebellion led by the prominent O'Neill family of Ulster, who wanted to recover its property from Protestants and overthrow the Puritan government then holding Ireland. The O'Neills had ordered their followers not to hurt anyone, but there was no stopping the crowd once it was unleashed. What started out as a political protest turned into an all-out attack on Protestant farmers as the Catholic commoners let their resentment bubble over. That November, Irish Catholics killed thousands of Protestants. No one knows how many died; estimates range from 2,000 (as suggested by some historians) to 150,000 (as claimed by Protestant pamphleteers). Many more lost their homes and property.

The attacks on Protestants by Catholics were bad, but they were nothing compared to the way that they were described by English propagandists in London. They called it a "massacre." Pamphleteers inflated the Protestant death toll to nearly 150,000, and used extreme creativity in describing the horrors that the Catholics had inflicted upon them. The English public had always suspected that the Irish were barbaric, and this confirmed their suspicions. Now they were out for blood.

It's hard to find accurate information about this rebellion. Many historians think that at least as many Catholics died as Protestants once the Protestants got into the fury of retaliation. In any event, it was the final nail in the coffin for Protestant–Catholic harmony in Ulster.

Civil War in England

The 1641 rebellion coincided with a crisis in the English Parliament that eventually turned to civil war. King Charles I was beheaded, and the leader who emerged from the crisis was one of the most puritanical Protestants in England—Oliver Cromwell. Cromwell had no problem believing that the Irish Catholics had committed any number of atrocities, so he put together one of the most lethal armies in Europe to punish them.

◀ Oliver Cromwell

The Irish Leadership

The Irish leadership at this time was split between the Old Irish—led by Owen Roe O'Neill, Hugh O'Neill's nephew—and the Old English, led by the earl of Ormond from the Butler family. Although O'Neill and Ormond agreed that Ireland should remain Catholic, they opposed Cromwell for different reasons. Whereas O'Neill wanted Ireland to be independent, Ormond opposed Cromwell because he saw him as a usurper against the real king, Charles II. This ideological difference made it difficult for them to work together and ultimately aided Cromwell's campaign of conquest.

Cromwell Lets Loose the Dogs of War

It took Cromwell until 1649 to clear up things at home sufficiently to launch his Irish campaign, but, when he came, he meant business. Cromwell's army of 20,000 was efficient, well armed, and prepared for a bloody war. The army's initial engagements were marked by extreme savagery; Cromwell wanted revenge for the supposed Catholic butchery of 1641, and he wanted to terrify the rest of Ireland into surrendering.

Here were some of Cromwell's less admirable achievements:

- He destroyed Drogheda, massacred the population, sent the heads of the leaders to Dublin on poles, and sold the survivors to slave plantations in Barbados.
- Also in Drogheda, he burned down St. Peter's Church to abolish the people who sought asylum inside; he later called his acts "a righteous judgment of God upon these barbarous wretches."
- Again at Drogheda, he had his soldiers kill the garrison commander by beating out the man's brains with the commander's own wooden leg.
- He massacred the people of Wexford, including 300 women seeking clemency at the town cross.
- He had all the Catholic citizens of Cork expelled from their homes.
- At Bishop's Rock in Inishbofin, off the coast of Connemara, he tied a priest to a rock and forced his comrades to watch as the tide washed over him.

Cromwell aimed to terrify the population, and he certainly succeeded. By 1653 the Irish resistance was completely destroyed.

Cromwell had a way with words. He coined the phrase "by hook or by crook"—meaning that he'd take Waterford either through Hook Head or the town of Crooke. He said that Catholics could go "to Hell or Connacht," a phrase used today in Ireland to describe a really raw deal (Connacht has some of the poorest soil in Ireland).

Cromwell's Legacy

One of Cromwell's goals in Ireland was to break the power of the Catholic Church, and for a time he succeeded. While on campaign, he had Catholic priests hunted down and banished. Throughout the country he had churches desecrated and their sacred books and art destroyed. The priests who escaped his army had to disguise themselves in order to remain on the island. Although Irish Catholicism was by no means destroyed, it would take decades to recover.

Once English control was firmly established in 1653, Parliament passed an act to confiscate all Catholic-owned land in Ireland. Cromwell wanted to transplant all Catholics to the western province of Connacht so that he could settle his own soldiers and Protestant supporters on the more fertile land of Munster, Leinster, and Ulster. Although the eventual settlement didn't force all Catholics off their land, thousands of families were forced to leave their homes and resettle on the rocky terrain of Connacht.

Cromwell lingers on in Irish memory. Up until modern times, Irish mothers would use Cromwell as a bogeyman to frighten their children—"eat your greens or Cromwell will get you!" He is also used to explain the sorry state of ruined buildings all across Ireland—"that used to be a beautiful castle, but then Cromwell showed up. . . ."

The Williamite War

The radical Protestant initiatives of Cromwell's Parliament took a backseat after Cromwell's death. His son, Henry Cromwell, carried the banner for a while, but the English were getting tired of the Cromwells and their Puritanism. In 1660 came the Restoration, in which Charles II reclaimed the throne.

Charles II was more lenient toward the Irish than Cromwell had been. He restored some former supporters to their previous positions—notably the earl of Ormond, who had joined him in exile. He was a Protestant, however, and while he didn't share Cromwell's enthusiasm for radical social engineering, he wasn't interested in restoring land or position to Ireland's Catholics.

E-SITE

St. Peter's Church in Drogheda proudly displays a blackened, shriveled reminder of Ireland's religious conflicts—St. Oliver Plunkett's head. Plunkett (1629–81) was archbishop of Armagh. In 1681 he was falsely accused of instigating a Catholic plot against the king. He was convicted of treason, hanged, and drawn and quartered. The Catholic Church made him a saint in 1975.

James II Succeeds Charles II

A wave of excitement went through Ireland when James II rose to the English throne in 1685. James II was the first Catholic monarch in England since Mary, Queen of Scots. Former landowners who had lost their positions and property thought that James would restore them to their former glory. James boosted these men's confidence when he appointed the earl of Tyrconnell, a Catholic, as his viceroy in Ireland.

To show James his support, Tyrconnell raised a Catholic army in Ireland. But Tyrconnell had misjudged—this wasn't the sort of support that James needed just then. The king's religion had made his reign shaky from the start. Anti-Catholic and anti-Irish sentiments were strong in England at that point, and an Irish-Catholic army was about the most alarming thing a good English Protestant could have imagined. Things went from shaky to really, really shaky, and in 1688 James fled to France.

William and Mary

Once James had run off, Parliament gave the crown to his Protestant daughter, Mary, and her husband, William of Orange, in what became known as the Glorious Revolution. It wasn't so glorious for Catholics, but it did result in the English Declaration of Rights—William and Mary had to grant their citizens certain basic rights if they wanted to remain on the throne. It was a crucial act in legal history.

In Ireland, however, people still supported James II. James borrowed an army from France's Louis XIV, a fellow Catholic, and sailed to Kinsale Harbor in 1689. He joined up with Tyrconnell's Irish army and began to set up a power base from which he could regain the throne.

William, meanwhile, was skillfully working the European political scene. Once he'd promised to treat Ireland's Catholics well, he got the support of the Danes, Germans, and Dutch. Even the pope supported him; although popes had lobbied for a Catholic monarch in England for more than 100 years, Pope Alexander VIII was fighting against Louis XIV, so he opposed Louis's ally James as well.

The Battle of the Boyne

King William III arrived in Ireland in 1690 with an international army of 36,000 soldiers. His forces swept through James's smaller Franco-Irish army at the Battle of the Boyne in July. James still had substantial resources that he could call up on his home territory, but he got spooked and fled to France again.

James's Catholic allies were left with the task of regrouping and facing William twelve months later at the Battle of Aughrim. This was another decisive victory for William.

The Irish army made its last stand at Limerick, but it had no chance of success. It sued for peace on the conditions that Catholics be spared religious persecution and that they have a guarantee of the same limited religious freedoms they'd had under Charles II. William agreed to the terms.

FACT

The defeated soldiers of James's army found jobs as soldiers of fortune in Europe. They were known as the "Wild Geese." In the following centuries, these men and their descendants fought all over Europe. Because of this, you can today find O'Rorkes in Russia, O'Donnells in Austria, and Murphys in Spain (not to mention the Hennessys, who moved to France and started making cognac).

The Aftermath of William's Victory

William did not stick to the terms agreed to at Limerick, however. As soon as he didn't need his European allies, he rolled back all his promises. A new round of confiscations robbed Catholics of their land, and a series of penal laws imposed harsh restrictions on the civil and economic rights of Catholics. This period of Irish history is known as the Protestant Ascendancy.

While the Williamite victory marked a downfall in the status of Ireland's traditional population, it also initiated an era of peace. The 500-year period from the arrival of Strongbow to William's total victory was marked by constant warfare. The English conquered, the Irish lords fought to take their land back, and then the English returned to conquer again. The fighting only got more vicious once the Protestant Reformation added a religious element to the conflict. The preceding years of Viking conquests hadn't been terribly peaceful either.

It is fair to say, then, that the Protestant Ascendancy brought to Ireland a kind of peace and prosperity that it had never known before. The shame is that the prosperity only applied to those at the top. Ⓔ

Chapter 8

The Protestant Ascendancy

During this period, the Anglican social elite dominated Ireland. They comprised about 25 percent of the population, but they owned most of the property and controlled law, politics, and society. For the island's native Catholic majority, however, it was a time of poverty and oppression.

1691 Treaty of Limerick

1695–1704 Penal laws instituted against Catholics

1775 American colonies rebel against British rule

1778 Volunteer movement gains steam

1798 Rebellion in Ulster and Connacht; Wolfe Tone's rebellion fails

1800 Act of Union abolishes Irish Parliament

1823 Catholic Association established

1829 Catholic Emancipation Act

1840 National Repeal Association established

Protestants Take Hold

The Treaty of Limerick of 1691 ended the violent wars that had ravaged Ireland in the seventeenth century. In the treaty, King William promised that Catholics would retain the right to practice their religion, and he gave the general impression that they would be treated fairly once they gave up their arms. Unfortunately, this proved not to be true. The king's true intention was to install a ruling class of Protestant landowners who would be loyal to the British Crown.

The victorious English government seized Catholic land to give to its Protestant supporters. The same thing had happened under the reigns of Elizabeth I, James I, and Cromwell. This time, however, the English were playing for keeps.

ESSENTIAL

About 1 million acres were confiscated from Catholic "rebels," leaving only one-seventh of Ireland's territory in Catholic hands. The Protestants who were now in power knew that the Catholics might try to take their land back, so they installed a system to maintain the status quo. The Irish Parliament instituted a new rule that all members had to take an oath refusing allegiance to the pope.

The Anglican Aristocrats

Members of the Protestant upper class had very mixed feelings about their new home and their place in it. Aristocrats who had moved from England felt as if they were living on a frontier, almost like colonists in the New World or in Africa. Some of them definitely didn't like Ireland and spent as little time there as necessary; these were known as absentee landlords, who lived off the proceeds of Irish land and labor but contributed nothing themselves.

But Ireland simply wasn't the place to be if you wanted to further a career in England, and this frustrated many gentlemen. Jonathan Swift in particular hated living in Ireland. At the same time, he was quite conscious of the problems facing Ireland, most of which were brought on by its colonial status. The older he got, the more he identified with his adoptive homeland, and this was the inspiration for many of his more biting critiques, such as his "A Modest Proposal."

The Penal Laws

The now-Protestant Parliament enacted a series of infamous penal laws designed to limit Catholic power by curtailing their economic and social rights. Catholics were not allowed to bear arms, send their children to other countries for school, acquire land from Protestants, or make wills. Instead of deciding for themselves how their children would inherit, Catholics had to divide their property equally among all their sons, which resulted in increasingly small farms. There was an insidious catch, however—if the oldest son converted to the Protestant Church of Ireland, he inherited everything.

FACT

One penal law prevented Catholics from owning a horse worth more than £5. In 1773, the Irish nobleman Art O'Leary was shot by an Englishman for refusing to relinquish his fine mare to him. The lament for him, composed by his wife, Dark Eileen O'Connell, is one of the finest and most heart-rending poems written in the Irish language.

Irish clergy were expelled from the country. The Irish were not allowed to maintain schools, and in 1728 they lost the right to vote. All Irish culture and music was banned.

The penal laws didn't outlaw Catholicism, but they did make life very difficult for Catholics. The purpose of the laws was to keep Catholics from achieving enough wealth or legal power to challenge their Protestant rulers, and in that they were successful. It took more than 100 years before Catholics were able to mount any serious opposition to their subjugated state.

The penal laws didn't just hit Catholics; Ulster was home to a number of Scottish Presbyterians (the Scotch-Irish) who also refused to accept the strictures of the Church of Ireland, and they too lost a good deal of political power. When push came to shove, though, the Ulster Presbyterians generally joined forces with their fellow Protestants against the Catholics.

What is the Church of Ireland?
The Church of Ireland is the Irish branch of the Anglican Church, the primary Protestant sect in England. During the Protestant Ascendancy, the king of England headed both churches. The Presbyterians of Ulster and Scotland are also Protestants, but they differ from the Anglicans on several theological points.

Catholic Life

In response to the penal laws, a few of the educated folks converted to Protestantism and kept their jobs and property. Most Catholics, though, were forced to give up their lands and their careers and move. Thousands ended up in the south and west of Ireland, especially in rocky Connacht.

Peasants who had been property owners now had to rent property from local landlords. Leases were often short, as little as one year, which made it impossible for people to accumulate belongings or store food from year to year. Throughout the 1700s, periodic famines killed many poor people.

The Protestants took over most of the existing large churches, but that didn't prevent Catholics from hearing Mass. Priests performed Mass out in the open countryside on large, flat stones called Mass stones; the people would post lookouts to spot approaching armies and warn the participants in time for them to escape. This could be a dangerous business; tales from this period tell of the English hunting priests for sport or of ex-priests turning in their former colleagues to collect bounties.

Relaxation (but not Repeal) of Penal Laws

As the 1700s wore on, the Protestants relaxed their enforcement of the penal laws. A Catholic middle class began to appear as Irish Catholics, forbidden from owning land, poured their energies into trade. Some of them were quite successful. As this happened, Protestants began to identify more with Catholics; they still didn't want to grant them equal rights, but they were united by their resentment of British government.

Nevertheless, the penal laws were kept on the books; Protestants were only too aware that their property had originally been in Catholic hands, and they wanted to keep the laws even if they weren't often enforced. Irish Protestants were particularly worried that the British Parliament might one day cave in to Catholic pressure and change laws to Protestant disadvantage.

The Second City of the British Empire

Dublin thrived in the eighteenth century, becoming the fifth-largest city in Europe. The ruling class supported arts and higher education and produced some of the most famous thinkers of the day.

The city of Dublin flourished during the Ascendancy. Aristocrats built themselves grand houses in the Georgian style. Urban planners designed a system of bridges and roads that allowed Dublin to expand into a city that stunned visitors from other countries, who didn't expect to find urban grandeur in Ireland.

E-SITE

One of the cultural highlights of the Ascendancy period was the world premiere of Handel's oratorio *Messiah*, which he conducted in 1742 in the Dublin Music Hall. You can still see the maestro's old pipe organ in St. Michan's Church.

The stability of the 1700s allowed professional and intellectual societies to develop and the arts to flourish. The Dublin Society was founded in 1731 to encourage the arts, manufacturing, and agriculture; its members helped develop a distinctively Irish style of architecture and sponsored many large projects, such as botanical gardens and drawing schools. The Royal Irish Academy, founded in 1785, encouraged the study of Irish culture and history.

Many of Ireland's most beautiful country estates, gardens, and urban architecture date to the Protestant Ascendancy period. One impressive estate is Powerscourt House in Enniskerry, near Dublin (its famous gardens weren't built until the nineteenth century). Phoenix Park, opened in 1747, is one of the largest city parks in the world—more than twice as big as New York's Central Park. The Custom House, built in the 1780s, was the first major project of the famous architect James Gandon. He followed this project with designs for the Four Courts, consisting of the High Court and Supreme Court of Ireland. Gandon also had a hand in renovating the cupola of the spectacular Rotunda Hospital, opened in 1757 as Europe's first maternity hospital.

Trinity College

Trinity College came into its prime in the 1700s. Queen Elizabeth I founded it in 1592 to provide an institute of higher education for Protestants in Ireland; for most of its history, it has been completely Protestant. (Catholics were eventually admitted in 1970; the majority of current students are Catholic.)

Many of the college's most important buildings were designed and built in the 1700s, including the Old Library, which now houses the Book of Kells. Trinity College was open to a variety of social classes; though everyone who went there was Anglican (and male), they were certainly not all noblemen. Many famous Irish men of this period got their start there.

FACT

One of Trinity's most famous graduates was George Berkeley. He was born in Kilkenny in 1685 and went to Trinity at the age of fifteen, where he proved to be a whiz at philosophy. As an Anglican bishop, he tried to convert Catholics to Protestantism, but he was relatively tolerant of their beliefs. He helped found the University of Pennsylvania, and Berkeley, California, was named after him.

Protestant Irish Nationalism

Once the Protestants had the Catholics under control, they started to examine their own situation vis-à-vis a larger power. Since Ireland had its own parliament, the Anglo-Irish questioned why the British Parliament had the right to pass legislation for Ireland.

The Protestants in Ireland began to see the Emerald Isle as their home, and they wanted it to be a nation distinct from Britain. Economics were a big concern; the British government regularly obstructed Irish economic development by restricting Irish trade. As Irish businessmen expanded their operations, they wanted to export their products, and British law often didn't allow that. Consequently, the Irish Protestants began to take a keener interest in the political process. This was the start of Protestant Irish Nationalism; its proponents became known as "patriots."

Now, the Irish Parliament, which the Normans brought to Ireland in the 1100s, was no paragon of democratic virtue. In the early eighteenth century, it consisted solely of members of the established Church of Ireland. The House of Lords was full of conservative bishops, and the House of Commons was composed of local clergy sent to Parliament on behalf of their wealthy patrons. Most of these men were more interested in feathering their own nests than in tackling constitutional issues, but at least they constituted a modicum of representational government independent of Britain.

Whatever Parliament did, though, the British were always ready to countermand it. Throughout the eighteenth century, the British made decisions for Ireland through officials sent to Dublin Castle from London; these decisions often took the place of anything the Irish Parliament decided.

Grattan's Parliament

The American War of Independence was bad news for British rule in Ireland. The Irish, both Catholic and Protestant, saw Britain's treatment of Ireland as analogous to its treatment of the American colonies, and they observed the American Revolution with keen interest. The American Declaration of Independence was greeted in Ireland with glee. The British responded by cracking down further on Ireland, trying to limit its trade with America.

In 1779, Henry Grattan, a young Irish Protestant, made a motion in Parliament to abolish the British restriction on Irish exports. He won this argument and proceeded to lead the Irish Parliament until the end of the century; the Parliament of this period is known as Grattan's Parliament.

Protestants and Catholics Join Cause

Many Irish people, both Protestant and Catholic, were fully behind the Nationalist patriots. In the late 1770s, groups of Protestant men, known as Volunteers, joined the Irish cause—by 1779 there were Volunteers all over Ireland. Their main goals were to secure Irish free trade and to fight English interference with Irish government.

Grattan and other leaders realized they couldn't achieve independence from Britain without the help of the Catholic majority. So in 1778, Grattan pushed a Catholic Relief Act through Parliament; this act repealed some of the prohibitions on Catholic property ownership and inheritance. Grattan continued to rally his supporters and in 1779 won free trade rights for Ireland.

Pleased with his success, Grattan drafted an Irish declaration of independence in 1780. This measure passed in 1782 and gave Ireland the right to govern itself through its Parliament and judiciary. England still sent a viceroy to Dublin and Dublin Castle was still answerable to the Crown, but it seemed to be a step forward.

The French Revolution, which began in 1789, gave more encouragement to Irish patriots; the Ulster Presbyterians were especially excited by the execution of Louis XVI and Marie Antoinette and the declaration of a French Republic. France seemed to be a model of religious tolerance, and the more idealistic Irish Protestant leaders accordingly decided that equality for Catholics would be good, or at least helpful to their cause.

Wolfe Tone's Rebellion

In 1791, a young Protestant named Theobald Wolfe Tone founded the Society of United Irishmen in Belfast. The United Irishmen's goal was to unite Irish people of all religions, to emancipate Catholics politically, to end the dominance of landlords, and to achieve political independence for Ireland. Wolfe Tone became secretary of the Catholic Association in Dublin, and through his efforts the Catholic population regained a number of the rights they had lost a century earlier. Catholic Relief Acts in 1792 restored the right to education, to practice law, to vote in local and parliamentary elections, and to bear arms. Catholics still couldn't sit in Parliament.

England didn't sit idle while this was going on. It formed militia of citizens and passed the Convention Act to prevent public assemblies. In 1794 the British government repressed the United Irishmen in Dublin. The result was that the Irish people met in secret, and more of them began to agitate for more extreme reforms.

Not All Protestants Agreed

Wolfe Tone decided that the key to success was attracting the poor to his movement, and he emphasized the United Irishmen's commitment to protecting Catholics. Catholics were ready for action, and many joined his cause. But other Protestants weren't nearly as sure that they wanted to align themselves with Catholics. This tension was especially bad in the north, where Catholics had flocked in the wake of the new free trade laws. Local Protestants feared Catholic competition in the profitable linen industry, and had been raised to fear Catholic theology as the teachings of the devil. The growing population didn't help, either, especially because Protestants saw Catholics as producing far more children than they did.

FACT

The Irish population exploded during the eighteenth century; travelers reported entering cabins packed with children and pigs. Many historians have credited the potato with making this possible—it was easy to grow on small plots of land and very nutritious.

This tension found an outlet in secret agrarian societies. Catholics joined secret agrarian societies such as the "Whiteboys" or the "Ribbonmen" to protest unjust taxes or other points of contention; Protestants had their own groups. In South Ulster, the tension turned into a clear-cut conflict between Catholics and Protestants. Protestants in that area formed an armed group called the Peep O'Day Boys, and the

Catholics responded with a group called the Defenders. These groups fought often; their most bloody battle was the 1795 Battle of the Diamond, in which the Protestants trounced the Catholics.

The victorious Protestants set up an organization called the Orange Order to protect their supremacy; they called themselves Orangemen. It included many government officials and leaders of the established church as members. The Catholics felt that the government was siding with the Orangemen and failing to protect them from Orange atrocities. This increasingly drove Catholics to side with Wolfe Tone and the United Irishmen, who were explicitly open to all religions and actively courted Catholic support.

1798 Rebellions and the End of Wolfe Tone

In the second half of the 1790s, Wolfe Tone planned an armed rebellion against the English. He got to work drumming up military assistance for this enterprise, traveling to America and to France to rouse support for the Irish cause. His first efforts met with little success. In December 1796, he tried to land in Ireland with a group of French soldiers, but bad weather prevented his landing. The British government increased its repression of the United Irishmen; it had a network of spies that kept the authorities in Dublin Castle well informed of Irish movements.

Things came to a head in 1798. The United Irishmen had planned a huge rebellion in Dublin and had collected more than 20,000 pikes to use against British soldiers. Before they could get started, British troops marched into Dublin. They arrested the leaders of the Dublin United Irishmen and searched houses all over the city, turning up quite a pile of pikes.

Many Irish decided to go ahead with their rebellion and started small-scale efforts all over the country. They were poorly armed and disorganized without their leaders in Dublin, and the British quickly put them down. Between 30,000 and 50,000 Irish people rebelled, and many of them lost their lives. The French sent a small group of troops to Ireland to help the rebels, but they were quickly captured. Wolfe Tone was among them, dressed as a French officer; the British took him to Dublin and sentenced him to death, but he committed suicide in prison before he could be executed.

The Act of Union

The British Parliament had no intention of letting Ireland rebel further. In 1800 they passed the Act of Union, which created the "United Kingdom of Great Britain and Ireland." This act dissolved the Irish Parliament and instead created seats for Irishmen in the British Parliament in London.

The Act of Union polarized Protestant–Catholic relations by forcing Protestants to align themselves with Britain. It also paved the way for the career of one of the most important patriots in Irish history: Daniel O'Connell, also known as the Liberator.

Daniel O'Connell, the Liberator

O'Connell came from an aristocratic Catholic family in County Kerry. As a boy, he studied briefly at a hedge school (see Chapter 10), where he learned Gaelic history. He then went to school in France, where he observed the French Revolution firsthand; it's thought that the bloody events he witnessed there contributed to his avoidance of violence later in his political career. He was one of the first Irish Catholics to practice law after Catholics won back that right in the late 1700s.

QUESTION?

How did the O'Connells manage to hold on to their estates when the Protestants came to power?
The O'Connells kept their property by smuggling brandy from the Continent for local Anglican gentry, which evidently entitled them to favorable treatment.

O'Connell was strongly opposed to a union between Ireland and Britain. In 1823, O'Connell established the Catholic Association, a political organization whose goal was to force Britain's Parliament to admit Catholics. The association was open to all Catholics, rich or poor, and quickly became very popular. Even the poorest could afford the symbolic dues of one penny a month. O'Connell was a brilliant orator, and his followers loved his style and his rhetoric, in which he claimed that the poor would soon inherit the Earth. He promised that if the Act of Union were repealed, the Irish would have rent security, unjust rents would be ended, votes would become secret, more people would be allowed to vote, and landlords would be taxed to support the poor.

◀ Daniel O'Connell, the Liberator

At this time, people who leased very small parcels of property (paying as little as 40 shillings a year) were allowed to vote. Votes weren't secret, and landlords could and did "influence" the votes of their tenants. This meant that landlords had an interest in keeping lots of tenants on their land, because they could then control blocks of votes. The more tenants they had, the more votes they controlled.

Generally tenants complied with their landlords' wishes. But in 1826, encouraged by O'Connell, poor Catholics stood up to their landlords and elected to Parliament many legislators sympathetic to the Catholic cause. It was a start.

Catholic Emancipation

In 1828, O'Connell himself ran for Parliament as a representative from County Clare and won. This presented a problem for the British because, since the days of Queen Elizabeth I, anyone taking public or church office was required to swear an Oath of Supremacy, which acknowledged the British monarch as the head of church and state. Anyone who refused to take the oath could be charged with treason. Catholics who believed that the pope in Rome was the head of the Church obviously couldn't swear this oath, so it kept them out of office. But O'Connell called the British bluff; he refused to take the Oath of Supremacy, and Parliament capitulated by allowing him into office without it.

They did this by passing the Catholic Emancipation Act in 1829; this act allowed Catholics to enter Parliament and hold other important political offices without taking the oath. This accomplishment won O'Connell his famous nickname, the Liberator.

Many members of Britain's Parliament had wanted to emancipate Catholics for some time already. The problem was that Protestants living in Ireland relied on British law to keep them in power, so any time the British Parliament would try to help the Irish Catholics, the Protestants would protest. O'Connell's election gave lawmakers the perfect opportunity to emancipate Catholics.

The Catholic Emancipation Act wasn't a perfect law; it mainly benefited the richer, middle-class Catholics. It actually made matters worse for the poor because it raised the rent requirement for voting to £10 a year. This disenfranchised most poorer property renters—now only about 1 percent of the Irish population could vote. It also took away any incentive landlords had to keep small tenants on their land and made the thought of using the land for profitable livestock more appealing. Landlords began getting rid of their tenants, which is one of the reasons the Great Famine was so devastating.

Continued Reforms

O'Connell's next goal was to get the Act of Union repealed, mainly so that the Irish Parliament could be reinstated. His poorer Irish compatriots wanted faster action than he could provide working in the British Parliament. They were disappointed that Catholic Emancipation hadn't been more profitable to them, and they began to take action for themselves.

O'Connell had kept agrarian secret societies, such as the Ribbonmen, quiet while he worked for emancipation, but now they rose up and again began to commit crimes against landlords. One continuing bone of contention was that Catholics had to pay tithes for the upkeep of Protestant clergy. In the 1830s, many Catholics refused to pay these tithes; this campaign became known as the Tithe War.

O'Connell kept working with the British Whig government to good effect. Through his efforts, Catholics won the right to be elected to important civic offices, and the Protestant Orange Order was quelled; the Orangemen didn't regain their strength until the 1880s. Tithes to the Church of Ireland were reduced, and some Poor Laws were passed to help the destitute. Most important for O'Connell, the Municipal Corporations Act of 1840 introduced more democratic local elections; as a result of this reform, O'Connell was elected mayor of Dublin.

E-SITE

In 1924, just after Ireland received independence, the city of Dublin honored O'Connell by renaming its major thoroughfare, Sackville Street, after him. O'Connell Street, which bisects the northern half of the city, impresses visitors with its Georgian architecture, its elegant shops and restaurants, and its surprising width—at one time it was the widest street in Europe.

The Fight for Home Rule Continues

These reforms were nice, but they didn't get to the root of Ireland's concerns—its continuing domination by the United Kingdom. In 1840, O'Connell founded the National Repeal Association, supported by the Catholic clergy and the Irish people. He declared 1843 "Repeal Year," and held "monster meetings"—huge and raucous gatherings—throughout Ireland to show the British government that he had ample support.

O'Connell's movement was undone by his insistence on nonviolence. The night before his last scheduled monster meeting, which was to have been held on the site of Brian Boru's famous victory at Clontarf (see Chapter 6), the British government made the gathering illegal, and O'Connell acquiesced rather than allow fighting to erupt.

That was the end of his great influence in Irish politics. His followers had seen him as a messiah, but now they felt that he had surrendered to the British. Many of them also disagreed with his insistence that Ireland was first and foremost a Catholic nation, arguing that politics should come before religion. These young men founded a new group, the Young Irelanders, which was to play an important political role in the second half of the nineteenth century.

Years of Peace and Resentment

Over a century and a half, from 1692 to 1840, Ireland lived through a time of unprecedented peace. There were no major wars, urban culture flourished, and high agricultural productivity led to a population boom. The positive aspects of the Protestant Ascendancy, however, could not cover up the fact that it was a society based on inequality and oppression. Resentment at this injustice flared up in the forms of Wolfe Tone's rebellion and O'Connell's independence movement. But true freedom was not to come about until after Ireland had endured its greatest tragedy—the Great Famine. Ⓔ

Chapter 9

Roman Catholic Church in Ireland

There can be no discussion of Ireland's history and culture without considering the role of the Roman Catholic Church. The Church has been integrated in Irish society for 1,600 years, and the word "Irish" has become almost synonymous with "Catholic." The Church has guided Irish nationalism and influenced the world's opinions of the Irish people, and it's still a major force in Ireland today.

Before the Reformation

In the Middle Ages (c.500–c.1500 C.E.), just about everyone in Ireland was Catholic, as was nearly everyone in England, Scotland, and Wales. At this time, almost all Western European Christians were Roman Catholic, led by the pope in Rome. Catholic churches were everywhere, in every town. Most people were baptized after birth, attended Mass, married in a church, and were buried in church cemeteries.

QUESTION?

What is a Catholic?
Catholics or, more precisely, Roman Catholics, are Christians who accept doctrine and authority from the pope and the Vatican in Rome, Italy. The term *Catholic* means "universal" or "all-embracing." Catholics are supposed to believe in the Trinity, the infallibility of the pope, and the intercession of saints. Catholicism is currently the largest Christian denomination.

Saints were a very real presence, and believers prayed to them to get help with their problems. Each saint had a different specialty; for example, someone with bad eyes would pray to St. Lucy, musicians would pray to St. Cecilia, and someone with a lost cause would pray to St. Jude for whatever help he could offer. The bones and physical possessions of saints supposedly could work miracles, and believers would travel to the places where these things were enshrined.

The liturgical calendar governed the course of the year. Each day was either an ordinary day or part of a ritual season like Lent or Advent. Every day had its own saint, which created a sort of family called the communion of saints. The liturgy was formulaic and ritualized and made it perfectly clear how a believer should worship.

Religious Leaders

On a local level, the Church was organized into geographical divisions called parishes, led by priests. Bishops oversaw larger territories that might encompass several parishes. A bishop had his seat in a cathedral. Each parish priest oversaw the spiritual life of the people in his area, called parishioners.

Priests said Mass (in Latin, which most people didn't understand) and provided sacraments:

- Baptism—accepting a new member into the Church
- Penance—confessing sins to the priest, repenting, and being absolved
- Eucharist—the ceremonial re-enactment of the Last Supper
- Matrimony—the union of a man and a woman in marriage
- Extreme Unction—anointing of the sick and dying

FACT

In the mid-1500s, the Council of Trent set the official number of sacraments at seven, where it stands today. The other two are Confirmation and Holy Orders. Confirmation makes an individual into a religious adult, and Holy Orders confers the status of priesthood.

Priests also ran schools, mediated quarrels, and helped the poor. In return, parishioners supported their priests with money and goods.

The Irish Church was run locally rather than externally, which made for lots of regional variation in practices. Outsiders tended to find Irish Catholicism both archaic and lax. Priests were respected, but they didn't control social structure; authority remained in the hands of chieftains and lords. The Irish mingled their Christianity with folk beliefs in fairies and changelings. Though the Catholic Church had decided in the eleventh century that its priests should be celibate, Irish priests continued to marry and have children. Divorce was allowed, and marriage between close relatives wasn't discouraged.

But however "unorthodox" their practices, the vast majority of Irish people were Catholic and knew it. They did not take it kindly when the English decided that they should change.

The English Become Protestant

The 1500s were a tumultuous time for Christianity. In 1516 the theologian Martin Luther declared that the Catholic Church had gone astray and become corrupt, and proposed a new form of Christianity. This was the beginning of the Protestant Reformation, which resulted in a new category of Christian: the Protestant. Protestants refused to acknowledge the supremacy of the pope in Rome. Protestantism quickly splintered into a profusion of groups with different beliefs, some of which harbored as much rancor against other Protestants as they did against Catholics.

The Reformation hit England during the reign of Henry VIII. Henry wanted to divorce his first wife, but the pope wouldn't permit it. So Henry announced in 1536 that he was now the head of a new church—the Church of England, or Anglican Church. Doctrinally, the Anglican Church is quite similar to the Roman Catholic one, but it does not acknowledge the pope. Henry also took the title "King of Ireland," and decreed that the Irish people should look to him as their supreme monarch.

Reformed England Meets Unreformed Ireland

Henry's interest in Ireland (and in England) was primarily political, not theological, but subsequent monarchs became much more interested in what people believed. Queen Elizabeth I began a concerted effort to transform Ireland into a Protestant land. During her reign, Irish people were required to attend Anglican churches and use the Protestant Common Book of Prayer. Preaching in the Irish language was outlawed. A number of extreme Protestants called Puritans moved to Ireland.

QUESTION?

Who were the Puritans?
Puritans were Protestants who wanted to purify the Church of England and to live a pure life themselves. They emphasized preaching as a means to educate people on how to live a biblically sanctioned life. It was a group of Puritans who landed in Plymouth, Massachusetts, in 1620.

In the early seventeenth century, King James I sent many Protestant clergymen to Ireland and banished Catholic priests; he fined people who refused to attend Protestant worship services and banned Catholic school-teachers. Priests were persecuted violently—some of them were drawn and quartered. But the Irish proved resistant to conversion. They refused to attend Protestant services and persisted in hearing Mass out in open fields.

Ireland and the Counter-Reformation

When the Protestant Reformation began to gather steam, the Catholic Church set about creating its own institutional reforms, in an effort to revitalize itself and keep its members. The Council of Trent (1545–63) modernized the Church in Europe, but Ireland was slow to implement these modernizations.

The pope watched the Reformation in England with great interest. He didn't want to lose Ireland, too. In 1606, the pope congratulated the Irish for sticking to their religion, and the Church leaders in Ireland decided it was time to modernize their parishioners.

The pope sent the Jesuits, a new group of Catholic missionary priests, to take on this project; the Jesuits found Irish Catholicism very strange. Not only was it full of odd Celtic rituals, the Irish Church itself was divided into an old Gaelic form, which rejected interference from Rome, and the (newer) Old English form, which embraced Roman doctrine.

The Jesuits worked on getting Irish priests to stop drinking and marrying, and encouraged the Catholic people to avoid Protestants. Although the Irish resisted change and persisted in holding their traditional wakes and casual marriages, the Catholic Church in Ireland did increase its presence and modernize some practices. The traditional Irish flexibility and adaptability proved useful in the survival of the institution.

The Calamitous Seventeenth Century

In 1600, Ulster was a stronghold of rebel Catholicism, led by the prominent O'Neill family. Beginning in 1606, Scots were allowed to settle in Ulster as part of the Ulster Plantation plan. These settlers were predominantly Presbyterians who feared Catholics.

The English government encouraged this settlement because it helped them control Ireland economically and socially, as the settlers imposed "civilized" values on the Irish "barbarians." As English settlers continued to arrive in Ireland, they took much of the best farmland for themselves. As a result, most Irish farmers and herdsmen saw their status continually diminished and deeply resented the occupiers.

QUESTION?

Who are the Presbyterians?
Presbyterians are Calvinist Protestants who believe in justification by faith, the authority of Scripture, and the priesthood of all believers. This group is governed by groups of parish representatives called presbyteries. The church was founded in Scotland in the mid-1500s by John Knox and quickly became Scotland's official religion.

The dispossessed O'Neills moved out into the hills and lived as outlaws, robbing and murdering travelers. They likened their Catholic troops to an army of Crusaders battling against the Turks, as they saw the Protestant invaders. This did not improve the Protestant opinion of them.

Tensions Leading Up to Violence

By the 1630s, the Catholics had regained much of their previous position in Ireland. Under King Charles I, they were allowed to worship fairly freely, they had reclaimed much of the land that had been taken away from them, and the number of Catholic priests had increased. But matters definitely were not peaceful.

The Protestant clergy resented the Catholic priests, who spoke Irish and were generally more popular with the Irish people. The Protestants thought the Catholic priests allowed the people to live in blind superstition. The Presbyterians in Ulster fervently believed that the Catholic Church was evil and its adherents idolatrous, and equated the pope with the anti-Christ. Groups of them swore to wipe out Catholicism. Ulster Catholics understandably felt threatened by this rhetoric.

Matters came to a head with the violent attacks of 1641, begun by the O'Neills as a political protest (see Chapter 7). Catholic leaders at home and abroad encouraged the rebels with the unfortunate suggestion that they kill the heretics or expel them from Ireland, which escalated the conflict into a bloody religious war.

Cromwell Takes Revenge

The English Civil War began the following year, and the Irish Catholics supported King Charles during the war. The Ulster Presbyterians supported Oliver Cromwell and the forces of Puritanism. Charles lost and was executed in 1649. Cromwell declared himself Lord Protector of England and immediately headed to Ireland, where he took revenge on the Catholics for supporting the king and for the violence of 1641 (see Chapter 7).

Religious Tensions in the North

Ulster Protestants were especially affected by the events of 1641 and were inclined to feel threatened by the Catholic presence. Because they were Presbyterian, they felt separate from the Anglican government as well and were never sure it wouldn't betray them; they resented any accommodation the government offered Catholics. This led to political separatism; as much as possible, the Ulster Protestants organized their own local government around their presbyteries.

Conservative Ulster Protestants were especially likely to evangelize and preach publicly. These preachers were extremely anti-Catholic and told their listeners stories of Catholic atrocities on Protestants. Protestants and Catholics were also separated economically—while the Protestants prospered through the linen industry, the Catholics were left out in the cold.

This combination of economic imbalance, social separatism, and Protestants' insecurity about their position has plagued Northern Ireland up to the present day. Protestants have long been the majority of the population, but they still aren't confident that Catholics will not be allowed to run roughshod over them. Even in the late 1990s, Protestants in Northern Ireland still claimed that the Roman Catholic Church was contrary to the word of

God, or was equivalent to the Whore of Babylon, or wasn't Christian at all—rhetoric that hasn't changed much since the days of Cromwell.

FACT

About 40 percent of Northern Ireland's population is Catholic; most Protestants there now belong to the Church of Ireland or the Presbyterian Church. The conservative evangelical Protestants, such as the Reverend Ian Paisley, tend to be most vocal in their anti-Catholic sentiments.

Catholic Revival and Nationalism

The post-famine period in Ireland ushered in something of a devotional revolution. In the late 1840s, the number of priests and nuns increased dramatically at the same time that the general population was shrinking from death or emigration. The Church itself underwent major reforms.

Cullen's Reforms

Father Paul Cullen became archbishop of Armagh in 1849, at the end of the Great Famine, and he spent the next thirty years modernizing the Irish Church. He called the famine a work of God intended to purify the Irish people, whose Catholicism was too steeped in superstition and whose clergy was too tempted by avarice and sex; he also thought there were simply too many Catholics for the existing clergy to serve. He professionalized the clergy and introduced a variety of new rituals, including novenas, stations of the cross, parish missions, and adoration of the Blessed Sacrament. These changes brought the Irish Church more in line with Rome.

Post-famine Catholics became more devout than their ancestors had been, and Catholic priests had more power over them. People enthusiastically joined new religious societies and embraced such devotional aids as the rosary, pilgrimages, shrines, processions, devotion to the Sacred Heart or the Immaculate Conception, and spiritual retreats. Older, "magical" events and events such as wakes, agricultural celebrations, and bonfires became less important.

Few Catholic churches had been built in the 1700s, but in the mid-1800s, Catholics once again started erecting churches and cathedrals. Middle-class Catholics willingly donated funds to help construct churches, symbolically reclaiming their role in the public sphere and their historical traditions.

Catholicism and National Identity

These reforms also gave the Irish a new cultural identity by which they could recognize one another. The older Gaelic society was almost completely gone, and the Church offered a replacement social structure. It went without saying that a post-famine Irish person was also Catholic; the two were almost synonymous. Emigrant Irish took this cultural trait with them, and Irish all over the world were assumed to be devout Catholics.

This religious identity merged into the Irish national identity. For Irish farmers and laborers, Catholicism became synonymous with political freedom, rebellion against tyranny, and empowerment of the working classes.

Catholicism in Today's Ireland

The Catholic Church has remained powerful in Ireland throughout the twentieth century. It played a major part in the emergence of the Irish Free State and still dictates much of the structure of the Irish family. There are still churches everywhere in Ireland, and priests in them say Mass regularly.

Ireland is more strongly tied to Rome than many other Catholic countries in Europe. When Pope John Paul II visited Ireland in 1979, people traveled for days and camped out overnight in the hope of getting a glimpse of him. Irish Catholicism also has an extraordinary number of links to its Celtic and medieval past. Some religious holidays have direct links to pagan festivals; for example, the annual pilgrimage to Croagh Patrick originated in the Celtic festival of Lughnasa.

E-SITE

Irish Catholics flock to shrines such as St. Brigid's shrine in County Louth or Glendalough in County Wicklow. The annual pilgrimage up Croagh Patrick draws hordes of the faithful to this steep, stony mountain in the bogs of County Mayo, where they crawl up the hill on their hands and knees.

School and Home

For most of the twentieth century, the Church controlled state-supported schools, which meant that almost all children were educated by priests, monks, and nuns. Some Irish remember the Catholic schools of their youth fondly. Others recall brutal physical punishments and being afraid to tell their parents for fear that their parents would beat them, too, so strongly did they believe in the Church's authority.

The Church has been present in family life as well. Irish often have crosses or religious pictures of the pope, Sacred Heart, or a favorite saint in their homes. Most Irish parents name their children after patron saints. Weddings and funerals almost invariably take place in the church; secular services are not popular. The Irish give more money to charity per capita than in any other European nation.

With the Church at the Helm

Up through the 1950s, many young Irish people chose religious vocations. Priests have long been honored and respected, and Irish priests have a reputation for being loving and devoted to their parishioners, though they can also be quite strict. Children and teenagers saw priests, monks, and nuns regularly, at church and at school, and the Church maintained a strong recruiting organization. Families who produced priests were praised, and many parents encouraged their children to seek a religious vocation. (Traditionally, it was a status symbol to have a priest or nun in the family, because it showed that the family had enough money to pay for religious education.)

Church and State

The Church has played a very active role in modern Irish politics. The Irish Free State was set up in 1922 to be a completely secular state, but its leaders saw the Church as an Irish institution that distinguished them from the English. The Catholic archbishop Charles McQuaid of Dublin helped Éamon de Valera draft the constitution, which is explicitly Catholic. It guaranteed the Church a "special position" as the guardian of the faith of the majority of Irish citizens (the clause was removed in 1972). It also prohibited divorce and abortion and said in no uncertain terms that a woman's place was in the home.

FACT

Irish politicians have often used Catholic symbolism to convey their political messages. The Easter Rebellion of 1916 was planned on that day to suggest national rebirth. The Good Friday Agreement (also known as the Good Friday Accords) of 1998 were set for that day to represent reconciliation.

The Church still has an extremely strong relationship with the government. Many Catholic voters insist that the government enforce their idea of what a family is. Ireland's leaders have therefore long kept very conservative views on issues such as contraception, abortion, divorce, and homosexuality.

Declining Popularity

Although the Catholic Church still plays a very important role for the Irish people, its power has been on the decline for decades. Fewer and fewer people now attend Mass. More significantly, the priesthood and the monastic vocations have lost much of their stature, thereby leading to a sharp drop in the number of people entering the religious orders.

Sex Scandals

The Irish Church has been plagued by some of the same sex abuse problems that have shocked North American Catholics; the term "pedophile priest" has become disturbingly common. Irish Catholics have accused the upper levels of the Church hierarchy of attempting to cover up the scandals of accused clergy. The Christian Brothers organization, which runs several Irish schools, has publicly apologized for the many cases of abuse that occurred in its schools.

Birth Control

Birth control and abortion have generated some of the biggest debates in Ireland. For decades, the use of birth control was considered a criminal act. In 1950, a government health minister proposed a "Mother and Child" plan that would have put the state into the Church's traditional role of providing health care for pregnant women and mothers. Church leaders were afraid that the state might provide family-planning information, so they blocked the plan. The Church leaders got their way, but the resulting national controversy demonstrated that many Irish people were willing to challenge Catholic positions on social issues.

Between 1968 and 1993 the Irish Parliament passed a series of laws that made contraceptives legal and available. They did this in part with the support of the Irish people, partly because of pressure from the European Union to protect people's right to privacy and partly to protect the population against sexually transmitted diseases. Church and conservative leaders opposed the new laws at every step, but the will of the people on this issue was clear. Abortion is still illegal, but thousands of Irish women travel overseas every year to terminate pregnancies.

A referendum in 1996 allowed divorce, to conform with European Union principles of human rights and property rights; this passed by a very small majority. Homosexuality is no longer a criminal offense in Ireland.

Conservative or Liberal?

Many young people in Ireland today feel alienated from the Church. They complain that the pope is too conservative and doesn't understand the needs of Catholic laypeople. They find that old-style Catholicism, with all its emphasis on shrines and the Virgin Mary, is irrelevant to modern people.

Ironically, though, one of the problems many modern Catholics have with the Church is that it has become too modern. The Second Vatican Council, convened by Pope John XXIII from 1962 to 1965, introduced a number of reforms into Church practice, including saying Mass in the vernacular and allowing laypeople to participate in Mass. Many Catholics had loved the old Latin Mass and the Gregorian chants in which it was sung and lamented its passing, as they did other forms of ritual that had been common and now are gone from Church practice. For some Catholics, that created a void that has not yet been filled.

Chapter 10

Preserving Irish Traditional Culture

By the end of the seventeenth century, England's political domination of Ireland was complete. Although the English tried to force their language and religion onto Ireland, the Irish culture proved resilient. The Irish people continued to speak their language, play their music, and transmit their beliefs to their children.

Traditional Life

There were great differences between the lifestyles of the Protestant Anglo-Irish ruling class and the Catholic Irish population. In Dublin and in their country estates, the Anglo-Irish gentry led lives very similar to their counterparts in England. The great mass of the Irish, however, led hardscrabble lives as small farmers and laborers.

Visitors to Ireland remarked on the obvious poverty of Irish farming families. Most families lived in small cottages, frequently with only one room and no floor. People wore simple clothes made of locally produced wool. Most heating came from peat, a brown substance from the bogs that burns for a long time but emits foul-smelling smoke. The diet of Irish farmers consisted of potatoes, milk, and a rare bit of meat.

The Irish exiled to Connacht had it particularly hard, because the rocky soil there is bad for farming. Their one blessing came from the abundant seafood in Irish waters. Fisherman would row out in currachs (COR-rahs), small boats made of pitch-coated cowhide stretched over a wooden frame. Fishing in these small craft was a dangerous business, but the seafood it produced added valuable protein and vitamins to the diet.

E-SITE

The Aran Islands, 30 miles off the coast of Galway, offer a glimpse into how the Irish used to live. You can see what *currachs* looked like, and marvel at the courage it took to go out to sea in the little boats. Scrawny cattle and sheep hunt for grass in the rocky fields, which are dutifully maintained by the islands' inhabitants.

Despite the poverty that most of the Irish experienced, they still managed to have fun. Through their language, music, dancing, and sports, they were able to express themselves in distinctively Irish ways.

The Irish Language

The Gaelic language of Ireland is one of the most distinctive in Europe. It's one of the few Celtic languages that survived the onslaught of

Germanic and Latin tongues. Some of the oldest vernacular literature in Europe was composed in Irish, and an extraordinary range of Irish stories have survived into the modern day. Irish is a lyrical language that seems particularly well suited to poetry and metaphor. But it's lucky to be around today. We have the efforts of many generations of stubborn Irish people to thank for its modern existence.

QUESTION?

Are "Irish" and "Gaelic" the same thing?
Sort of. The term *Gaelic* is used to describe several languages spoken by the old Celtic populations of Ireland, Scotland, Wales, and France. "Irish" is the name of the language spoken specifically in Ireland. In Irish, *Gael* means an Irish person, and *Gaeilge* is the name of their language.

Irish Imperiled

In 1500, the great majority of Ireland's inhabitants still spoke Irish as their first language. The Anglo-Norman families like the FitzGeralds and Butlers spoke English, but the farmers and laborers outside the Pale predominantly spoke Irish. With the plantations and conquests of the sixteenth and seventeenth centuries, however, the language trends began to change.

Thousands of English-speaking families moved onto Irish land. English policies actively promoted the adoption of the English language. There's a story that schoolteachers would hang sticks from students' necks and notch them every time they spoke Irish; for every notch the student would receive a beating. The most powerful force against Irish was the fact that all the wealthy and powerful people spoke English, so a person needed to speak English to have any opportunities for advancement. Between 1700 and 1900, Irish went from being the majority language of the island to a minor tongue spoken by disenfranchised groups in the West.

While the Irish were pressured to speak English, it was hard for them to learn to read it. The penal laws prevented most Irish children from attending school. But the Irish had a resourceful response to this problem; they created hedge schools—informal schools taught in the open or in barns by volunteer schoolteachers. These schools taught English, Irish, Latin, history, geography, and whatever else they could manage. They didn't have many books and couldn't meet all the time, but they did prevent the Irish people from becoming totally illiterate.

Irish Survives

Although it suffered, the Irish language didn't die out. It lived on in remote places with little English presence, particularly in the West. The English didn't bother to put schools in backwards outposts like the Blasket Islands off the Dingle coast. The province of Connacht, which Cromwell had seen fit to leave to the Irish, remained the bastion of the old Gaelic language. The area where Irish continued to be spoken as a first language was called the Gaeltacht.

E-SITE

The Gaeltacht still exists today, but it's a pale shadow of its former self. It's now restricted to a small portion of seven counties along the west coast. At the end of the twentieth century, perhaps 21,000 people spoke Irish as their primary language. But you can still hear people speaking Irish quite naturally in Galway pubs, in Donegal, and in a few other places.

Over the years, the Irish government has instituted a number of programs to preserve the Irish language. Irish is the official language of the Republic of Ireland and a mandatory part of the curriculum for all Irish schoolchildren. For a while, all civil servants had to pass examinations in Irish before they could take their posts. The government has provided a number of incentives to promote Irish language initiatives in the Gaeltacht, such as Raidió na Gaeltachta, an all-Irish radio station.

Irish Music

There has been a major upsurge of interest in traditional Irish music in recent years. Bands like The Chieftains and Clannad have helped develop a worldwide interest in the lyrical sound of Celtic music. Musicians throughout Ireland and its emigrant communities have found opportunities to play for adoring crowds in Irish pubs everywhere. These musicians are continuing in a Celtic music tradition that goes back many centuries.

Celtic Praise Poets

Poets and bards were big shots in Celtic societies. A good poet could grant either fame or shame to Celtic nobles, so when one showed up at court and started to sing, everyone gathered to listen. These bards often played harps and other musical instruments. Brian Boru's harp—the symbol of Ireland—was supposedly played to rally his troops.

The singing poets continued their cultural influence after the Norman Conquest. The Anglo-Norman nobles, like the old Irish nobles before them, recognized the power of a good song, so they often sponsored these bards in their courts. Over time, however, the power of the bards waned. With books and letters available, nobles no longer needed poets to spread their fame.

The Elements of Traditional Music

Irish music is a free-form style. The length, pace, and musical composition of a given piece will change from night to night and from group to group. Traditional musicians almost never play from written music; in the past, many of the best musicians couldn't even read music. As in American jazz, most pieces revolve around group performances that highlight the virtuosic improvisations of individual musicians.

FACT

One of the best-known Irish songs is "Danny Boy." Interestingly, the lyrics aren't Irish; an Englishman named Frederic Weatherly composed them in 1910. The music is from an older tune called "Londonderry Air," which was transcribed by Jane Ross of County Derry around 1855. Its origins are unclear, but it may have been a traditional harp song.

Despite the free-form style, Irish music has a distinctive sound that makes it immediately identifiable (although Scottish and Welsh music sound similar). The distinctiveness comes largely from the mix of instruments used. The traditional instruments of Irish music are:

- Harp
- Bodhrán drum
- Fiddle
- Flute
- Tin whistle
- Accordion
- Bagpipes or uilleann pipes
- Pretty much anything that can jam

Traditional music performances are informal. They generally take place in pubs, with the musicians performing only for free beer and the cheers of the crowd. Members of the audience can join in if they have a fiddle, a good voice, or even just a set of spoons to add to the music.

Ballads

The Irish love of poetic language mixed with humor and tragedy to produce the beautiful Irish ballad. The ability to compose and perform a beautiful ballad has been highly prized in Ireland for centuries. The ballad is generally sung by a single person, who may or may not be accompanied by instruments. Ballads range from a handful of lines to many hundreds of lines in length. They can tell stories of lost love, injustice and revenge, or what happened when the singer went to get a beer.

Before There Was Riverdance

Dancing has been an important form of artistic expression and social interaction in Ireland for thousands of years. The Celts and the druids had their own forms of folk dancing. Some say that the prevalence of ring structures in modern Irish dancing has to do with the way the ancient druids danced around sacred oak trees—either that, or it's just easier to dance in a circle.

The Evolution of Irish Dance

The Vikings, the Normans, and the English all probably contributed to the development of dance in Ireland. By the sixteenth century, three dances were spoken of as distinctively Irish: the Irish Hey, the Rinnce Fada, and the Trenchmore. Sir Henry Sidney, Queen Elizabeth's lieutenant in Ireland, saw some comely Irish lasses dancing Irish jigs in Galway. He wrote, "They are very beautiful, magnificently dressed and first class dancers." Whenever royalty or important guests visited Ireland, it was customary to meet them with fancy dancers.

FACT

The best way to hear a range of traditional music is to attend a Fleadh (flah), a traditional music festival. The festivals attract musicians and dancers from all over the country. The largest, the Fleadh Nua, is held over five days every May in Ennis.

The steps toward the development of contemporary Irish dance are unclear. It is known, however, that dancing was an important part of the social lives of the native Irish population. Festivals, weddings, and wakes were all occasions for dancing. Towns would have dance competitions, and wandering dance masters would go from town to town, teaching all the latest steps. It was through the influence of these itinerant masters that the Irish forms of the jig, reel, hornpie, and polka developed.

Today, thanks in part to Riverdance, Irish step-dancing is the most recognizable form of Irish dance. In this style, dancers hold a rigid posture, keep their arms mostly by their sides, and step and kick about for all they're worth. Many Irish dancers maintain that their ancestors developed this rigid-armed style of dancing so that if English people looked in through a window they wouldn't be able to tell that the Irish were dancing. There may be a grain of truth to this, but most dance scholars think that the style was adapted from French dances imported in the eighteenth century.

The *Céilí*

The most authentically Irish form of dance is the *céilí*, or *ceilidh* (kay-lee), which is similar in form to folk dancing in many other parts of the world. A *céilí* is essentially a dance party in which everyone dances to traditional Irish music, spinning, exchanging partners, waltzing around, and generally having a good time. *Céilí* dance arrangements generally involve four or more dancers at a time. Irish-American organizations throughout the United States host *céilís* from time to time. The steps are easy to learn, so if you're interested you should ask at your local pub.

Parties to Raise the Dead—Irish Wakes

For the Irish, a funeral wasn't just an occasion for mourning. It was also an opportunity to get together with friends, meet members of the opposite sex, and play wild games. This both honored the dead person and allowed the living to rejoice in their continuing life.

The corpse and his or her family would be separated from the party by a screen so that the mourners could grieve and weep without distraction. Meanwhile, all the guests would drink whiskey, sing, smoke, and play various party games. These games involved mock marriages and some games that the clergy condemned as downright obscene—not unlike the games played at some teenage parties today. Flirtation was allowed but fornication was not; the Irish did not approve of sex outside of marriage.

ESSENTIAL

With the great boom in Irish tourism, all sorts of things have been called "traditional culture." Generally speaking, "traditional" refers to the cultural practices of the common people who weren't part of the Protestant Ascendancy ruling class. But remember that there have been many types of Irish people, and many kinds of Irish culture.

Irish Beliefs of the Supernatural

The Irish people have maintained a set of unique beliefs and superstitions that have lived on until the modern day. There is an abundance of stories and superstitions about the mischief of the fairies. The Irish term for the fairies is *sídhe* (shee); in English they are called by a number of terms, such as "wee folk" or the "good people." Irish legends suggest that there is an extraordinary diversity of charming and terrifying fairies frolicking in the countryside:

- Changelings—fairy children left in place of stolen mortal babies; the fairies were said to leave sickly babies after stealing healthy ones.
- *Bean sídhe* (banshee)—a female spirit associated with the ancestors of old Irish families, who wails terribly whenever someone in the family dies.
- *Gruagach*—a female spirit that guards livestock but requires an offering of milk.
- Selkies—gentle spirits that are seals by day but humans by night; they sometimes marry human fishermen.
- *Lianhan shee*—a sort of love goddess who invites men for trysts in Tír na nÓg (the home of the fairies); loving the *lianhan shee* almost invariably results in disaster.
- Leprechauns—short, mischievous creatures known for their skills in making shoes and hiding gold; if a mortal traps one at the end of a rainbow, he can take his pot of gold.
- *Cluricauns*—similar to leprechauns, except they don't make shoes and they like to steal shepherds' dogs and goats for impromptu midnight races.
- Pooka—a spooky spirit who appears as a black eagle, goat, or horse; he has the irritating habit of picking up unwary travelers for terrifying midnight rides, sometimes into the sea.

It is widely suspected that the fairies came from one of the races that inhabited Ireland before the Celts arrived. There is an abundance of rings of stones throughout the Irish countryside. Local legend generally attributes these "fairy rings" to Ireland's mystical inhabitants from the past.

Superstitious locals have avoided the rings for centuries. Less superstitious archaeologists usually attribute the rings to Ireland's Stone Age inhabitants.

FACT

The spirit world of Ireland has inspired a number of artistic creations, from the poems of Yeats to a particularly deplorable movie series about a nasty leprechaun. A good movie for kids is *The Secret of Roan Inish*, about a young girl's attempts to communicate with selkies. You'll never look at seals the same way again.

Irish Superstitions

The beauty of Irish superstitions is that the Irish adopted all the superstitions of Christian culture without giving up their old Celtic beliefs. The result was a whole cornucopia of beliefs about how to avert disaster, placate the fairies, or attain wealth and love.

A great many superstitions dealt with relations with the spirit world. The wee folk were notoriously mischievous, so a wise person kept a number of practices in mind—only calling them "the good people," for example. People called out a warning whenever they threw water out of the house, for fear of hitting an unsuspecting fairy. To stay on the fairies' good side, sensible housewives always left out little plates of food or milk for the little people to enjoy. If someone should be so unfortunate as to cross paths with hostile fairies, it was well known that throwing dust from under one's feet would force the fairies to give up any human captives. When gathering wood for a fire, people would never take anything growing on a fairy mound.

A number of beliefs dealt with specific holidays. On Halloween it was customary to put up Parshell crosses—two sticks tied together with twine— to keep spirits at bay (the Parshell cross looks suspiciously like the spooky sticks in the film *The Blair Witch Project*). On May 1, a woman could achieve great beauty by rolling naked in the morning dew. St. Stephen's Day—December 26—was also known as Wren Day because local boys would hunt down a wren and then parade it around town on a stick for good luck. On Whit Sunday it was considered unwise to go anywhere near water, because it was widely known that the spirits of drowned people would rise up on that day and try to pull down the living.

Irish Sports

The Celts were an active, warlike folk, so when they found themselves at peace, they invented warlike sports to keep themselves fit. Although they'd beaten their Celtic swords into ploughshares, Irish farmers continued to play these exciting sports. In the late nineteenth century, the Gaelic Athletic Association (GAA) revived them. GAA matches still gather roaring crowds from across the island.

ESSENTIAL

The Irish people kept their language and traditions alive during several centuries of British dominance. Because of their efforts, there was an identifiable "Irish culture" for Irish patriots to revive in the nineteenth century as a unifying force for their country. Today, the continuing rebirth of Irish traditional culture makes Ireland a fascinating place to visit.

Hurling

One of the most unique Irish sports is hurling, an ancient game played by two fifteen-member teams armed with curved wooden sticks called "hurlies." They use the sticks to smack around a hard leather ball (*sliothar*), at speeds of up to 80 miles per hour, until it goes through a hoop. With all the swinging and smacking, injuries are common; it's said that the ancient Celts used the sport as a training tool to give their warriors strong bones. The All-Ireland Hurling Final, held every year at Croke Park in Dublin, excites fanatical enthusiasm.

The woman's version of hurling is called *camogie. Camogie* matches tend to be somewhat less violent than the men's matches, but they are popular anyway.

Gaelic Football and Other Sports

Hurling is an ancient sport, and forms of it have evolved into a number of popular modern sports. The Scottish form of hurling is called shinty. Since shinty involves hitting a ball around with a stick, it is thought to have inspired that other Scottish sport, golf. Hurling and shinty enthusiasts emigrated to Canada, where they adapted their favorite sport to the ice and called it hockey. Unlike the Celts or the Irish, however, the Canadians had the sense to wear pads.

FACT

The hero Cuchulain wasn't just Ireland's greatest warrior; he was also the best hurler. In one version of the story of how he got his name (see Chapter 3 for another version), he accidentally killed Culain's hound when he got too enthusiastic in a hurling match. He offered to serve in the dog's place, and thereafter he was known as Cu Culain—"Culain's hound."

A marginally safer form of hurling evolved into Gaelic Football, the GAA's other major sport. It's kind of like soccer, except the players use their hands, and it's kind of like American football, except the players don't wear pads. Games are fast and furious.

Chapter 11

Storytelling— An Irish Tradition

I rish storytellers are famous for their wit and inventiveness. The extraordinary range of Irish stories comes from a folklore tradition more than 2,000 years old, which successfully blended Celtic, Christian, and English influences to create some of the most distinctive oral literature in all of Europe. Although the traditional format for Irish storytelling is dying out, its legacy continues in books and in poetry.

Ireland's Rich Folklore Heritage

Ireland has one of the richest folklore traditions in the world. Folklorists have hypothesized that in 1935 the parish of Carna, in west Galway, held more unrecorded folktales than did the rest of Western Europe combined. There are many reasons for this rich heritage, but two main factors stand out. First, Irish culture kept a Celtic base for more than 2,000 years, while incorporating the traditions and beliefs of Christianity, the Vikings, the Normans, and the English. These layers of culture piled on top of one another to create a rich tapestry. Second, the tradition of oral composition and performance has been strong in Ireland all those years.

E-SITE

The Irish genius for glib speech and storytelling is called the gift of the gab. To acquire this eloquence for yourself, kiss the Blarney Stone at Blarney Castle in County Cork. Of course, the word *blarney* can also mean "deceptive nonsense," so don't believe everything you hear in County Cork.

In ancient Celtic society, professional singers and poets called bards were extremely important. The Celts didn't write, so bards memorized vast amounts of poetry and performed it live. Their poems and songs were often the only record of a king's deeds or misdeeds, and their performances were the best entertainment around. People were accustomed to listening to stories told aloud and appreciated skilled storytellers.

As time went on, more people learned to read and write and the bards became less important. But the Irish populace remained mostly illiterate, so they kept up the tradition of oral storytelling. Bards evolved into wandering storytellers called *shanachies,* or *seanachaí* (SHAN-uck-ee), who went from town to town, entertaining the townsfolk. *Shanachies,* like their bard predecessors, were always welcome; people paid them with food if money wasn't available. When there wasn't a *shanachie* around, ordinary people entertained themselves by telling stories around the fire. A good storyteller knew hundreds of tales and could perform them with gusto and eloquence. In this informal way an ancient oral literary tradition quietly continued into modern times.

Folkloric Revival

For centuries, Irish folktales were unknown to the outside world. During the Protestant Ascendancy, the ruling class had nothing but disdain for the stories of Irish farmers. Not only were the stories in the barbaric Irish tongue, but also they were all about fantastic heroes and fairies, which the English dismissed as a bunch of superstitious nonsense.

In the early nineteenth century folklore suddenly became fashionable. The brothers Grimm in Germany started collecting and studying folktales (which you can read in *Grimm's Fairy Tales*) and declared folklore a vital expression of a culture's heritage. Soon, enterprising Irish scholars began to explore the countryside, looking for stories of value. They found a gold mine.

QUESTION?

How does someone collect folktales?
The key step is to find the people who know the most stories, especially older folks. Good folklorists collect stories in the original language and record the exact words used by the storyteller. They cover a wide geographical area and try to get several versions of the same story.

The First Collections

The first volume of Irish folktales was *Fairy Legends and Traditions of the South of Ireland*, published in 1825 by Thomas Croker from Cork. Croker and other early scholars of Irish folklore visited the Anglicized areas of Ireland in the east and recorded stories in English; this limited the value of their work because it ignored the great majority of Irish folktales, which were told only in Irish. In the mid-nineteenth century, Jeremiah Curtin, an Irish-American who had learned Irish, traveled throughout the Irish-speaking enclaves in Connacht and discovered hundreds of previously unrecorded stories. He recorded them in their original language and advanced the study of Irish folklore a great step forward.

At the end of the nineteenth century, Irish folklore studies became respectable. Oscar Wilde's parents, Sir William and Speranza Wilde, were important figures in this field and eccentric luminaries on the Anglo-Irish scene. The intellectuals of the Celtic Renaissance drew their inspiration from the Irish language and its folklore. Douglas Hyde's *Beside the Fire*, William Butler Yeats's *The Celtic Twilight*, and Lady Augusta Gregory's *Visions and Beliefs of the West of Ireland* not only established Irish folklore as one of the great oral literature traditions of Western civilization, but also provided an immense source of pride for the growing Irish Nationalist movement.

FACT

Yeats's story collections advanced the study of Irish folklore, but poetry was his most powerful tool for spreading awareness. Irish mythology and folklore influenced his poetic works, most noticeably "The Wanderings of Oisin" and "The Rose." Through his poems, Yeats was able to share his love of Ireland's mystical past with the world.

The Irish Folklore Commission

Even as Yeats and Lady Gregory collected tales in the cottages of Sligo and Connemara, they recognized that the storytelling tradition was dying out. They knew that if the Irish language died, a vast literary heritage would die with it. To prevent that from happening, in 1935 the Irish government created the Irish Folklore Commission. In the following decades, Irish-speaking collectors scoured the countryside to record stories of saints, heroes, and spirits. Currently, more than a million and a half pages of folklore reside in the commission's collection. Since 1971, the work of the commission has been carried on by the Folklore Department at University College Dublin.

Tales of the Supernatural

One of the most popular themes for stories was the spirit world. Ireland was widely known to be inhabited by all manner of fairies. The fairies were notoriously mischievous, and a vast array of stories described the mysterious tricks they played on unsuspecting mortals.

The Leprechaun

The leprechaun is perhaps the most famous of Ireland's little people. In one story, a man came down from his fields one day and he went to look after his old mare, who had served him well for many years. When he approached the stable, he heard a loud hammering sound. He peeked in through a window and spotted a funny little man sitting under his mare, hammering away at some shoes and whistling the prettiest tune you ever heard. The man realized what he had in his stable—a leprechaun.

◀ A leprechaun

Leprechauns are famous for their shoemaking abilities, but they're even more famous for their gold. The man knew this, so he snuck in the backdoor and tiptoed up behind the little man. The leprechaun was so busy making his shoes that he didn't notice the man until the man had caught the leprechaun fast. "I have you now," the man said, "and I won't let you go until I have your gold!"

"Stop, you're squeezing too hard!" said the leprechaun. "Let me go for a moment and I'll get you the gold." Eager for the gold, the man released the leprechaun, who, quick as a wink, ran out the door. All the man had left was the little shoe that the leprechaun had been making. The man didn't get any gold, but his wife said that it was the prettiest shoe she'd ever seen.

The Coin That Came Back

Some fairies were thought to be helpful, in their own mysterious ways. One story tells of a man who started feeling faint while in church. He walked outside to clear his head, and a gentleman approached to ask if he was all right. The man explained that he was feeling faint. The gentleman handed him a florin (a valuable coin) and told him to go have a whiskey at the local pub (Irish whiskey, of course, has amazing curative powers). The man thanked him and walked to the pub.

He paid for his drink with the florin, took the change, and drank down the whiskey. In no time at all he was feeling better. The man went home thinking nothing of it.

The next day he was going fishing, so he went to the store to buy some tobacco for his trip. When he reached into his pocket to get some money, he was surprised to find that the same florin was in his pocket. He paid with the florin, took the change, and walked away smoking, wondering what had happened. On the way home after fishing, he stopped by the bakery for some bread. He discovered that the same florin was in his pocket again.

The man continued in this way for some time, paying for everything with the florin and always finding it back in his pocket. He was happy with his good fortune, but something about the strange coin never seemed right to him. One day he went into the pub where he'd bought the first glass of whiskey. He threw the florin down on the counter and yelled, "May the devil go with you!"

He never saw the coin again. To the end of his days, he always said that it was a fairy man who had given it to him.

The literature on Irish folklore is vast and rewarding. The essential books on the subject are *Irish Myths and Legends*, by William Yeats and Lady Gregory; *Folktales of Ireland,* edited by Sean O'Sullivan; and the mother epic, the Táin Bó Cuailnge (the Thomas Kinsella translation is good).

Christian Stories

Not all Irish stories were about pagan subjects. The saints and priests also became material for a formidable body of tales. Christian-themed stories were sometimes intended to teach a moral lesson, sometimes they described the triumph of good over evil, and sometimes they just told exciting and glorious accounts of Ireland's many saints.

St. Patrick and the Phantom Chariot

St. Patrick was Ireland's greatest saint, and accordingly, he was the subject of the most stories. The exciting thing about Patrick's life was that he came to Ireland at a time when pagan worship was still in full force. Not only did he have to convince the natives that Christianity was good for them, he also had to do battle with pagan priests and demons who weren't so happy about giving up their island. Fortunately for Patrick, he was on good terms with the powers up in Heaven, and consequently, he could bring down some serious Christian firepower on the pagans.

Lots of Patrick legends feature him meeting up with heroes from Irish epics. He supposedly met Ossian, son of Finn MacCool (see Chapter 3), and converted him to Christianity. In one famous story, he asked High King Laoghaire for permission to preach to the Irish. He picked a shamrock and used it to explain the nature of the Trinity—three leaves but one single stalk indicating the unity of three (Father, Son, and Holy Spirit) in one (God). The king was so impressed that he let Patrick preach, although he did not convert himself.

In another story, Patrick recruited Cuchulain, pagan Ireland's greatest hero, to help convert Laoghaire. The high king was proving stubborn, so Patrick put things on terms that his pagan audience could relate to. He summoned Cuchulain to rise up from hell in his phantom chariot, which the dead hero promptly did. Cuchulain described the pains of hell to the nonbelievers. Laoghaire and his court were suitably impressed, and they all promptly converted to Christianity. For his help, Cuchulain was rewarded with a free pass to Heaven. In Irish this story is called Siaburcharpat Con Culainn ("The Phantom Chariot of Cuchulain").

St. Kevin and the Lady's Leap

St. Kevin was the ascetic supermonk who founded the thriving monastery of Glendalough (see Chapter 4). Kevin wanted nothing more than to live a life of isolation and chastity, but unfortunately for him, he was a magnificently beautiful man. A princess named Kathleen saw him one day and was overcome with lust for him. He thought he would be safe in Glendalough, but the wily princess found him there, so he decided to live in a cave over the Upper Lake. He lived there peacefully with his rocks and his dog.

Kathleen was smart; she recognized Kevin's dog, and one day she followed the dog to Kevin's cave. Kevin was sleeping, so the wicked woman began to take advantage of him. He woke up enraged and threw her out of the cave and into the lake, where she drowned. Ashamed of his violent act, Kevin spent the rest of his life in atonement, teaching monks and taking care of animals.

Historical Figures

Contemporary political figures were also fair game for storytellers. Popular priests or unpopular landlords inspired stories that the people could really relate to. Two of the most popular subjects for stories were Daniel O'Connell, the Irish Catholics' greatest hero, and Oliver Cromwell, their wickedest enemy.

FACT

Another famous subject for stories was Jonathan Swift (1667–1745), a great storyteller in his own right. Swift was notorious for using his biting wit to destroy enemies. A true story about him deals with his last will—he left aside money to build a hospital near Dublin for "ideots and lunaticks" because "No Nation wanted it so much."

Daniel O'Connell's Hat

Daniel O'Connell helped bring political emancipation to Ireland's Catholic population in the early nineteenth century (See Chapter 8). His adoring Irish fans called him "the Liberator" and told many stories about his intelligence, daring, and quick wits.

One story tells about his first days in the British Parliament. It was customary for members of Parliament to remove their hats when they entered the building. O'Connell, however, was particularly fond of his hat, so when he entered for the first time he kept it on, explaining that he had a bad headache. The next day he complained of the same headache, and on the third day he kept his head bowed down the whole time to show the pain in his head.

On the fourth day he marched into Parliament with his head held high, with the hat still on it. Everyone could see that he no longer had a headache, so they asked him to remove the hat. He pointed out the custom that whatever stands for three days in Parliament becomes law, so he kept the hat on. For the rest of his career in Parliament, he wore a hat while everyone else went around bareheaded.

Oliver Cromwell

The favorite bad guy for Irish stories was Oliver Cromwell, the British Protestant general who authorized wholesale destruction in his 1649 Irish campaign (See Chapter 7). From roasting priests to demolishing castles, he inflicted as much mischief in Irish stories as did the worst of the wee folk. It was common knowledge to some storytellers that Cromwell was the son of the devil, or at least a good friend of his. Other stories talk about how the devil himself came to claim Cromwell's soul when he died.

For the Irish storyteller, Cromwell served two major functions: he provided a helpful plot device as the character that everyone loathed; and speaking ill of him allowed the storytellers to express their own resentment of Britain's treatment of Ireland.

Irish Wit and Humor

The Irish have always had a good sense of humor, and that definitely came out in their stories. After hard days in the fields, often all a farmer wanted was a pint and a light story to take his mind off his troubles. *Shanachies* and other storytellers obliged these desires with amusing stories about animals, mishaps, and the fools we call humans.

Why Cats Sleep Inside

There's a story about why cats get to stay inside by the fire while dogs have to sleep out in the cold. Long ago, there were a cat and a dog who argued over who would get to stay inside. Their owner overheard the argument and decided to settle the matter.

"We'll have a race," he said. "You'll start five miles from the house, and whoever gets to the house first gets to stay inside the house from then on. The other can look after the place outside."

So the next day the two animals went to the place where the race was to start. They both ran as fast as they could. The dog, with his longer legs, got far ahead of the cat. But an old beggar saw the dog running at him with his mouth open, and he thought the dog was going to bite him. The beggar hit the dog with a stick. The dog was angry, so he barked at the man and tried to bite him for satisfaction.

When the dog finally got to the house, the cat was licking her paws by the fire. From that day on, cats have stayed inside the house while dogs have slept outside in the cold.

The Legacy Continues

Today, the Irish storytelling tradition has died out in some ways, but it has been reborn in others. Although few people these days are interested in eking out a living as a *shanachie,* the old stories have found a form of greater permanence in the many books written on Irish folklore and in the collections of the Irish Folklore Commission. Elements of the traditional stories have inspired a number of modern writers, such as Yeats, Joyce, and Seamus Heaney.

Chapter 12

The Great Irish Potato Famine

An Gorta Mór, the Great Potato Famine of the 1840s, is one of the pivotal events in Irish history. Millions emigrated, and the resulting demographic shift led to a decreasing population. The famine also ignited anger at the British government, which eventually built into the Irish independence movement.

1845 Potato blight hits Ireland

1846 Potato blight hits again

1846–1847 Harsh winter

1847 Death of Daniel O'Connell

1848 Rebellion of Young Irelanders; third potato blight

1850 Tenant League formed in Dublin

1858 James Stephens founds Irish Republican Brotherhood (IRB)

1858–1860 IRB spreads rapidly

Potatoes, for Better or for Worse

Potatoes came to Europe from the New World in the early sixteenth century. Sir Francis Drake is thought to have introduced the potato to England, and shortly afterward Sir Walter Raleigh tried planting them on his Irish estates.

When the potato reached Ireland, it created a revolution. It was very easy to grow; farmers could plant them in the spring and leave them alone for months while they went off and worked elsewhere (anywhere that scarce wages might be offered). People grew potatoes on any patch of land that could sustain them, even the most marginal of fields.

FACT

There are many varieties of potato, and the Irish had definite preferences among them. Richer people ate the more desirable types, such as "minions" or "apple potatoes." Poor folk grew and ate "lumper" potatoes, which were watery and tasteless but grew well on poor farmland. Unfortunately, the lumper was especially susceptible to the blight that caused the famine.

A Good Source of Nourishment

Potatoes are extremely nutritious; they are full of vitamins, protein, calcium, and iron, especially when washed down with buttermilk, the potato's traditional accompaniment. The potato, in fact, is perhaps the only crop that can provide a balanced diet by itself, which kept the Irish healthier than other people living on one starch such as rice or millet or even bread (made of wheat). It was relatively easy to store over the winter, which was important because most tenant farmers had no buildings in which to store vast quantities of grain. Unfortunately, you can't store potatoes for much more than a year, and this would have devastating consequences for the Irish in the famine years.

A Potato Economy

Patterns in land ownership made Irish farmers dependent on the potato. Most farmers had to rent from landlords (who were usually

English), who demanded cash payments. The farmers had to use most of their time and land to produce cash crops to cover the rent, and consequently they only had small amounts of time or land left to grow their own food. Given these constraints, the potato was the only crop that could provide sufficient nutrition to feed the growing Irish families.

And grow they did; between 1700 and 1800 the population doubled from somewhere around 2.5 million people to about 5 million people. By the early 1840s, the population stood at 8.2 million; ironically, it was densest in the poorest areas. The potato helped make this possible, but population growth also made people more dependent on the potato. Fathers would split up their land between their sons, making families depend on smaller and smaller plots of land. The system worked, but only as long as the potatoes were plentiful.

QUESTION?

What did people eat besides potatoes?
Not very much. They might supplement their diet with foraged berries or shellfish if they lived in the right area. Most families kept a pig, to fatten it up on leftover potatoes and then sell it at the beginning of the summer, which was the only time of year the potatoes ran low. Then they would buy oatmeal to tide themselves over until the potatoes came back.

A Fungus Among Us

So there the Irish were, planting their potatoes every spring, digging them up every fall, and eating rather well, all things considered. But in the autumn of 1845, all that changed.

In October of that year, farmers walked out to their fields to harvest their crops. They plunged their shovels into the ground and then shrieked in horror—the potatoes were black and rotten, completely useless. The crop they had counted on for generations had finally failed them.

No one knew what to do. Experts offered advice, suggesting that the fungus killing the potatoes was attracted to moisture. Farmers tried to dig dry pits, but the spores traveled through the air and soaked into the ground after rain, which has always been plentiful in Ireland. It took only one infected plant to spread the blight over acres of potatoes. There was no escape.

FACT

The potato blight was caused by a "vampire" fungus called *Phytophthora infestans.* It might have originated in the United States and traveled to Europe in the holds of ships carrying produce. By the end of the 1800s, scientists had figured out that farmers could control it by spraying plants with copper compounds.

The Hardest Hit

The west and southwest of Ireland bore the brunt of the famine. Those areas, including Mayo, Sligo, Roscommon, Galway, Clare, and Cork, were the poorest regions of the island, and the most dependent on subsistence farming. Not coincidentally, these were also the areas that Catholic Irish had been sent to during the Protestant plantation. Poor laborers were hardest hit, followed by the smallest farmers.

Famine Here to Stay

The worst part of the potato blight was that it didn't go away. After the 1845 crops failed, people counted on the potatoes of 1846 to pull them through, but those potatoes rotted away, too. For some reason the crop of 1847 survived, but not enough fields of potatoes had been planted to produce enough food for everyone who needed it. And in 1848 the blight reappeared with a vengeance.

Life During the Famine

The poor Irish who had lost their potatoes faced terrifying difficulties. They called the time an Gorta Mór, which means "the Great Hunger," or an Droch Shaol, "the Bad Times."

The poorest farmers, already living at a subsistence level, were the first to feel the effects. Within a few months of the bad harvest, the people in the hardest-hit areas were already dying of starvation. Travelers reported seeing skeletal people with their mouths stained green; they had tried to ward off hunger by eating grass. In some places in western Ireland, piles of corpses filled the ditches.

The first thing the stricken farmers did was try to eat their diseased potatoes. This made them terribly sick with stomach cramps, diarrhea, and intestinal bleeding. Some very old and very young people died from this disease.

There was some food to be found on the land, and the Irish were very resourceful at scrounging it. They trapped birds and stole eggs from nests, gathered shellfish from the shores, and caught fish. Coastal people ate seaweed. They would take blood from cattle and fry it. They ate rats, worms, nettles, and chickweed. When the opportunity presented itself, they stole food from wagons and barges. But none of it helped much.

With Famine Comes Pestilence

The malnourished Irish were very vulnerable to diseases. In fact, more people died from illness than from actual starvation.

Typhus appeared in the winter of 1846. The Irish called it the black fever because it made victims' faces swollen and dark. It was incredibly contagious, spread by lice, which were everywhere. Many people lived in one-room cottages, humans and animals all huddled together, and there was no way to avoid lice jumping from person to person. The typhus bacteria also traveled in louse feces, which formed an invisible dust in the air. Anyone who touched an infected person, or even an infected person's clothes, could become the disease's next victim. Typhus was the supreme killer of the famine; in the winter of 1847, thousands of people died of it every week.

Another fever appeared at the same time, the relapsing fever called yellow fever because its victims became jaundiced. This fever also came from lice. A victim would suffer from a high fever for several days, seem to recover, and then relapse a week later. Many people died from this fever as well.

Scurvy became a problem. This disease comes from a deficiency of vitamin C, and it causes the victim's connective tissue to break down.

The Irish called scurvy black leg, because it made the blood vessels under the skin burst, giving a victim's limbs a black appearance. The cure for scurvy is fresh food—meat, vegetables, or fruit—none of which was available to the poor in Ireland.

The modern obsession with cleanliness isn't just a matter of cosmetics or pride. Dirty clothes and sheets can harbor disease. When someone died of typhus, anyone who took and wore that person's clothes without washing them first could catch the fever from dust lingering in the clothes.

There were other diseases, too. Some Irish children fell victim to an odd disease that made hair grow on their faces while it fell out of their heads. Some observers commented that the children looked like monkeys. Cholera was always a problem in unsanitary, crowded conditions; it broke out in workhouses throughout the famine years.

Deaths in the Family

When people died, the living were left with the problem of what to do with the bodies. There were not enough coffins to hold the dead, even if the poor had money to pay for them. Stories abounded of entire families dying, or of mothers losing all their children and carrying the bodies to the cemetery on their backs, one by one. Visitors reported seeing dead bodies stacked in ditches and dogs devouring corpses in the fields; to their horror, they also observed people killing and eating those same dogs.

When someone came down with typhus, relatives and neighbors feared that they would contract the disease, too. Sometimes all healthy members of a family would leave a sick person alone in a house, hoping to escape the contagion. They hadn't abandoned the sufferer; they would push food in through the windows on the end of a long pole. When there was no longer a response from inside the house, they would pull the house down on top of the victim and burn the whole thing.

Landlords and Evictions

Most of the victims of the famine did not own the land they lived on. Instead, they rented houses and farmland from large landholders. When the potato crops failed, they could no longer pay their rent. Some landlords were understanding; many actually helped their tenants, handing out food and concocting jobs that would allow them to earn wages.

But other landlords were less accommodating. Scores of poor Irish were evicted from their homes. This wasn't all due to cruelty and greed; many landlords themselves faced bankruptcy and starvation as their rents stopped coming in. Some landlords decided that grazing sheep or cattle would be a better use of the land, and the peasants and their potato plots had to give way for the livestock.

The result was that many poor Irish found themselves not only starving, but homeless as well. Some of them moved into workhouses, but many dug holes in hillsides or made huts out of peat and lived in them as best they could. Others simply wandered the roads until they dropped dead.

FACT

One of the most bitter comments about the Irish potato famine came from economic theorist and "father of communism," Karl Marx. He remarked that in the time of Cromwell, the English had supplanted the Irish Catholics with Protestants, but during the famine they supplanted them with cattle.

Help for Victims

One of the things that made the Irish famine especially bad was a lack of help for the starving. The British government was reluctant to help too much, partly out of fear that the poor would depend on aid and not try to help themselves. The mid-nineteenth century was the heyday of laissez faire economics, which taught that the free market would solve all problems and that the government should never intervene. Unfortunately, that approach led to tragedy for the Irish population.

Governmental Response, or Lack Thereof

Politicians quickly got word that the Irish peasantry had nothing to eat. Many English were not particularly impressed with the Irish plight. A number of them thought that the famine was a punishment for Ireland's sin of overpopulation. According to population theorist Thomas Robert Malthus, Ireland had far too many people for its land to support, and the best solution was to get rid of most of them. The famine would take care of that.

The truth was, the factors that contributed to the Irish famine were far more complex than mere overpopulation. There was plenty of food in Ireland. The island grew and exported more than 1 billion pounds of grain every year. Many Irish actually sold this food willingly so they would have the money to pay rent. Ireland also was not allowed to import rice or corn from the British colonies. This was the effect of the Corn Laws (the British call wheat "corn"; they call corn "maize"), which set artificially high prices for British grain and locked out cheaper imports until the entire British crop was sold. This was a problem for the Irish, who had no money.

Prime Minister Robert Peel initially took pity on the starving Irish, and, unbeknownst to his own government, ordered Indian corn from the Americas to be delivered to the island. This corn was only a last resort for the sufferers; it was difficult to grind and cook, not nearly as filling as potatoes, and it lacked vitamin C. It ran out quickly, too, and was not replaced.

Peel resigned in 1846, and for the next four years the man he appointed to oversee famine relief, Charles Edward Trevelyan, handled matters. Trevelyan didn't have a very high opinion of the Irish, and in fact only visited Ireland once; he thought distance helped him maintain objectivity. He was a firm believer in laissez faire and thought donated food actually exacerbated the problem by relieving the Irish of the obligation to feed themselves. Unfortunately, in some places, no one had either food or money, so feeding themselves was completely impossible. Irish crops continued to be exported, which led to great resentment on the part of the Irish people.

Workhouses

When people got truly desperate, there was a place that they could go: the workhouse. These houses had been established in the early 1840s to provide relief to the poorest people. Opponents of workhouses feared that the Irish would abuse the system, using the workhouse if they weren't truly desperate. But supporters countered that they could solve this problem by making workhouses so unpleasant that only people with no alternative would enter them.

Unpleasant they were. Anyone who owned land had to give it up before entering a workhouse, which forced many families to choose between staying on their farms and starving or giving up their land for a chance to eat. People who entered a workhouse were segregated by sex, which meant dividing up families. They were forced to live there, essentially sentencing themselves to prison. They had to give up their own clothes and wear pauper's uniforms, which marked them as destitute. They had to work at menial jobs to earn their keep—men broke up rocks, women knitted, and children either had lessons or learned to do various industrial tasks. Families only got together on Sundays.

The Irish people did everything they could to avoid the workhouse. They found the splitting up of families especially hard to bear. The unpleasant regimen did succeed in keeping people away from public charity in the early 1840s and even into 1846, before the second bad potato crop.

FACT

Although it was probably not common in practice, Irish folk memory recalls Protestant soup kitchens that would only give food to Catholics if they renounced the Catholic faith. The families who converted were called "Soupers," and they bore a stigma from it for generations.

But after the second nonexistent potato harvest in the autumn of 1846, people were more willing to surrender their dignity in the hopes of not starving. Poorhouse food was bad and often inadequate, but at least it was food. By mid-October, most workhouses in the worst-hit areas were full and turning away inmates.

Crowding did nothing to improve the workhouse atmosphere. The stench became overpowering as hundreds of unhealthy people contributed their bodily products to the building. Typhus, cholera, and other diseases thrived in this environment, and many people died.

Public Works

Not everyone could fit in the workhouses, and many people refused to even consider the possibility. The government provided an alternative for them: working for pay on public projects. Local relief committees made lists of people who needed help, and then one member of each needy family was allowed to work for pay.

This was a nice idea, but ineffective in practice. The projects in question involved hard physical labor—digging ditches, breaking and moving rocks to build roads—and the workers were already malnourished. The winter of 1846 to 1847 was especially harsh, and the workers had no adequate clothes. Many of them fell sick and dropped dead on the job. In fact, 1847 was such a bad year that it became known as "Black '47."

E-SITE

Old famine roads from these make-work projects are still visible in western Ireland, where many of them have been converted into hiking trails or highways. The Dingle Peninsula contains a number of these roads and some famine fences. Some roads travel by prehistoric tombs and other ancient Irish artifacts.

The wages for public works would have been generous in the days of plentiful potatoes, but during the famine food prices went through the roof. A week's wages were barely adequate to buy half a week's sustenance for a family of any size, and many Irish families were large. Families were desperate to keep someone on the works to collect money, though, so they would often deprive nonworkers of food to keep up the strength of the wage-earner. Children would go hungry so their father could eat.

In many cases, the person going out to work was also the person who would have planted the next year's potato crop at home. Without that labor, the next year's harvest suffered.

Private Charity

At the start of the famine, the government insisted that charity was best done by private institutions. The Quakers in particular rose to the occasion, opening soup kitchens to feed paupers. Some landlords helped their tenants, providing food, clothes, or housing. Irish peasants helped one another when they could; many stories from the famine years tell of housewives who gave away their last cabbage in the garden or last drop of milk from the cow, only to have their supplies miraculously renewed the next morning. These are nice stories, but unfortunately usually not true.

British "Charity"

In 1847, the government stopped the public works programs and announced that from now on, private aid would be the solution. The British still feared that too much aid to the Irish would prevent them from ever going back to work. The British decided that Irish landlords must be responsible for the famine, so it would be their job to fix it. Local governments were supposed to organize charitable soup kitchens paid for by taxes collected by local relief committees.

But as the famine years progressed, Ireland had less and less food and money. Landlords went bankrupt as their tenants failed to pay rents, and property taxes went up, ironically, to provide money to feed the starving. In an effort to lower their property values and thus their taxes, some of them evicted the peasants still living on their land and tore down their huts. Britain sent more and more soldiers to Ireland to enforce evictions and see that taxes were collected. This combination of military might and no food made the Irish even more resentful of the occupying British government. Though there was more food available now, no one had the money to buy it.

Matters were made even worse by a financial crisis in Britain in 1847. Wheat prices plummeted, railroad stocks fell, and many businesses went bankrupt. The British had less money to help the Irish, even if they had wanted to.

The winter of 1848 to 1849 was a nightmare for the Irish. They had gambled on the potato crop, spending every cent they had to buy seed potatoes that they planted in the spring; after all, the blight hadn't attacked the 1847 crop, so they had reason to hope that it was gone. But they were terribly wrong; the blight was still around and it devastated potatoes all over the island. Landlords kept evicting peasants, and the British government kept raising Ireland's taxes in the vain hope that this would help the island pull itself up by its bootstraps. The poorest people shrank down to human skeletons before dying. Some turned to crime as an alternative to starvation—in prison or on a ship heading to Australia there would at least be something to eat. Wealthier people gave up on Ireland and left for other countries.

The Results of the Famine

Ireland was a different place after the famine. The population was drastically reduced—an island of 8.2 million people in 1841 was reduced to 6 million in 1851. At least 1 million of those people had died. The rest fled the country, hoping for a new life in another land.

QUESTION?

When did the famine end?
Various historians give different dates, ranging from 1847 to 1850. In 1851, workhouses were still full and mortality was still high. By 1852 conditions seemed more or less back to normal. So the famine lasted about five years.

After the famine, there were fewer tiny landholdings, farms of 5 or fewer acres. By 1851, many more farms consisted of 30 acres or more. Fathers stopped dividing their acreage among all their sons and instead passed the entire farm to just one of them. This made it easier for a farmer to support his own family but caused problems for the children who didn't inherit. It also forced inheriting sons to wait longer to come into property, which delayed marriages. Farmers used more of their land to grow livestock; not surprisingly, they didn't grow nearly as many potatoes as they had before.

A New Start in a New Country

Many Irish left their beloved homeland during the famine years, hoping to find something better in the United States, England, Canada, or Australia. Emigration posed its own risks. Many emigrants died en route to their destinations. Others found that their new homes were little better than the barren farms they'd left behind. Nevertheless, many Irish emigrants quickly grew roots in fresh soil and flourished. For better or for worse, the Irish were now permanently planted around the world.

Young Ireland's Movement Toward Independence

Daniel O'Connell had worked hard on behalf of the starving Irishmen, petitioning Parliament to put a stop to grain exports and to provide public work for people in need. He continued his support of nonviolent means of dealing with the Crown, but at the same time a group called Young Ireland appeared. This was a group of younger men who were more interested in gaining Irish independence than in improving the existing system. After O'Connell died in 1847, the Young Irelanders were ready to use violence to fight for an Irish republic.

FACT

The year 1848 was a great year for revolutions in Europe; they happened in France, Italy, Germany, Poland, Denmark, Slovakia, the Czech Republic, Hungary, Croatia, and Romania. Although each was unique, they all were attempts to correct government abuses and give more representation to the people.

The Young Irelanders tried to foment a rebellion in 1848. They weren't prepared for it, and it fizzled quickly. Some of their leaders were captured and transported to Australia; others fled to the United States. Prominent among them were William Smith O'Brien, Thomas Francis Meagher (MAH-her), John Mitchel, and John Boyle O'Reilly. These men and others like them were responsible for spreading word throughout the world of Britain's handling of the famine. They also became prominent citizens of the New World and Ireland; for example, Meagher fought as a general for the Union Army in the American Civil War and went on to become governor of Montana. Mitchel later returned to Ireland and became mayor of Tipperary.

The Start of the Fenian Movement

The famine did a lot to foster a feeling of unity among the Irish against the English. Dedication to the Catholic Church increased and priests grew more powerful. The Irish especially hated the landlord-tenant system, which had forced so many of them out of their homes. People across the country formed societies to protect tenants by fixing rents and getting farmers to promise not to take over the lands of evicted tenants. Irish politicians began pushing the tenant agenda in Parliament, and their efforts formed the start of Ireland's independence movement.

On St. Patrick's Day, 1858, a former Young Ireland leader named James Stephens founded the Irish Republican Brotherhood. Around the same time, another rebel named Jeremiah O'Donovan Rossa founded a similar Phoenix Society in Skibbereen. These movements spread rapidly during the late 1850s. Though they were strongly condemned by the Catholic Church, these independence movements continued to gather steam and plan insurrections that would lead to an Irish republic.

Looking Back at What Happened

The great famine has inspired more than its fair share of historical interpretations, many of which are wildly contradictory. The Irish used to say, "God gave us the potato blight, but the English gave us the famine." There is some truth to this statement, but it's not entirely fair to the English. They didn't understand the scope of the problem and some of their policies made matters worse, but the fact remains that many people would have starved even with better help. In the hardest-hit areas there was simply nothing to eat, and there was no easy way to deliver food there, even if it had been available. But whether or not the English were to blame for the famine, Irish Nationalists definitely believed they were. This spurred them to action, and the rest is history. Ⓔ

Chapter 13

The Immigrant Experience

Irish demographics reveal two startling facts: There are around 70 million people worldwide who claim Irish descent, and Ireland today has barely half the population that it had 160 years ago, a decline unmatched in the modern world. These facts are explained and connected by the undeniable social reality of nineteenth-century Ireland—emigration.

Why They Left

No one kept careful track of how many people left Ireland in the nineteenth century, but it certainly was a large number. People started leaving long before the Great Famine began in 1845; in the thirty years that preceded it, at least 1 million people left Ireland. Between the start of the famine and 1870, another 3 million or so emigrated. A decreased population and a lower birthrate decreased the flow of emigrants in the following years, but a significant proportion of the population continued to leave well into the twentieth century.

The two overpowering causes for emigration were hunger and poverty. The Great Famine and the half-dozen other potato failures of the nineteenth century sent millions of Irish people overseas. People saw the death and suffering around them; rather than wait for death in a land with no food, they picked up everything and sailed across the Atlantic.

QUESTION?

What is the difference between an emigrant and an immigrant?
An "emigrant" is a person who leaves a country; an "immigrant" is someone who moves to a new country. Therefore, an emigrant from Dublin would be an immigrant in New York. In this chapter, we use the term "emigrant" when looking at people from the perspective of Ireland, and "immigrant" when speaking about them in their new country.

But long before the famine struck and years after its end, young Irish people were leaving their homeland. The basic economic facts of Ireland were not promising: the island was small, with few natural resources beyond farmland; most of the best land was tied up in the hands of the Anglo-Irish aristocracy, and the rest was split up among more people than it could support; and English policies inhibited the development of Irish industries, which might have provided a way off the farms. Young Irish men and women realized that if they wanted any hope of a better life, they had to go overseas. If families were lucky enough to own land, younger sons often emigrated in order to clear the way to inheritance for the oldest.

Some young people left Ireland as seasonal migrants. Instead of setting up a new home in the New World, they would travel to another country for seasonal work, in agriculture or the fisheries, and then return home when the work was done for the year. The sons of small farmers were especially likely to do this; their periodic wages helped the family hold on to its property.

There were also noneconomic reasons to leave Ireland. Some people, particularly a number of Nationalist revolutionaries, emigrated to avoid legal trouble and to drum up support for their cause in the New World. Others left to join family and friends overseas.

FACT

The only significant non-English-speaking destination for Irish emigrants was Argentina. From 1840 to 1885, around 11,000 families moved to the Rio Plata area in Argentina and Uruguay. They were known as *gauchos ingleses* or *irlandeses*, and they even had their own newspaper, the *Hiberno-Argentine Review*. Today, Irish descendants make up about 1 percent of the Argentine population.

Where They Went

Where people went changed over time. During the nineteenth century, the vast majority of Irish emigrants went to the United States. Many also went to Canada, with a substantial proportion of those winding up in the United States after a few years. England and Scotland were always viable options, because the trip over was less expensive and less permanent. More distant English colonies, like Australia and South Africa, also saw a good number of Irish immigrants, although many of the newcomers to Australia weren't there of their own free will—the English sent prisoners and rebels to Australia.

Where people were from in Ireland played a part in where they wound up. Most of the people from the southwest and west ended up in the United States, while families from the north more commonly went to Canada. A longstanding tradition of migrant laborers going seasonally from Donegal to Scotland made Scotland the favored destination for Ireland's northwest. People in the east were more likely to head over to England.

The number of emigrants dropped significantly in the twentieth century. A trend of anti-immigrant sentiment swept the United States, making it less popular as a destination. From the 1930s on, an increasing percentage of Irish immigrants moved to British cities such as Liverpool, London, and Edinburgh. These cities offered the job prospects of an industrialized society, but they were close enough to home that people could make the trip back for the holidays. Large Irish communities developed in these cities, offering emigrants cultural continuity, a chance to practice their religion, and a degree of political influence.

The Hardships of Emigration

Choosing to emigrate was not an easy decision. In a culture in which family and community ties were so strong, the decision to leave it all behind was heart-wrenching. Emigrants knew that they would probably never see their loved ones again. Friends and family often held mock wakes for emigrants on the night before their departure, symbolic of the permanent separation that was coming between them.

The Journey

The price of the passage was the first difficulty most emigrants faced. Tickets for the overpacked transport ships weren't very expensive, but the people who wanted to leave were usually poor. Sometimes landlords and government programs assisted poor people with the price of a ticket.

FACT

The majority of Irish immigrants were young, single men and women. Emigrants usually traveled by themselves, because it was easier to pay for one ticket at a time. (The famine years were one of the few times when whole families emigrated together, all at the same time.) Once overseas, if they found work, they would send money back to bring over family and friends.

The voyage overseas could be perilous, and it became especially dangerous during the famine years. The ships carrying emigrants during the famine became known as "coffin ships." The death rates onboard these ships were appallingly bad; for example, one-fifth of the people who traveled from Cork to Quebec died in the process.

The owners of ships that specialized in transporting poor passengers fleeing the famine did not pay much attention to shipboard conditions. Dozens or hundreds of emigrants were packed into cargo holds with poor ventilation, little light, and rudimentary sanitation at best. Food was generally inadequate—think rancid meat and flour full of weevils. Under these conditions, diseases such as typhus and cholera ran rampant. Their immune systems already weakened by hunger, poor emigrants fell easy prey to the pathogens that lurked in the murky cargo holds.

Arrival and Quarantine

Reaching port was just a first step; many Irish died after arriving in the New World but before they could legally set foot on the mainland. Canada was closer to Ireland than the United States, and many ships docked there. It was easier for ships to land in Canada for another reason—the United States put far more restrictions on emigrant ships, particularly in the matter of health. A ship full of feverish passengers couldn't land in the United States, which didn't want to take care of ailing paupers.

Many ships traveled up the St. Lawrence River to the quarantine island of Grosse Île, near Quebec City. In the summer of 1847, thousands of Irish immigrants crowded into the small hospital there; many of them died quickly, which freed up beds for the next round of sick people. Bodies were stacked high in the hot summer sun. Towns on the river would try to send boats to the next place upstream; no one wanted to keep these crowds of sick Irish.

Surviving the voyage and the quarantine didn't guarantee further survival. Immigrants who wanted to continue to Boston, New York, or other U.S. destinations would sometimes walk across the border from Montreal. This finished off many more people, especially those faced with a Canadian winter.

E-SITE

A memorial erected by the Ancient Order of Hibernians in 1909 at Grosse Île reads (in Irish): "Thousands of Children of the Gael died on this island having fled from the laws of foreign tyrants and artificial famine in the years 1847 and 1848. God's blessing on them. Let this monument be a token to their name and honor from the Gaels of America. God Save Ireland!" Canada recognized it as a National Historic Site in 1996.

The Immigrant Experience in the United States

For centuries, the United States has loomed in the Irish consciousness as the place to go for a new life. The United States offered the things that the Irish could not find at home: land, economic opportunities, and freedom from English control. With land resources vastly greater than those of Ireland, the United States seemed like a place of limitless possibilities. For people who chafed under British rule, the United States stood out as the colony that had made itself free.

Early Immigration

After Cromwell sacked Ireland in the mid-seventeenth century, he sent Irish prisoners over to the West Indies as slave labor. Many of these forced immigrants eventually made their way to the English colonies in the New World; the Catholic colony of Maryland was a popular destination.

Irish immigrants had arrived in America in a steady stream throughout the eighteenth century. Most of the first voluntary Irish immigrants came from Ulster in the north of Ireland. These immigrants were generally, although not exclusively, Protestants. They were known as "Scotch-Irish" or "Scots Irish," because of the large number of Scots who settled in Ulster during the plantations of the seventeenth century. They quickly became an established component of U.S. society. Several U.S. presidents, including Andrew Jackson, James Polk, and Woodrow Wilson, were of Scotch-Irish descent.

The Great Wave

In the nineteenth century, when a rapidly expanding population combined with a series of potato failures, millions of Irish decided to make the trip to the New World. Although the Scotch-Irish immigrants continued to arrive, the vast majority of the new arrivals were Catholics from the south of Ireland. Irish immigrants began to arrive in the United States' eastern cities in large numbers in the 1820s and then flooded in during the years of the famine. They headed for the big cities—New York, Philadelphia, Boston, Baltimore, and Chicago—and they usually stayed there.

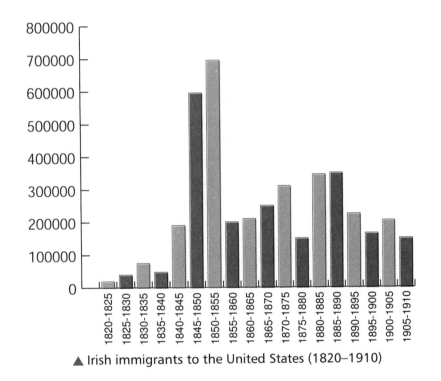

▲ Irish immigrants to the United States (1820–1910)

These new immigrants tended to have a tougher time of it than their Protestant predecessors, and they faced a great deal of anti-Irish prejudice from the people already living in the United States. This was for a number of reasons: they came in far larger numbers; they were mostly poor farmers and unskilled laborers; they came at a time when most land in the East was already settled; and they were Catholics moving into a mostly Protestant land. Immigrants who deluged U.S. cities in the late 1840s were especially unwelcome because of their extreme poverty and poor health.

Irish immigrants tended to be intimidated by the prospect of farming in the vast and unpopulated lands of rural United States, which bore little resemblance to the close-knit farming communities they'd known back home. Instead, they sought the apparently more lucrative work of building U.S. cities.

The massive influx of newcomers caused a strain with the existing populations, who were often of English and Protestant heritage. In the years when the majority of the Irish arrived, U.S. cities had not yet figured out how they would handle immigrants. Consequently, the immigrants wound up figuring it out for themselves.

E-SITE

To get a feel for what it was like to arrive in the United States, visit the Ellis Island Immigration Museum in New York City. The exhibits are excellent, but most Irish immigrants didn't arrive there—Ellis Island wasn't opened until 1892. Prior to that, immigrants arrived at Castle Garden, which today is a National Park site.

Irish Power

Most of the immigrants were uneducated and unskilled, so at first they could only take on menial tasks. But hard work in the United States was better than starving to death back in Ireland, so the Irish immigrants quickly developed a reputation as hard workers. The great wave of Irish immigration happened at a time of tremendous growth in U.S. cities and industries. Factories, apartment buildings, bridges, and railroads all needed to be built, and Irish immigrants were there to build them. In 1847, a New York newspaper wrote, "There are several sorts of power working at the fabric of this Republic: waterpower, steampower, horsepower, and Irish power."

Because so many Irish-Americans were in the building trades, they quickly took hold of a tool that was still rare back in Ireland—labor unions. The strong Irish sense of community allowed them to quickly grasp the strength of unity and collective bargaining. Irishmen soon led unions for bricklayers, carpenters, and plumbers. Many Irish families are still active leaders in the labor movement.

The textile industry also employed many immigrants, particularly women. Irish women also often found work doing laundry or serving as maids and cooks.

Machine Politics

Irish immigrants arrived in cities that often did not want them and did not have an infrastructure in place to take care of them. To address these problems, immigrants fell back on the tribal cohesiveness that had governed their rural communities in Ireland. While the Irish newcomers did not have status, they did have numbers. This allowed them to focus their power on a political level, almost exclusively through the Democratic Party. The resulting political organizations were the first of America's political "machines"—organizations that used tight community organization to take power over local government, and then used government patronage to maintain their power.

The Tammany machine in New York was the prototype for this style of politics. Bosses Tweed and Croker oversaw tightly controlled political organizations that offered favors—food, clothing, social services—in exchange for votes. Once in power, they exchanged jobs for kickbacks. The patronage jobs were largely in law enforcement and construction, which contributed to Irish dominance in the building trades. It was during this period that the stereotype of the Irish police officer became popular. The machine organizations were undeniably corrupt, but they did provide services to immigrant communities that they would not have had otherwise.

FACT

The original Tammany Hall was the headquarters for a Manhattan patriotic organization named after an Indian chief. Around the time of Andrew Jackson, the organization became associated with the Democratic Party and Irish immigrants. Today, the term *Tammany* is a byword for a corrupt political machine.

The Irish Mob

While some immigrants responded to their tough conditions by becoming cops, others chose an alternate path. The Irish mob sought to make money from the chaos of the United States' fast-growing cities. The Irish relied on old traditions of family and community loyalty, as well as a tradition of rural terrorism. Irish mobsters organized gambling, prostitution, and protection rackets in urban immigrant communities.

The Irish mob families never achieved great success, but they did manage to survive well into the twentieth century. The Irish mob operated alongside the Mafia in several cities, notably Boston and Chicago. Many of them were active rumrunners during Prohibition.

The progressive gentrification of the Irish immigrant community, however, tended to undercut the appeal of crime. As more and more Irish families moved into the middle class, the gangsters lost the support networks and opportunities offered by an insular immigrant community. Once second- and third-generation Irish-Americans found that they could go to college and become professionals, the power of the mob began to die out.

There are a number of good movies about the Irish mob. Before *The Godfather* made Mafia movies popular, the James Cagney style of Irish gangster was Hollywood's prototypical tough criminal. For classic Hells Kitchen action, see *Angels with Dirty Faces* (1938) or *The Public Enemy* (1931). For a more recent film treatment, see *Miller's Crossing* (1990).

Anti-Irish Sentiments

Catholic Irish immigrants often met with hostility and contempt from the more established American populations. The Irish represented competition for jobs and political power. Also, as Catholics, they presented a challenge to a predominantly Protestant country. Many employers refused to hire the Irish, and some landlords wouldn't rent to them.

One area where the Irish clashed with established groups was the question of alcohol. The Puritan tradition in the United States generally frowned on alcohol, whereas Irish culture viewed it as a harmless indulgence. When the Temperance movement arose in the mid-nineteenth century, Irish saloons were some of its first targets. Political cartoons of the time depicted Irishmen as red-face buffoons, enslaved by the bottle.

Interestingly, some of the worst anti-Irish discrimination came from the Scotch-Irish, who wanted to make clear that they were a different group from the impoverished newcomers. They created social organizations that specifically excluded Irish Catholics, and they derided the social pretensions of the "lace curtain Irish"—Catholic immigrants who had managed to make it into the middle class.

Although the Irish had to overcome a great deal of social stigma, they eventually became a part of the American mainstream. This was partially due to the influx of more immigrants, but it was mostly due to economic advancement. The sons and daughters of manual laborers were able to become doctors, merchants, and teachers. Although some of the old prejudices died hard, by 1960 the Irish-American community had progressed to the point that John F. Kennedy, a Catholic of Irish descent, could become president of the United States.

FACT

Alfred E. Smith, an Irish-American, was the first Catholic nominated for the presidency by a major party. Smith rose from the ranks of the Tammany machine to become governor of New York. In 1924 he led a fight within the Democratic Party to condemn the Ku Klux Klan for its violence and anti-Catholic prejudice, but lost. He lost the 1928 presidential election to Herbert Hoover.

Irish Communities in Other Destinations

Irish emigrants didn't restrict themselves to America. Many of them simply crossed the Irish channel to Great Britain. Others traveled to the opposite side of the globe to settle in Australia and New Zealand.

British Isles

After the United States, England and Scotland were the top destinations for Irish emigrants. The trip was shorter and cheaper, so it was both easier to get there and easier to get back. The Irish went there in great numbers to pursue jobs in the textile mills, coal mines, and other businesses of the burgeoning Industrial Revolution. They primarily went to the industrial cities, like London and Liverpool. The total Irish population in England—including both immigrants and their children born in England—numbered as much as 1.5 million people by the late nineteenth century.

Like America, England offered jobs. Unlike America, however, it did not offer much social mobility. English society had strong class lines, and elements of old anti-Irish and anti-Catholic prejudices still operated. Irish immigrants usually lived in large city slums. They rarely exercised much political power, and they generally remained in low-level jobs. This situation did not begin to improve until the early twentieth century.

The Land Down Under

Irish people had been settling in Australia unintentionally for decades before large-scale emigration began—Australia was Great Britain's biggest prison, and many Irish were sentenced to life there. Their crimes often seem paltry compared to such a major punishment. For the offense of stealing clothes or threatening a landlord, an individual could be sentenced to exile on the other side of the Earth for the rest of his or her life—a sentence known as "transportation." Occasionally, family members left behind in Ireland managed to join their loved one in Australia, but usually a man or woman who left was gone for good.

Ironically, criminals transported to Australia were sometimes much better off than the poorer immigrants who voluntarily chose to sail away from Ireland. Prison ships were subject to much stricter standards than commercial ones (which often weren't subject to any), and all ships carried a doctor onboard to minister to the prisoners. The convicts were fed and clothed. Men and women traveled on separate ships, and women often brought their children along with them. Australia itself was a land of immense opportunity; convicts who were deemed harmless found numerous jobs available to them, and many of them became quite prosperous.

Relatively few Irish intentionally emigrated to Australia or New Zealand, largely because the long journey was four times more expensive than passage to the United States, but those who went found a vast and sparsely populated land. They encountered some of the old English prejudices, but in a land where most of the people had arrived as prisoners, being Irish or Catholic was not a serious impediment to social advancement. Many Irish immigrants soon became wealthy through farming and wool production.

The Impact of Emigration

This outflow of people had a tremendous impact, both on Ireland and on the destination countries. By 1890, some 3 million Irish-born people lived in other countries. In Ireland, it meant that the remaining population had a better chance of getting by, but it also meant a degree of stagnation. By taking away the youngest and most vigorous members of the workforce, emigration deprived Ireland of the surplus manpower that could have fueled an industrial revolution. Instead, Irish muscles powered the factories of England and the United States.

ESSENTIAL

The wide-scale emigration took a huge psychological toll on those remaining in Ireland. Everyone living on the island would have known someone, and probably many people, who had gone away forever. It seems likely that this constant sense of loss would have contributed to the sense of fatalism and morbidity that has appeared in so much of Ireland's art and literature.

Another impact of losing the young population was that it made revolution in Ireland unlikely. With its youngsters gone, the remaining population tended toward conservatism. While Ireland in the late nineteenth century certainly had its share of revolutionaries, one has to wonder what would have happened if all the angry young men running the political machines in Boston and New York had stayed home. It is noteworthy that Ireland's final revolt against England happened during World War I, when ordinary emigration policies had been suspended.

The Story Continues

The story of Irish emigration isn't over. You'll still frequently run into authentic Irish accents in the many pubs of Boston and New York. Thousands of young Irish men and women emigrate every year. The difference, however, is their reason for leaving. Today, Irish people emigrate for education, or for job relocations, or because they've always heard how much fun Boston is. The days of people leaving because of hunger and poverty are over. Ⓔ

Chapter 14

E The Road to Independence

The Ireland that dragged itself out of the Great Hunger was changed forever. Lingering resentment began to take shape, leading to an organized political movement for independence. Eventually, the forces of Irish Nationalism won their independence but the violent path they chose has left scars to this day.

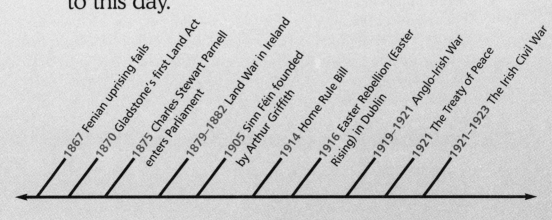

1867 Fenian uprising fails

1870 Gladstone's first Land Act

1875 Charles Stewart Parnell enters Parliament

1879–1882 Land War in Ireland

1905 Sinn Féin founded by Arthur Griffith

1914 Home Rule Bill

1916 Easter Rebellion (Easter Rising) in Dublin

1919–1921 Anglo-Irish War

1921 The Treaty of Peace

1921–1923 The Irish Civil War

The Rebirth of Nationalism

The Irish Nationalist movement rose out of the anger people felt about the famine and the continuing economic disparities of their island. It first manifested itself in agrarian secret societies—groups of farmers and laborers who secretly gathered in the countryside to enforce their own views of justice, usually against landowners and their agents. Groups like this had existed for over a century, but in the 1850s their campaigns of rural terrorism and economic sanctions became more aggressive and targeted specifically the English. The most powerful of these secret societies was the Irish Republican Brotherhood (IRB), known commonly as the Fenians.

FACT

The name "Fenian" referred to Finn MacCool's legendary band of warriors, the Fianna, who defended Ireland in the distant past. (See Chapter 3 for the stories of Finn's legendary exploits.)

The Fenians

The principal mover behind the Fenians was James Stephens, a fiery orator with a gift for organization and a vague notion of an independent Irish nation. John O'Mahoney, the head of the powerful U.S. Fenian chapter, was his ally. Stephens and O'Mahoney built the Fenian Brotherhood into a secret, semirevolutionary society with thousands of members. They founded the newspaper *Irish People* to express their desire for land reform and Irish independence.

Fenians in Ireland were mostly Catholic farmers and shopkeepers who had little political power. So the Fenian leaders decided that their greatest chance for success lay not in politics but in armed revolt, just like Wolfe Tone had envisioned in 1798. Working with O'Mahoney, Stephens actively recruited Irish-American Civil War veterans to come fight for Ireland.

The 1867 Uprising and the Manchester Martyrs

In 1867 the Fenians took action. They didn't have enough weapons to pose any real threat to British military power, but they hoped that an act of armed defiance would encourage the people to rise up against England. They launched several raids to steal weapons from police and coast guard stations; unfortunately for them, the people did not rally to their aid as they had hoped, and most of their fighters got caught. The English quickly broke up the Fenian military organization and imprisoned its leaders. They executed Fenian leaders William Allen, Michael Larkin, and Michael O'Brien on dubious legal grounds. These men became known as the "Manchester Martyrs."

The 1867 Uprising didn't have much of a material impact. But the Fenians and the Manchester Martyrs had planted Nationalist ideas in the minds of the Irish people, and these ideas gradually transformed themselves into action.

The Home Rule Party

The Fenians kept (quietly) calling for armed revolt. But in the following decades the banner of Irish Nationalism moved away from the rifle and into the realm of politics.

After the famine, both Catholics and Protestants had begun to feel that the English could not rule their island effectively and justly. Although they had their own differences, an uneasy coalition of conservative Protestants and liberal Catholics got together and formed the Home Rule Party. This party got a bunch of its members into Parliament at the same time that a liberal, Prime Minister William Gladstone, was emerging as a giant in British politics.

Gladstone's Involvement

Gladstone realized that Ireland's complaints against England were justified and that England's presence in Ireland was based on a tradition of injustice; at the same time, he felt that the Home Rulers were too radical. He tried to defuse the Home Rule movement by enacting landmark legislation to address Irish grievances—killing home rule with kindness. His first act, in 1868, declared that the Protestant Church of

Ireland was no longer the official religion of the entire country. Most Irish loved this. The act was cheered in Dublin but condemned in Belfast, where the population was mostly Protestant.

Gladstone's most important reforms were his Land Acts of 1870 and 1881. Before these acts, the average Irish farmer rented his farmland (usually from an English landowner) and lived in constant fear of eviction. The Land Acts granted these farmers protection against unreasonable rents and unfair evictions, and made it easier for them to buy land. Over time, the Land Acts greatly improved the lives of many farmers, and Gladstone's strategy might well have defused the Home Rule movement, if not for the emergence of one Ireland's most charismatic leaders—Charles Stewart Parnell.

Parnell's Fight for Ireland

Parnell was handsome, impassioned, and articulate, and he took Parliament by storm. People didn't know what to make of him; he was a wealthy, Protestant landowner, but at the same time he supported the radical Nationalist politics of poor Catholic farmers. He entered Parliament in 1875 as the representative for County Meath. His confident oratory and uncompromising dedication to land reform instantly made him a leader of the Home Rule Party. When he felt that Irish issues were being ignored in Parliament, he recruited his fellow Irish MPs to obstruct parliamentary proceedings until his issues were heard.

The Land War

Parnell was president of the Land League, a farmers' organization that called for relief of exorbitant rents, more lenient eviction policies, and easier land ownership for small farmers. Gladstone's Land Acts had made some progress on these fronts, but that progress was too slow for Parnell. His Land League insisted that farmers evicted from their property should hold their ground, and it tacitly condoned the use of boycotts and violence against landlords who took possession of an evicted tenant's land. This period of rural intimidation and economic sanction became known as the Land War.

FACT

A famous Land War episode involved a landlord named Captain Boycott, who was notorious for evicting tenants. After the Land League persuaded local farmers not to harvest his crops, fifty Ulster farmers were shipped in for the harvest, as well as 6,000 British troops to protect them. This case gave us the word "boycott"—a protest in which people refuse to do business with the boycotted party.

Gladstone didn't approve of Parnell's obstructionist policies and endorsement of Land League violence; he had Parnell arrested and thrown in Kilmainham Jail in 1881. Parnell continued to run his political machine from jail, and he achieved unprecedented popularity in Ireland for his defiance of the Prime Minister.

Both Parnell and Gladstone, however, realized that they needed to work together to achieve real reform. They carried on secret negotiations through two intermediaries, Captain Willie O'Shea and his wife, Katherine (Kitty). Gladstone and Parnell eventually reached a settlement called the Kilmainham Treaty, in which Parnell restrained Land League violence in exchange for his release and Gladstone's cooperation on a more powerful Land Act.

The Issue of Home Rule

In the 1885 election, Parnell's Home Rulers took 85 of the 103 Irish seats in Parliament. It appeared that some form of constitutional solution to home rule was in sight. In 1886 Parnell and Gladstone brought forth a Home Rule Bill to finally give Ireland a form of independence.

ESSENTIAL

"Home rule" meant different things to different people. While the Fenians called for complete separation, Parnell wanted an Ireland with its own Parliament, responsible for its own economic and social affairs, but still a part of the British Empire. For most Irish people, this limited form of independence was perfectly acceptable.

The Problem of Ulster

There was a big problem, though—the Protestants in the northern part of Ireland (Ulster) didn't want home rule. The rise of the Home Rule Party called attention for the first time to a phenomenon that Irish Nationalists had traditionally ignored and would continue to ignore to their detriment—the loyalty of Ulster Unionists (those who wanted Ireland to remain part of the United Kingdom). That's why Protestants had founded the Orange Order during the time of Wolfe Tone (see Chapter 8). That's also why they created the militant Ulster Defence Association after Gladstone disestablished the Protestant Church in Ireland in 1868.

Many Irish in Ulster supported the concept of home rule. But there were also many who thought it would inevitably lead to a complete separation from Britain and a subsequent loss of position by the dominant Protestant population. These folks were totally against home rule and threatened to oppose it wholeheartedly, even with violence if they had to.

Parnell's Fall

The 1886 Home Rule Bill didn't pass; it had too much opposition from Ulster and the British House of Lords, who still liked the idea of Ireland as part of the British Empire. Parnell regathered his forces and prepared to try again, but personal affairs suddenly intruded—Willie O'Shea divorced his wife, Kitty, and named Parnell as her lover. It was a huge scandal. Remember, the O'Sheas had served as Parnell's intermediaries for the Kilmainham Treaty. The trial revealed that Parnell and Kitty had been carrying on a passionate affair since then. Captain O'Shea had known about the affair for years; Kitty had already had three children with Parnell.

The case shocked both liberal Englishmen and Catholic Irishmen. Gladstone ended his alliance with Parnell, fearing that his own party in England wouldn't support him if he stuck with the Irishman. Parnell fell from power.

Parnell didn't give up. He married Kitty O'Shea and began a fierce campaign to retake his position in the party. His charisma and political skill were such that he might have actually succeeded, but a fever killed him suddenly in 1891. Kitty was beside him when he died. With Parnell's death, the Home Rule movement lost its momentum, and it didn't truly regain it for another twenty-five years.

Political Stalemate and Celtic Revival

The Home Rule Party continued to press for a parliamentary solution, but without Parnell, it lacked the organization to push it through. The remaining members kept fighting with one another, which diffused their political power. Gladstone sponsored a second Home Rule Bill in 1893, but the same opposition from Conservatives and Ulster Unionists killed it. Ironically, the success of the very Land Acts and other liberal measures that the Home Rule Party had pushed for had taken the wind out of its sails. The state of civil rights and living conditions for the Irish people had significantly improved in recent years, so the need for home rule seemed less intense.

Celtic Revival

While political efforts at nationalism were stuck in a rut, arts and culture saw a huge surge of interest in all things Irish. The English traditionally thought of the Irish as uncouth barbarians, but a new generation of the Irish looked into their island's past and proved the English wrong.

Intellectuals like William Butler Yeats, Douglas Hyde, and Lady Augusta Gregory called for the preservation and appreciation of Irish storytelling, Celtic art, and the fast-fading Irish language. Hyde founded the Gaelic League to promote the Irish language. By 1906 there were more than 900 branches, with more than 100,000 members. In 1903 Yeats and Gregory founded the Irish National Theatre at the Abbey Theatre in Dublin and promoted the production of distinctively Irish plays.

Athletics were another focus of nationalist energy. The Gaelic Athletic Association, founded in 1884, promoted the distinctively Irish sports of Gaelic football and hurling.

In these expressions of Irish culture, many Irish people realized for the first time that their people had a history and culture every bit as worthy as the English. While these movements had little direct political impact, they provided Irish people with an identity and a rallying point for their nationalist feelings.

E-SITE

The Irish National Theatre still stages first-rate productions. You can visit the snazzy new Abbey Theatre on the banks of the Liffey River. This isn't the building frequented by Yeats and Synge, though; that one burned down in 1951.

The Founding of Sinn Féin

Although the independence movement had entered a period of contented inaction, radical Nationalism hadn't disappeared. The IRB (the people who organized the Fenian uprising) was still around, but its call for armed revolt seemed more and more like the talk of cranky old men.

The movement for an independent republic took a quiet step forward in 1905 when a publisher named Arthur Griffith founded a new political party called Sinn Féin, Irish for "ourselves alone." Griffith promoted the Nationalist cause in a newspaper called the *United Irishman,* after Wolfe Tone's old organization. Sinn Féin was a relatively small party throughout the prewar years, but it provided radicals and intellectuals with a place to discuss aggressive alternatives to the slow constitutional path to home rule.

The Decision to Divide Ireland

Home rule made no progress in the Conservative-controlled Parliament of the first decade of the twentieth century. But when the Liberals swept back into power in 1910 behind Prime Minister Herbert Henry Asquith, Ireland was at the top of their agenda. In 1912 Asquith brought forward the third Home Rule Bill, which reached further than any of its predecessors and enjoyed wide popularity among the Irish people.

Ulster Volunteers and Irish Volunteers

There was one section of the Irish population, however, that still opposed home rule—the Ulster Protestants. Seeing the latest Home Rule Bill as the final step toward separation, the members of the Orange Order rose up against it. They organized the Ulster Volunteer Force (UVF), a paramilitary group committed to defending Ulster's union with England. The UVF began drilling and stockpiling weapons. By 1914 there were estimated to be more than 100,000 men ready to fight for the UVF.

In response, Nationalists in the south began their own paramilitary organization called the Irish Volunteers. The Volunteers was initially organized by the remnants of the IRB, although its politics were generally closer to the moderates of the Home Rule Party. The Volunteers claimed to have more than 100,000 members as well, though it had fewer weapons than its rivals in the North.

Dealing with the Ulster Problem

The Ulster dilemma froze the Home Rule Bill in its tracks. Although the Liberals may have had sufficient votes to push the bill through, it was politically very awkward to push away a big group of loyal British subjects, especially when those subjects were threatening to fight to stay in. A leading solution to this problem was to grant home rule and then use the British army to enforce it in Ulster. This proposal faltered when the mutiny at the Curragh revealed that British army officers were opposed to fighting Ulster troops.

FACT

The mutiny at the Curragh showed that the Ulster problem was tougher than people had thought. Sir Arthur Paget, the chief of military forces in Ireland, told his officers that they could choose to exempt themselves from enforcing Irish home rule on Ulster. Most of his officers immediately exempted themselves, thereby calling into question the government's power to enforce any resolution.

The second set of options revolved around some form of partition, in effect dividing Ireland into two states. There were nine counties in the traditional province of Ulster, but only six of them had large Protestant populations, and in 1910 only four of them had Protestant majorities. Unionists and Nationalists suggested different partition plans. Some supported having all of Ulster split off and stay with the United Kingdom, which might have facilitated reunification in the future. Others thought it would be better if only those counties with Protestant majorities broke away from the Irish nation. Both sides spent the next four years wrangling over various proposals, but none met the approval of both the Unionist and the Nationalist sides.

World War I Changes the Game

In August 1914, outside events suddenly changed the whole debate. World War I was breaking out in Europe, and Parliament wanted to solve the Irish problem quickly so that it could concentrate on the coming war. John Redmond, the leader of the Home Rulers, offered the United Kingdom the use of the Irish Volunteers for home defense in exchange for a provisional acceptance of the Home Rule Bill, leaving aside the Ulster question for the time being. Asquith's Parliament agreed, and the bill was put on the books with the proviso that it would not go into effect until a year had passed or the war was over. Both sides saw this as a way to move forward on the Ireland issue without coming to a final decision on Ulster.

To some Irish Nationalists, England's enemy was their friend. The IRB's Roger Casement went to Germany and asked for a brigade of Irish prisoners of war to fight against England. The prisoners told him to go to hell. The Germans weren't impressed, but they sent him home with a boatload of weapons anyway. The boat sank, and British troops captured Casement. He was executed for treason in 1916.

The act was immediately received as a tremendous step forward for Ireland, and Nationalists felt free for the first time in decades to express British patriotism. Thousands of young men from all parts of Ireland came forward to serve in the war, including many members of the UVF and the Irish Volunteers. In the early days, morale was high.

As the war ground on, however, Irish opinions began to turn. Not only did the war delay the enactment of home rule, but each month brought new lists of Irish casualties from the battlefields of Europe as well. The British military didn't accept Redmond's offer to use the Volunteers, nor did it arm them for home defense. It was rumored that the English draft would soon spread to Ireland. To make matters worse, a change in government put Ulster Unionist leaders in the British Cabinet, making Nationalists suspect that home rule might be delayed indefinitely. It was in this environment that the radicals in the IRB and Sinn Féin decided to make their move.

The Easter Rebellion (The Easter Rising)

On April 24, 1916, Easter Monday, a group of armed Irish Volunteers moved into the General Post Office in Dublin and occupied the building. Patrick Pearse (or Pádraig MacPiarais), a schoolteacher and Sinn Féin activist, read the Proclamation of the Irish Republic, a statement declaring Ireland's independence. Simultaneously, armed Volunteers took over other significant buildings throughout the city.

E-SITE

The General Post Office on O'Connell Street is one of Dublin's most famous landmarks. Today it is both a monument and a very busy post office. You can still see bullet holes in the wall, left there from the Easter Uprising. In Ireland, "going postal" has a whole different meaning.

The uprising was a surprise for Unionists and Nationalists alike; with home rule already on the books, armed revolution seemed a little extreme. British troops were quickly sent into the city, and soon much of central Dublin was in flames. The Volunteers lacked either the arms or the organization to put up a real military resistance to the British army, and after a week the last of the rebels surrendered. The fighting killed 450, and afterward more than 1,000 Irish were sent to prisons in England.

At the time of the Easter Rebellion, most Irish people—even Nationalists—didn't think violence was the answer to Ireland's problems. Most people were content to let the constitutional procedures take their course. Ensuing events, however, soon led to a change in opinions.

In May of 1916 the British army began executing leaders of the rebellion. They shot or hanged sixteen men. Most Irish thought that they had decided to execute the prisoners much too hastily and without fair trials. In addition, there were reports of bad treatment of imprisoned rebels. The British released the remaining prisoners by Christmas in 1916, primarily as a gesture to help bring the United States into the war, but that did little to quiet emotions in Ireland.

Independence to All but Six

Prime Minister Asquith appointed David Lloyd George (who would replace Asquith as prime minister later that year) to resolve the Irish home rule question once and for all. Lloyd George, relying heavily on the advice of Unionist associates, settled on a compromise in which Ireland got home rule but the six majority Protestant counties in the north remained part of the Union (the British Empire).

To southern Nationalists, this was unacceptable. To make matters worse, the British army seized the weapons from Irish Volunteer groups in the south but allowed UVF forces to keep theirs. People in the south began to believe that the Home Rule Bill on the books was a charade.

This gave Sinn Féin its big chance. Led by Éamon de Valera, a half-American mathematician who had taken part in the Easter Rebellion, Sinn Féin began to take Parliament seats away from the traditional home rule candidates. Sinn Féin's stated goal was an independent, unified Republic of Ireland. While the party was vague about how exactly it wanted to accomplish this, its message struck a chord with a young Irish population that was tired of World War I and the endless stalemate of the home rule debate.

Sinn Féin's parliamentary successes were limited to Nationalist hotbeds until the British government gave them two great boosts: first, it extended army conscription to Ireland, an act the Irish had dreaded for years; second, it arrested de Valera and other Sinn Féin leaders on vague and insubstantial charges of a plot against the government. Both actions were highly unpopular, and they convinced the majority of the Irish that the British government was not serious about letting Ireland run its own affairs.

The War of Independence

While Sinn Féin was taking the road of politics, a twenty-seven-year-old Easter Rebellion veteran named Michael Collins was exploring an alternate path. Working with the IRB and the Irish Volunteers, he began organizing a paramilitary force that could put guns behind Sinn Féin's claims of independence. This force became known as the Irish Republican Army—the IRA.

FACT

The War of Independence was also known as the Anglo-Irish War. It lasted for two years (1919–21), during which the Irish resistance fighters waged guerilla warfare against the British soldiers and police.

IRA Versus the Black and Tans

Most Irish people deplored the IRA killings. Collins knew that simply assassinating a few individuals would never drive the English out, but he probably calculated that his systematic terrorism would provoke the English into an overly aggressive response. And that's exactly what happened.

The British shipped thousands of soldiers to Ireland and created a new police force called the Black and Tans to help keep the peace. The Black and Tans were composed primarily of former British soldiers who had neither the police training nor the familiarity with Ireland that the sensitive situation demanded. These men found Ireland very stressful—the people who murdered their fellow officers were indistinguishable from the people they were supposed to protect. So they responded with a campaign of reprisals that matched the IRA's in brutality, beating or killing hundreds of innocent civilians in an attempt to intimidate the IRA. The IRA responded with more bullets.

This period of guerilla strikes and police reprisals is known as the Anglo-Irish War. Both sides lost hundreds of men. The IRA made little military headway, but the war's impact on the opinions of the Irish people was devastating to the British. The peacekeeping strategy backfired—the brutal and often indiscriminate reprisals of the Black and Tans convinced people that Sinn Féin was right after all and that Great Britain was a repressive occupier that would only relinquish Ireland if forced out.

Michael Collins (1890–1922) played several extraordinary roles for the Nationalists: spymaster, guerrilla leader, minister of Finance, diplomat, and, finally, tragic martyr. His exploits were legendary. Liam Neeson portrayed his life in the unabashedly patriotic movie *Michael Collins* (1996).

The British Call for Peace

The conflict was simultaneously playing havoc with British politics. English civilians were shocked by the daily stories of police brutality in Ireland. In composing the Treaty of Versailles at the end of the war, Britain claimed that World War I had been fought to protect to the rights of small countries to determine their own fates, and yet it had a small country in its own backyard demanding its own rights. The English began to think that enough was enough.

Prime Minister Lloyd George called for a cease-fire and treaty negotiations. The fact that he was offering a treaty was significant; only sovereign nations can sign treaties with one another, so his offer made clear that independence was on the table. The Sinn Féin and IRA leaders agreed to the cease-fire, and a group of ambassadors led by Arthur Griffith and Michael Collins went to London in 1921 to negotiate.

Both sides agreed that Ireland would take a dominion status similar to that enjoyed by Canada—independent, but still a part of the British Empire. The chief sticking points were whether the Irish would have to swear an oath to the king, and the final settlement of the Ulster question.

The Resulting Treaty

After skillful negotiating by a British team including Lloyd George and Winston Churchill, the Irish contingent largely gave in on both points. The final Treaty of Peace between Great Britain and Ireland did not demand that Irish citizens swear allegiance to the king, but it did require them to recognize his dominion over Ireland. More significantly, the treaty established the six-county *partition* of Ulster pushed for by Unionists since 1914. This action, called Partition, created the political entity called Northern Ireland.

Collins signed the treaty, saying it was the best that Ireland could achieve under the current conditions. After a bitter struggle, it was passed by the Dáil (the new Irish Parliament). Not everyone was happy, however; Éamon de Valera condemned the treaty, as did the majority of radical Nationalists in the IRA. These Nationalists said that they had fought for a united Ireland, and they wouldn't take one cut into pieces. And so the Irish Civil War (1921–23) began.

QUESTION?

Was violence necessary to achieve independence?
This question is still debated today. Collins and de Valera thought it was. But given that home rule was already on the books, and also considering the increasing independence of other British possessions since 1914 (Canada and India are just two examples), Irish independence probably would have come about without violence.

The Irish Civil War

Like all civil wars, this one was marked by bitterness and atrocity. Collins was forced to organize an official military response against the same IRA men he had fought beside for years. Hundreds died, and Collins himself was killed in an ambush. The anti-treaty forces, however, did not have the support of the populace, and it was soon clear that they could not win. To stop the bloodshed, Éamon de Valera announced that it was time for Ireland to accept the treaty and move on.

Ireland had peace and independence at last, but not without a cost. The scars of the Civil War haunted Irish politics for decades. More significantly, the division between the Irish Free State in the South and Northern Ireland had become real and immovable. Unionists in Northern Ireland, appalled by the violence of the Anglo-Irish and Civil Wars, resolved more strongly than ever to remain part of the United Kingdom. This unnatural division between North and South has plagued people on both sides of the border to this day.

Chapter 15

E The Path to Republic of Ireland

W hen the Irish Civil War ended, Ireland had peace and independence at last. Over the next fifty years, the people of Ireland worked through the difficult questions regarding their relationship with the United Kingdom, the role of the Catholic Church in their government, and the thorny question of Northern Ireland.

1923 Cease-fire; Irish Free State joins League of Nations

1926 Founding of Fianna Fáil

1932 Fianna Fáil wins general election

1932–1938 Economic War with the United Kingdom

1937 Éamon de Valera's new constitution

1939 Ireland declares neutrality in World War II

1949 Birth of the Republic of Ireland

The Irish Free State

The Ireland that emerged from the Anglo-Irish Treaty in 1921 was known as the Irish Free State. In many ways, it had the independence that Irish Nationalists had dreamed about for years. It had its own Parliament, the Dáil Éireann (doyl ay-ran), which was responsible for Ireland's social and economic affairs. It inherited a British government infrastructure that allowed it to jump quickly into efficient self-government. Police and Irish home defense forces were now entirely under Ireland's control, with a new, unarmed police force known as the Garda Síochána (GAR-dah sho-HA-na).

But the Free State still maintained a number of ties to England. It was still subject to British international policy, a point made clear by the naval bases that the British navy maintained at Irish ports. A British "governor" continued to serve in Dublin, although the role was largely symbolic. The most powerful symbolic gesture was that Irish civil servants were required to swear the Oath of Fidelity (also known as the Oath of Allegiance) to the British Empire before they could serve. These remnants of the old relationship with England played a powerful role in the course of Irish Free State politics.

FACT

The Irish Free State flew the same green, white, and orange flag that the Republic of Ireland flies today. The three colors represent the hope of many Irish people for their island's reunification: green is the traditional color of Ireland, orange represents the Protestant population in the north, and white signifies the hope for peace between these two groups.

Free State Politics

The civil-war beginning of the Irish Free State accounts for the curious political divisions of twentieth-century Ireland: the fundamental political divisions in Ireland developed around those who supported the Anglo-Irish Treaty and those who opposed it, rather than on the Liberal/Conservative or Labor/Business lines seen in the political systems of most modern democratic states.

The victorious pro-treaty faction created a political party called Cumann na nGaedheal (ku-man na gah-yehl), which had been the original name of Sinn Féin in 1900. Cumann na nGaedheal formed the basis of the Free State government. Its leader, William T. Cosgrave, tried to establish a stable Irish state within its constitutional boundaries as a British dominion.

But the opponents of the Anglo-Irish Treaty were still an important force. The opposing party, Fianna Fáil (fee-AH-na foil), was created in 1926 by Éamon de Valera and his supporters. Fianna Fáil maintained that the provisions of the Anglo-Irish Treaty—the Oath of Fidelity and the partition of Northern Ireland—were unacceptable compromises. Although de Valera had called a halt to military opposition to the treaty, he still believed that Ireland needed to assert its independence. Fianna Fáil had limited influence in the early days of the Free State because its members refused to swear the Oath of Fidelity to the British Empire and thus could not take their seats in the Dáil.

The priority of the Free State government under Cumann na nGaedheal was to create a stable government. In 1924 a contingent of old IRA men within the Free State Army voiced objections to the new government. Rather than risk a military coup, the Free State government immediately removed all objectionable officers from power and placed the army under the command of a loyal Garda commander. They made clear from the start that the Irish Free State was going to be ruled by civil rather than military powers.

Conflict over Partition

A potential crisis arose when the Boundary Commission met in 1925. This was a joint meeting between English and Irish diplomats to re-examine the Northern Ireland border. When Michael Collins had negotiated the Anglo-Irish Treaty back in 1921, he had not wanted to partition Ireland and had been led to believe that the Boundary Commission would bring additional northern Catholics into the Free State. Collins, however, was dead at this point and could not defend his position on the treaty. When it became clear that Ulster Unionists were unwilling to grant any additional land to the Free State, the Free State government pulled out of the talks rather than risk another destabilizing conflict.

In 1923, Ireland joined the League of Nations and then, in 1955, the United Nations. Both were important steps for Ireland to demonstrate its independence. Éamon de Valera served as president of the League of Nations Council in 1932 and as president of the Assembly in 1938. Irish peacekeepers have been active with the UN since the 1950s.

De Valera Rises to Power

Éamon de Valera dominated twentieth-century Irish politics. He led Sinn Féin (1917–26), the Irish provisional government (1919–22), the anti-treaty forces (1922–25), and then Fianna Fáil (for the next fifty years). He served for sixteen years as Taoiseach (prime minister) and nineteen years as president. He retired from politics at the age of ninety-one and died two years later, in 1975. Throughout, de Valera was known as a fervent patriot, a devout Catholic, and an incorruptible servant of his people.

An Interesting Character

De Valera was born in New York in 1882 to an Irish mother and a Spanish father—hence his unusual name. This made him an American, which he used to his advantage throughout his political career. When he was three, his father died and his mother sent him to Ireland to be raised by his grandmother in Bruree, County Limerick. He studied mathematics in Dublin and became a teacher. He also came to love the Irish language and became involved with the Gaelic League, which led to his extreme Nationalism.

De Valera was an intellectual and he looked the part—tall, thin, and bespectacled. He didn't stand out from the crowd until he ended up in prison after the Easter Rebellion; subsequently, his eloquent letters and well-thought-out arguments for Irish independence began to inspire a generation of young men, and they soon chose him as their leader.

Fianna Fáil Enters the Political Mainstream

In 1927 Fianna Fáil politicians agreed to take the Oath of Fidelity after an IRA assassination of a top Free State administrator threatened to renew factional violence. De Valera decided that the time had come to work within the constitutional framework in order to achieve his party's goals. This strategy became increasingly effective after the British Parliament passed the Statute of Westminster, which gave imperial dominions—Canada, India, South Africa, and the Irish Free State—the right to disregard parliamentary actions that they did not believe should apply to them. Pushed to its logical conclusion, the Statute of Westminster effectively allowed dominions to make themselves independent in all but name. This was the chance de Valera had been waiting for.

E-SITE

The Irish people have treasured de Valera's memory. In his childhood home of Bruree there is a museum devoted to him, which contains items from his schooldays—letters, glasses, a medal, a lock of hair, and a desk carved with his initials. You can also visit the cottage where his grandmother raised him.

The Fianna Fáil Path to Independence

The 1932 general elections returned a majority of Fianna Fáil delegates to the Dáil. A few months afterward, de Valera announced that Ireland would no longer pay land annuities to England. These annuities were part of the Anglo-Irish Treaty: farmers who had benefited from English government loans to buy land were supposed to repay the loans to the Free State government, who would then hand the money over to England. But de Valera maintained that the land had been stolen from the Irish in the first place, so Ireland had a moral justification for withholding the annuity payments.

The act was popular in Ireland, but the British Treasury was not amused. It immediately began a system of retaliatory trade measures to punish Ireland. British tariffs increased the cost of Irish cattle imports by up to 80 percent. British markets constituted 96 percent of Irish exports at this time, so the tariffs were costly, although they were partially offset by not having to pay the land annuities. This period of trade retaliation was known unofficially as the Economic War.

Withholding the land annuities was a powerful statement of independence, but Fianna Fáil wanted to go further. In 1933 it passed legislation that removed the requirement for civil servants to swear the Oath of Fidelity. Again, the British did not like to see another breach of the treaty, but the Statute of Westminster made the Irish action perfectly legal.

The Opposition—Fine Gael

There were some in Ireland who thought that Fianna Fáil was going too far too fast. The old Free State politicians of Cumann na nGaedheal were still around, although their party had lost much of its power. In 1933 Cumann na nGaedheal joined together with two smaller groups, the Centre Party and the National Guard, to form Fine Gael. The newly empowered Fine Gael advocated a more moderate position toward England than Fianna Fáil, and it tended to appeal more to large landholders and business interests, whereas Fianna Fáil traditionally appealed to small farmers and laborers. These differences aside, by European political standards the parties were, and still are, fairly close together ideologically. Fine Gael and Fianna Fáil have continued to this day as the two major parties of Irish politics.

FACT

The oldest political party in Ireland is the Labour Party, founded by trade union activists in 1912. Labour is currently Ireland's third largest party. In the past, it has joined in coalition governments with both Fianna Fáil and Fine Gael.

A New Constitution

Fianna Fáil took a further step in 1936 by removing references to the Crown and the British governor-general from the Irish Constitution. This was a direct challenge to the basis of the Anglo-Irish Treaty, but its reception in England was probably mitigated by the crisis over Edward VIII's abdication. In any event, it was clear that Ireland was in charge of its own constitution.

In 1937 de Valera made this point official by passing a new constitution that officially ended the Irish Free State of the Anglo-Irish Treaty. This new constitution established a number of key points: Ireland was now officially a nation called Éire; the nation of Éire consisted of the entire island of Ireland, including the six counties of the north; and it allowed for religious freedom but reserved a "special relationship" with the Catholic Church. The constitution also created the position of an Irish president. The first person to fill that role was Douglas Hyde, the scholar and patriot who forty years before had rallied nationalist feelings around the Gaelic League.

The reaction in England was resignation; the government under Prime Minister Arthur Neville Chamberlain was unwilling to fight the move, which was, after all, technically legal under the Statute of Westminster. The people in Northern Ireland were outraged by both the new constitution's claim to the entire island, and by the pro-Catholic position of the new country. If the two states had been far from reunification before, this step put them that much further apart. But by this time, de Valera and his Nationalist supporters had mostly given up hope of a near-term reunification of Ireland.

The economic war with England came to an end in 1938, with the British Treasury giving in. In exchange for a £10,000,000 lump payment, the Treasury excused Irish farmers from any further land payments.

Ireland's Neutrality in World War II

The great test of Irish sovereignty came in 1939, when England and Germany went to war. The United Kingdom expected that Ireland would join the war against the Axis powers. Ireland refused. In addition, de Valera refused to allow the British navy to use its former naval bases on Irish soil. In Ireland, World War II was known as "the Emergency."

Why Ireland Stayed Neutral

Ireland received a great deal of criticism for its choice of neutrality. Many English considered it a betrayal of their long-term relationship, and their government initiated an unofficial economic war of sanctions against Ireland. Americans were shocked that Ireland would not take an official stance against Germany. De Valera's government was under immense internal pressure as well, from a population whose sentiments were overwhelmingly on the side of the Allies.

But de Valera wanted to prove a point: Ireland was no longer a part of the British Empire, and the most decisive way to demonstrate that fact was to maintain firm neutrality in the war. One of the traditional arguments of the Republican movement had been that Irishmen should not have to die for another country's empire. It was a tough stance to take, but de Valera was not going to lose his chance to take it. Moreover, Ireland was in no condition to fight; years of warfare had reduced it to a state of poverty with an army of only 7,000 poorly equipped soldiers.

The War Years

Despite the official stance of neutrality, Ireland did support the Allied cause in a number of quiet ways. Thousands of Irish citizens were allowed to volunteer for Allied armies. While downed German airmen were interned, downed Allied soldiers were promptly handed over to Northern Ireland. When Axis bombing set Belfast ablaze in 1941, de Valera promptly sent fire trucks from Dublin, Drogheda, and Dundalk to help combat the fire. Ireland also suffered its own war wounds: a German bombing raid intended for Liverpool lost its way and bombed Dublin, killing thirty-four civilians.

When the war was over, both British and American diplomats harbored resentment against Ireland's seemingly unfriendly stance. But to de Valera and his government, Ireland had demonstrated once and for all that it was in charge of its own destiny.

Meanwhile, Northern Ireland used the war to show its dedication to the United Kingdom. Thousands of Northern Ireland's citizens volunteered to fight. Belfast's shipbuilding industry played an important role in supplying warships for the British navy. Because of its economic importance to the Allied war effort, Belfast was the target of heavy German bombing; more than 1,200 people died in the "Belfast Blitz." Northern Ireland's sacrifices had a significant impact on its relationship with the British government in later years.

FACT

In 1945 de Valera shocked international observers by visiting the German embassy in Dublin to express his condolences on the death of Adolph Hitler. The Americans and English could not understand the gesture, but de Valera viewed it as the appropriate action for the head of a neutral state.

A Republic at Last

De Valera steered Ireland through the dangerous days of the Emergency, but he was not the one to cut Ireland's last ties to England. In 1948, after sixteen years of Fianna Fáil dominance, Fine Gael joined with the Labour Party and a radical Nationalist group called Clann na Poblachta (klan-na po-blah-ta) to create a coalition government.

It was a strange coalition: the moderates, leftists, and nationalists of the three parties could agree on little more than a common desire to unseat Fianna Fáil. The Taoiseach in charge of this new government was John Costello, a Dublin lawyer who had served with Fine Gael for years.

In a meeting with the prime minister of Canada in 1948, Costello revealed that Ireland intended to declare itself a republic. The following year, with a unanimous vote of the Cabinet, Ireland officially removed itself from the British Commonwealth. Ireland was now officially the Republic of Ireland. It has continued in this form to the present day.

The British Reaction

The United Kingdom was surprised and angry. Parliament responded with the Ireland Act of 1949, which stated that Northern Ireland was still part of the United Kingdom and would remain so until the people of

Northern Ireland consented to leave. This act directly contradicted the constitution of Ireland, which claimed Northern Ireland as part of the nation. In addition, the United Kingdom guaranteed to the people of Northern Ireland that their social security benefits would not be allowed to fall behind Britain's.

The effect of the Ireland Act was to seal the partition between Northern Ireland and the Republic more solidly than ever before. Politicians on both sides recognized this fact, and many criticized Costello's government for making an essentially symbolic gesture that ruined any chances of undoing Partition. British Prime Minister Clement Attlee remarked, "The government of Éire considered the cutting of the last tie which united Éire to the British Commonwealth as a more important objective than ending Partition."

But what was done was done. The island of Ireland was now home to a British state and an independent republic, both looking anxiously across the border and wondering how they ended up so far apart.

Ireland under the Republic

By 1950, Ireland had finally resolved its long-standing questions about its government and its relationship with England. In the following years, the Irish government focused increasingly on economics. The country was still one of the poorest in Europe, and despite its political claims to independence, the Irish economy was heavily dependent on England for both import and export markets. These economic realities were underlined by Ireland's high rate of emigration. The Irish population had continued to drop in every census since the Great Famine of the 1840s.

Fianna Fáil regained power from Fine Gael in 1951 and held on to it for most of the next fifty years. Both parties, however, agreed on the basic solution to Ireland's economic problems: foreign investment, foreign loans, and a planned economy. The plan was to use foreign capital to build industries that would finally relieve Ireland's chronic unemployment.

The plans were successful. Ireland benefited from American Marshall Plan funds, and American and English businesses showed enthusiasm for investing in Ireland. The economy slowly developed, and by the 1960s the Irish standard of living was creeping toward the standard of Western Europe. The rate of emigration slowed down. The 1966 census showed, for the first time in more than 100 years, an increase in population.

FACT

Ireland doesn't have much wood or coal, so whenever the Irish have needed a power source, they've always turned to peat—the combustible organic matter stacked meters thick in Ireland's abundant bogs. In keeping with tradition, modern Ireland has fueled its growing industries with electricity from highly efficient peat-burning power plants.

Ireland eagerly took part in the developing multinational organizations of the postwar years. The Republic joined the UN in 1955 and the European Economic Community in 1972. In these platforms, Ireland put forth the image of a small country, related to England but not tied to it, ready to take its own place in the international community.

Trouble Brewing in the North

While the Republic of Ireland worked out its path of independent development, Northern Ireland embraced its role as a loyal province of the United Kingdom. Northern Ireland's industries successfully pursued further economic ties with England, and the standard of living in the North continued to outpace that of the South. As described previously, Northern Ireland played an important role in World War II. In part because of its sacrifices during the war, the United Kingdom rewarded Northern Ireland with substantial welfare funding, allowing the North's standard of living to rise further above that of the South.

A Divided Society

Northern Ireland's image as a peaceful and prosperous British province, however, concealed a tension beneath the surface. There were still Irish Nationalists who wanted to undo Partition. Fianna Fáil maintained that Northern Ireland was part of Ireland, as shown by territorial claims in the 1937 constitution. The Protestant politicians of Northern Ireland staunchly denied these claims. In 1954 they passed the Flags and Emblems Act, which made it illegal to fly the tricolor Irish flag in Northern Ireland. Although politicians in the Republic often spoke of reuniting their country, the majority of them realized that, in practical terms, their claims were little more than rhetoric.

Seamus Heaney (1939–present) is Northern Ireland's greatest poet. Born into a Catholic family in rural County Derry, Heaney poured the tensions and divisions of his society into some of the most evocative poetry of the century. He is currently a professor at Harvard University. His works, including *North* and *Seeing Things*, earned him the Nobel Prize for literature in 1995.

One group that did not accept Northern Ireland's status was the Irish Republican Army (IRA). Remnants of this organization had existed ever since the Civil War, even though the Free State had outlawed it. From 1956 to 1962, IRA terrorists in the Republic waged a guerrilla war across the border against Northern Ireland's police force and soldiers. The conflict claimed nineteen lives. In the end, however, the IRA ceased the effort after it acknowledged that it had no support from the people of either the Republic or Northern Ireland.

The situation would change, however, in the late 1960s. Although Northern Ireland was generally prosperous, beneath the surface was a profound inequality that split along religious lines. The Catholic minority of Northern Ireland was kept as an underclass by an entrenched system of discrimination in employment, housing, and education. Anger at the continuing inequality would spark a wave of civil rights protests. These protests set in motion the bloody conflict known as the Troubles. (E)

Chapter 16

The Troubles

For more than three decades, a bloody conflict known as the Troubles has raged in Northern Ireland. By 1999, it had claimed the lives of 3,636 people and injured 36,000 more. Most of those people were civilians. The recent success of the peace process, however, suggests that Ireland may be ready to leave tragedy behind.

1968 Derry Civil Rights March

1972 Bloody Sunday; Stormont government falls

1974 Ulster Workers' Council strike

1981 Hunger strikes

1985 Anglo-Irish Agreement

1988–1993 Gerry Adams and John Hume hold secret peace talks

1994 Gerry Adams visits United States; IRA cease-fire

1996 Canary Wharf bomb breaks the cease-fire

1998 Good Friday Agreement

The Roots of the Troubles

During the years when King Henry VIII and Queen Elizabeth I extended English control over most of Ireland, the northern counties of Ulster were regarded as the most "savage" part of the island. In the early 1600s, King James I (of King James Bible fame) decided to cure Ulster of its Catholicism by displacing the Irish and settling English and Scottish Protestants there. This settlement became known as the Ulster Plantation.

Different Paths

As a result, the northern and southern regions of the island developed along different lines. While the predominantly Catholic population in the rest of Ireland continued in the traditional Irish jobs of farming and animal husbandry, the largely Protestant population in Ulster embraced the industrial revolution. Belfast became a center of the shipbuilding and linen textile industries. By the nineteenth century, the average person in Ulster was considerably wealthier than his southern counterparts. When the Great Famine struck, the wealthier northern counties showed lower rates of eviction, emigration, and starvation than did Ireland as a whole.

The central conflict of the Troubles is the dispute between Unionists (who think Northern Ireland should remain in the United Kingdom) and Republicans (who want Northern Ireland to join the Republic of Ireland). Most Protestants are Unionists, while most Catholics are Republican.

The prosperity of the north, however, was mostly prosperity for Protestants. The Scots and English who had settled there were keenly aware that their land had been seized from the Irish, and they never lost their anxiety that the previous inhabitants might try to take it back. As in the Protestant Ascendancy, they enforced a social and legal code designed to repress Catholics. Even after O'Connell's reforms had begun to liberate Ireland's Catholics, the people of Ulster dutifully maintained an unofficial system of repression.

Northern Ireland—Protestant State

Ulster Protestant anxieties rose as the Irish Nationalist movement grew. As described in Chapter 14, Unionists in the north blocked the passage of a series of home rule bills, and they formed a variety of organizations, such as the United Orangemen and the Ulster Volunteers, to resist any change that might harm their position of social and economic dominance. The havoc of the Anglo-Irish War and the Irish Civil War further polarized the Protestant stance—they felt that the north was their country, and they didn't want to budge.

Northern Ireland was created in 1921 as a semiautonomous state, still tied to the British Empire—this was part of the agreement that Michael Collins and other Irish Nationalists made with the British. Northern Ireland ruled itself through an independent administration at Stormont, outside Belfast. The north's economic development continued to outpace the Republic of Ireland's. For nearly fifty years the region remained largely peaceful, but just beneath the orderly veneer smoldered the coals of deep-seated resentment.

FACT

For many, the voice of hard-line Unionism is the Reverend Ian Paisley. A cofounder of Ulster's Free Presbyterian Church, Paisley has loudly opposed any concessions to Northern Ireland's Catholic community, including every major peace proposal since the 1960s. Although he's been accused of having ties to paramilitary groups, Paisley has been elected to the British and European Parliaments.

Northern Ireland's approximately 550,000 Catholics never shared equally in the state's prosperity. They officially had all the rights guaranteed by the British Constitution, but unspoken rules kept them a distinct underclass—many companies wouldn't hire Catholics, and many landlords wouldn't rent to them. Most of them worked in low-paying, unskilled jobs. Although Catholics made up 31 percent of the labor force, they only accounted for 6 percent of mechanical engineers, 8 percent of university teachers, and 19 percent of doctors.

Protestants dominated the local government and the Royal Ulster Constabulary (RUC)—the police. Northern Ireland received millions of pounds a year from the British government to invest in infrastructure, but a disproportionate amount of this money went to Protestant areas. It was a civil rights movement waiting to happen.

A Civil Rights Movement Gone Bad

The Troubles began in the late 1960s, when Catholics tried to use peaceful protest to demand equal treatment. But the Protestant population had other ideas and responded with violence. The Irish Republican Army and various Unionist paramilitary groups jumped into the fray, which quickly escalated into something resembling a local war.

The Derry March—the Troubles Begin

In the late 1960s, a population of young, educated, and unemployed Catholics looked west and saw the success of the Civil Rights movement in the United States. They created the Northern Ireland Civil Rights Association (NICRA), intending to use peaceful protest to bring attention to discrimination in employment and housing.

One of NICRA's first efforts at peaceful protest was the Derry March of 1968, which many people consider the start of the Troubles. The protesters planned to march from Belfast to Derry, imitating Martin Luther King's 1966 march from Selma to Montgomery. The 600 marchers proceeded peacefully for four days, but when they reached Derry, a mob of Protestants attacked them with stones, nails, and crowbars. The RUC escort—which was composed primarily of Protestants—did little to protect them. Riots broke out in the Catholic Bogside neighborhood, which the RUC put down brutally.

The Derry March was an inauspicious beginning to the Unionist–Republican debate. It established an unfortunate precedent of mass violence between the sides, and it told the Catholic population that it could not trust the RUC to look after its safety. When Protestant paramilitary groups subsequently launched campaigns of arson and intimidation against them, the Catholics turned to a group that was more than willing to fight back—the IRA.

Paramilitary Violence

The IRA had kept calling for a united Ireland since the War of Independence, although its agitation hadn't been taken seriously for years. The outbreak of violence in Derry was exactly what its members had been looking for: an excuse to strike back at the Unionists and the police forces, which the IRA saw as the agents of British imperialism.

The IRA took on the role of police and defense force for Northern Ireland's Catholics. If someone sold drugs in a Catholic neighborhood, he could be maimed or even killed by the IRA. If Unionist paramilitaries burned down a Catholic house, the IRA would bomb a Protestant pub. A stream of guns and bombs started flowing into the neighborhoods of Belfast and Derry.

Members of the IRA weren't just out to defend Catholics—they also wanted to drive out the English. To that end, they began a campaign of terror against the RUC—and later, against British soldiers.

The Unionist paramilitaries, meanwhile, were waging their own campaign of terror. Groups like the Ulster Defence Association (UDA) and the Red Hand Commandoes used the same tactics of murder and bombing. The UDA's attacks were generally meant to intimidate activist Catholics or to retaliate for IRA killings, which were usually in retaliation for UDA murders, which were generally retaliations for earlier IRA murders . . . and so on.

Of the paramilitary groups, the IRA always received the lion's share of news coverage. There were two reasons for this. First, Irish descendants in other countries have tended to sympathize with the IRA cause, even while condemning its methods. The news plays to them. Second, the IRA chose the United Kingdom as its enemy, whereas the UDA targeted neighborhoods and individuals. When the British government tried to control the Troubles, it moved against the group that had targeted it—the IRA. This led to increasing coverage of the IRA's role in the conflict, and it also led many Catholics to perceive that the British government was biased against their side. This perception of British bias grew much worse after one of the most notorious events of the Troubles—Bloody Sunday.

Bloody Sunday

To control the increasing power of the IRA, the British government sent the army into Northern Ireland and began a policy of internment. This meant that police or soldiers could seize a suspected terrorist without formal charges and hold him or her indefinitely. By 1972, hundreds of Irish Catholics were being detained on these terms.

NICRA protested internment by holding a march through Derry's Bogside neighborhood on January 30, 1972. The local RUC chief recommended that the march be allowed to proceed as planned. An unnamed authority, however, decided instead to use the event to send in British paratroopers to arrest IRA members.

FACT

To get a feel for the emotions that the Troubles inflicted in the Republic of Ireland, listen to "Sunday Bloody Sunday" by the Irish band U2 (*War*; 1983). It's a powerful testament to the pain and frustration caused by the seemingly unending conflict.

Shots Are Fired

The march went on as planned and was relatively uneventful until around 4 P.M., when the soldiers arrived. They moved past the barricades and opened fire on the crowd. The march immediately dispersed in panic, and the troops followed to pursue the "arrest operation." The precise order of events that followed has been disputed for the last three decades, but the indisputable fact is that the soldiers shot thirteen civilians dead on the spot and injured another man who later died of his wounds.

After the troops had moved out, British authorities immediately issued statements that the men killed were IRA members who had fired on the soldiers. But in the days that followed, these claims were retracted. Subsequent investigations determined that none of the men killed were carrying weapons. Investigations also failed to establish that there was any concentrated IRA presence at the scene or that the soldiers had been fired on first. What is clear is that not a single soldier was injured during the operation.

The Widgery Report

Bloody Sunday was the first time in the Troubles that British soldiers had opened fire at unarmed civilians. People throughout Ireland were outraged by the atrocity; on February 2 a mob attacked and burned the British embassy in Dublin, and in Australia, dockers refused to unload British cargo ships. The British government appointed Lord Widgery, lord chief justice of England, to investigate. Widgery determined that none of the victims could be proved to have had weapons, and that while some of the soldiers might have acted irresponsibly, they did not act illegally. In compiling this report, Widgery reviewed the reports of soldiers and RUC officers but ignored the statements collected from more than 500 civilians at the scene. No soldiers were punished. The Widgery report was met with outrage—some even refer to it as the Widgery Whitewash.

Stormont Falls

Bloody Sunday ignited Catholic fears of government bias. The British government decided that the situation in Northern Ireland had gone beyond the local government's ability to control. It suspended the Northern Ireland Parliament in Stormont and imposed direct rule from London. The fifty-year experiment in home rule was over.

ESSENTIAL

By the late 1990s, new information on Bloody Sunday suggested that the soldiers had fired intentionally on unarmed civilians. It also appears that investigators intentionally whitewashed events from the beginning, even to the point of revising soldiers' statements.

A Failed Hope for Peace

By 1972, Northern Ireland was in chaos: the body count from paramilitary violence was rising daily, British soldiers were patrolling the streets, and the entire state was divided along seemingly unbridgeable social lines. The British government, faced with governing this mess, began proceedings to restore Northern Ireland home rule on more stable grounds.

It was a gargantuan political puzzle. Negotiators had to bring together Catholic and Protestant politicians who were increasingly at each other's throats. They had to find some way to neutralize the paramilitaries without actually asking them to the talks. And they had to include the views of the Republic of Ireland and England, who had still not exorcised the ghosts of their own dispute from fifty years before.

An Attempt to Compromise

Despite these tough conditions, the negotiators ironed out an agreement in December 1973 in Sunningdale, England. The principal point was the restoration of Northern Ireland home rule, with power shared between Catholics and Protestants. It called for the creation of a Council of Ireland to promote cooperation between Northern Ireland and the Republic. The English agreed to release political prisoners and reform the RUC, while the Irish agreed to suppress the IRA and to scale back their claims to Northern Ireland. People hoped that the compromise agreement would lay the ground for lasting peace.

No Compromise Here

Sadly, it was not to be. Unionist groups felt that the arrangement ceded too much to Catholics. The Ulster Workers' Council, a working-class Loyalist group, called a general strike in Belfast that lasted for thirteen days. The strike—and the paramilitary violence that accompanied it—brought Northern Ireland to a standstill. The local government decided to withdraw from the Sunningdale Agreement. The United Kingdom concluded that if it couldn't reform Northern Ireland, it would try to contain it. For the next two decades, Britain treated the Troubles as primarily a security problem with the IRA.

FACT

The film *In the Name of the Father* (1993) is the slightly fictionalized account of Gerry and Giuseppe Conlon (played by Daniel Day-Lewis and Pete Postlethwaite), a father and son who were unjustly convicted of a 1974 IRA bombing in London. The movie portrays the ferocity of the IRA, the anger of the British, and the ways in which the Troubles scarred lives on all sides of the conflict.

Dark Days in Northern Ireland

In the following decades, the Troubles remained a source of pain and dismay for rational people throughout the world. The cycle of killing, retaliation, and counterkilling continued despite all attempts to stop it. Britain discovered that it could patrol the streets and throw thousands in jail, but as long as there was an angry young Catholic with a gun or a bomb, the violence would continue. The Catholic minority learned that they could talk to the politicians all they wanted, but as long as the Protestant working class wanted to maintain its position of superiority, the intimidation would continue. A shadow had fallen over Northern Ireland.

The Hunger Strikes

One of the more notorious episodes of the Troubles was the so-called Dirty Protest of IRA prisoners. The IRA prisoners wanted to be treated like prisoners of war, which would allow them to wear their own clothes, but the British insisted that they were common criminals. To protest, the prisoners refused to wear prison clothes or to clean their cells. For months, they huddled under blankets, wallowing in filth. International journalists called their conditions appalling, but British Prime Minister Margaret Thatcher replied that if they chose to live in squalor, that was their problem.

In 1981, after it became clear that the dirty tactics wouldn't work, the prisoners adopted a more extreme approach. Bobby Sands, a charismatic twenty-seven-year-old prisoner, announced that he would not eat until he received prisoner-of-war status. Every ten days, a fellow prisoner joined him on the hunger strike. The British thought he was bluffing; Prime Minister Thatcher refused to give in to the moral blackmail tactics. The IRA's Gerry Adams pleaded with Sands to call off the strike, as did the Catholic bishop of Derry. While Sands wasted away, he won an election for Parliament as a Sinn Féin candidate.

But he never took his seat in Westminster. After sixty-six days without food, Bobby Sands, MP (member of Parliament), died. Riots struck throughout Belfast, and 100,000 people attended his funeral procession. In the following months, nine more hunger strikers died. Finally, the prisoners called off the strike—they had decided not to lose any more lives in a futile gesture. Three days later, Britain granted the IRA prisoners most of their demands.

FACT

Some Mother's Son, the 1996 movie by Terry George, explores the painful moral questions of the IRA hunger strike. Two women find their sons starving to death in the Maze prison; when their sons lose consciousness, the mothers have to decide whether to let them die as they wish, or to have them fed intravenously. The movie ultimately asks whether the cause is worth dying for.

The Flow of Guns

One factor that kept the Troubles going for so long was the abundance of weapons available to the IRA. One major source of weapons was the United States. Thousands of Irish-Americans, infuriated by what they saw as the continuing English oppression of the Irish people, gave the IRA money to buy weapons.

One of the largest shipments of weapons came from an unlikely source—Libyan dictator Colonel Qaddafi. In an attempt to destabilize the United Kingdom through terrorism, he sent the IRA four shipments of machine guns, ammunition, and explosives—hundreds of tons of weapons in all.

The supply of weapons almost certainly prolonged the conflict. The IRA maintained that it could defeat England on military grounds by making its presence in Northern Ireland so costly that it would have to pull out. The abundance of weapons made this strategy seem possible—as long as the IRA didn't run out of guns and bombs, it thought it could continue the campaign for as long as it took.

The Anglo-Irish Agreement

There was a glimmer of hope in 1985, when the United Kingdom and the Republic of Ireland tried to break through the deadlock of violence by clearing up their own interests in Northern Ireland. Prime Minister Thatcher and Garrett Fitzgerald, the Taoiseach (Irish prime minister) signed the Anglo-Irish Agreement, which stated that "any change in the status of Northern Ireland would only come about with the consent of a majority of the people in Northern Ireland." It was a historic statement, making clear that Ulster's fate would be determined by democratic processes within Ulster, and only by those processes. The agreement also established an intergovernmental conference that gave the Republic an official consultative role in the affairs of Northern Ireland.

While the Anglo-Irish Agreement laid the grounds for peace as far as England and the Republic were concerned, it was not well received in Northern Ireland. Unionist MPs resigned in protest, and Unionist workers called a province-wide strike. The IRA wasn't impressed either; later that year, it issued a threat of violence against all civilians, Catholic or Protestant, who worked with the RUC. The following year, a massive IRA bomb killed eleven people at a Remembrance Day ceremony in Enniskillen. Peace was not at hand.

QUESTION?

Why were the Troubles so hard to end?
There are many answers: the ready supply of weapons; the centuries-long history of the conflict; the stubborn unwillingness of hard-liners on either side to compromise. But perhaps the toughest problem was the culture of brutality the Troubles created—as long as people could cheer when a bomb went off, the Troubles could not end.

The Peace Process

For decades, it seemed that the best anyone could hope for was a contained level of violence. But a spark of hope appeared in the early 1990s when Gerry Adams, head of the IRA's political arm Sinn Féin, revealed that he'd been in peace talks with John Hume, head of the Social Democratic Labour Party (SDLP), the moderate Catholic party. If the IRA was ready to talk, perhaps there was a chance for peace.

The Politics of Cease-Fire

In January 1994, President Bill Clinton granted Gerry Adams a visa to visit the United States for the first time; previous administrations had always banned Adams because of his associations with terrorists. Adams's visit was historic for two reasons. First, it allowed him to gather the political support of Irish-Americans, which increased Sinn Féin's status in later negotiations. Second, it forced him to act as a politician, rather than as a spokesman for terrorists. He knew that if he wanted to keep the support of the United States, he needed to exchange the rifle for the negotiating table.

To demonstrate that it was serious about the peace process, the IRA declared a unilateral cease-fire on August 31, 1994. In October the Unionist paramilitaries followed suit. In 1995, representatives of the United Kingdom and Ireland met to iron out a framework for a peace settlement. The document they came up with called for points similar to the Sunningdale Agreement:

- Northern Ireland remained part of the United Kingdom, but only so long as the majority still desired it.
- Northern Ireland would return to a form of independent government.
- The parties would create a "north–south" body that (hopefully) would lead to stronger ties between the Republic and Northern Ireland.

The framework was not an actual settlement, nor was it popular with either Republicans or Unionists. Efforts to turn the framework into an actual settlement were agonizingly slow. British Prime Minister John Major insisted that the peace process could move forward only if the IRA agreed to decommission their arms. Gerry Adams refused; he viewed Major's position as a trick to break the IRA's power without granting any concessions.

The Cease-Fire Ends

On February 9, 1996, the IRA announced its dissatisfaction with the process by exploding an immense bomb at Canary Wharf in London. The resumption of violence was met with appalled condemnation on all sides. The British government attacked the IRA and scored a number of successes. It appeared that the nasty conflict of the 1980s and early 1990s was back again.

Fortunately, two political changes in 1997 got the peace process back on track. First, Sinn Féin won its largest percentage of the vote ever, which many interpreted as popular support for a resolution of the conflict through peaceful means. Second, Labour Prime Minister Tony Blair swept into power with a crushing victory over the Conservatives. Blair immediately put out feelers to Sinn Féin to get the peace process started again.

Good News on Good Friday

After a touch-and-go period, Prime Minister Blair brought all the major parties together in 1998. Extremists on both sides threatened to scuttle the talks, but last-minute heroics by Blair, U.S. Senator George Mitchell, and President Bill Clinton kept the negotiators at the table. The Good Friday Agreement of April 10, 1998, laid the groundwork for what many hope will be a lasting peace.

FACT

Moderate Catholic leader John Hume shared the 1998 Nobel Peace Prize with Unionist leader David Trimble for their part in the Good Friday Agreement. This was the second peace prize granted for work on the Troubles; Betty Williams and Mairead Corrigan-Maguire won the 1976 Nobel Peace Prize for organizing Peace People, a grassroots organization in Northern Ireland dedicated to ending the violence.

The Good Friday Agreement

The Good Friday Agreement adopted many of the provisions of previous peace attempts, such as the Sunningdale Agreement. One of the unfortunate ironies of the situation is that it took so long to reach essentially the same solution as was rejected in 1974. But maybe it took years of violence to make people accept the necessary compromises:

- Home rule returned to Northern Ireland, with a representative assembly sharing power between Catholics and Protestants.
- The RUC was reorganized and renamed the Police Service of Northern Ireland.
- The IRA and UDA agreed to maintain the cease-fire.
- Assuming the cease-fire held, the IRA and UDA agreed to a gradual process of decommissioning their weapons.
- Political prisoners were released.
- The Republic of Ireland amended its constitution to remove its territorial claim to Northern Ireland until the people of Northern Ireland agreed to rejoin.

To go into effect, the agreement required the approval of a majority of the people in Northern Ireland and the Republic. In a May 1998 referendum, it drew the support of 94.4 percent of voters in the Republic and 71.1 percent of people in Northern Ireland. While this result gave a great boost for the peace process, one element of the vote still gave people pause—while 96 percent of Catholic voters in Northern Ireland supported the Good Friday Agreement, only 52 percent of Protestants voted in favor.

A Fragile Peace

Today, the peace process continues to move forward. Catholics and Protestants share power, the RUC has been reorganized and renamed the Police Service of Northern Ireland, and the paramilitary groups have demonstrated a commitment, however reluctant, to put their weapons away for good. But it's been a rocky path, and the road ahead does not look much smoother.

Bombing in Omagh

Thirteen weeks after the Good Friday Agreement was reached, disaster struck. A Republican splinter group calling itself the Real IRA detonated a massive bomb in the Northern Ireland town of Omagh. Its death toll of twenty-eight was the largest single loss of life in the entire conflict.

If the bomb had gone off five years earlier, it would most likely have launched a wave of attacks and counterattacks—this is almost certainly what the Real IRA intended. But this time, the UDA and the IRA both kept the cease-fire. Gerry Adams released a statement condemning the attack, saying that "violence must be a thing of the past." The peace had passed its first major test.

Testing the Peace

Sadly, it wasn't the last test. Although the leaders have decided to move forward, there is still a great deal of anger left in the people of Northern Ireland. Every summer the peace gets tested in the Marching Season, when the Orange Order and Apprentice Boy parades antagonize Catholic neighborhoods. These are Unionist groups that march through Catholic neighborhoods on dates significant to their history, such as the Protestant victory in the Battle of the Boyne (See Chapter 7).

FACT

The Orange Order is named in honor of William of Orange, the English King who defeated James II in the battles of the Boyne and Aughrim (1690 and 1691). William's victory sealed Protestant domination over Ireland for the next two centuries. The Apprentice Boys are named after a group of apprentices who sealed the gates of Derry against James II's army.

The Orange Order claims that the marches are part of its cultural heritage; Catholics claim they are triumphalist gestures designed to humiliate them. In an attempt to prevent Catholic riots, the newly installed Parades Commission has voted to prevent marches through traditionally troubled areas. The resulting police blockades have sparked Protestant riots.

Hope for the Future

Despite difficulties, the peace has held. The discrimination that angered Catholics so much in the past has largely been addressed through government reforms and the force of social change. Many Protestants remain angry about the concessions their government has made to the Catholic minority—the Reverend Ian Paisley led the fight against the Good Friday Agreement. But the majority of them seem to have decided that there is room enough in their little state for both populations to live and thrive.

Although the path forward seems tortuous at times, the majority of Northern Ireland's people seem to have realized that the peace, however imperfect, is vastly better than the Troubles that came before. We can only hope that the voices of reason will continue to prevail. (E)

Chapter 17

Ireland's Contribution to Literature

I rish writers have made extraordinary contributions to English literature, producing four Nobel Prize winners Although many of Ireland's greatest writers left their island to work in other countries, their work demonstrates the love of wit and poetry that has characterized the Irish people for centuries.

1726 Jonathan Swift's Gulliver's Travels

1895 Oscar Wilde's The Importance of Being Earnest performed in London

1897 Bram Stoker's Dracula

1907 J. M. Synge's Playboy of the Western World sparks a riot

1922 James Joyce's Ulysses published in Paris

1924 George Bernard Shaw's Saint Joan performed in London

1953 Samuel Beckett's Waiting for Godot performed in Paris

1958 Brendan Behan's The Borstal Boy

1975 Seamus Heaney's North

Irish Literary Tradition

The full story of Irish literature begins long before the English ever arrived in Ireland. The Celtic epics described in Chapter 3, such as the Taín Bó Cuailnge, represent one of the great oral literary traditions in world history. In the Middle Ages, Irish bards were famous for the originality of their poetry. It is very unfortunate that relatively little of that poetry survives today.

Few Irish writers stood out during the years of English domination. After all, most of the Irish were uneducated farmers who had little opportunity to express themselves in writing. Moreover, the most talented writers went to England to pursue the greater opportunities there. This trend of writers leaving the country has continued into the modern day, but within the last 150 years the growth of Irish consciousness has created a greater distinction between the cultures of Ireland and England, in the minds of both the Irish and the rest of the world. This distinction has allowed people to talk about a body of Irish literature that can stand shoulder-to-shoulder with the literature of England or the United States.

International Recognition

Irish writers often receive literary awards for which they compete with writers from all over the world. In the last century, four Irish writers won the Nobel Prize in literature:

- William Butler Yeats, 1923
- George Bernard Shaw, 1925
- Samuel Beckett, 1969
- Seamus Heaney, 1995

E-SITE

Yeats's majestic *The Wild Swans at Coole* was inspired by Coole Park, Lady Gregory's estate in County Galway. Lady Gregory's house was ruined in the Civil War, but the natural beauty of the area remains. Today it is a national park with a useful visitors center. Three miles north is Thoor Ballylee, a thirteenth-century tower that Yeats used as a retreat.

Irish Writers in England

Between 1600 and 1900, the people with the best opportunities to write and publish in Ireland were members of the Anglo-Irish ruling class. These people generally identified themselves as British and frequently went to London to take advantage of the greater number of theaters and publishers there. It is important to note, however, that these Anglo-Irish writers often maintained emotional ties to Ireland that surfaced in the content and style of their work.

Jonathan Swift (1667–1745)

Ireland's first great contributor to English literature was Jonathan Swift. Born in Dublin to Protestant English parents, Swift faced financial challenges after his father's early death. After an education at Trinity College, he moved to London to serve as secretary to Sir William Temple. With Temple's help, Swift obtained appointments with the Church of England in both England and Ireland. In 1713 he became the dean of Saint Patrick's Cathedral in Dublin, where he remained for the rest of his life; when historians of the Protestant Ascendancy refer to "the dean," they are talking about Swift.

Swift's *Gulliver's Travels* can be appreciated at many levels; it is at the same time an amusing adventure story and a scathing critique of humanity's flaws. The book was an extraordinary success in its own day, and its popularity has continued into modern times.

In his early career, Swift used his talents for satire and allegory in addressing political causes. His work skillfully articulated the positions of the Tory Party while skewering his enemies. As his career progressed, he increasingly identified with Ireland. His "Drapier's Letters" (1724), which helped block an English coinage scheme that would have debased the Irish currency, made him a hero in Dublin. "A Modest Proposal" (1729) satirically argued that Irish families could address poverty and overpopulation by selling their children as food. It was a bitterly ironic attack against Whig policies of ignoring Irish social problems.

Swift's greatest work was not so much an attack on a political enemy as a criticism of human irrationality. *Gulliver's Travels* (1726) is a satire in the form of a fantastic travel journal. Lemuel Gulliver, a ship's physician, voyages to four exotic lands: Lilliput, where no one is more than 6 inches tall; Brobdingnag, a land of giants; Laputa, an empire run by wise men; and Houyhnhnmland, where the Houyhnhnms and the Yahoos live.

Bram Stoker (1847–1912)

Abraham "Bram" Stoker was born to a middle-class family near Dublin. After a successful stint at Trinity College, he entered the civil service in Dublin. His life took a turn for the dramatic, however, when some amateur theater criticism he had written came to the attention of Sir Henry Irving, one of the pre-eminent actors in England at that time. The two met and immediately became friends. Soon afterward, Stoker quit the civil service and moved to London to serve as Irving's full-time manager.

E-SITE

St. Michan's Church in Dublin is charming on the surface, but underneath it lie crypts of ancient creeping horror. Originally built during Viking times, the limestone catacombs boast an unusual combination of cool, dry air that has somehow preserved dozens of corpses within. It is thought that the St. Michan's mummies inspired Bram Stoker's story of a man who would not die—Count Dracula.

While working in the London theater scene, Stoker wrote a number of eerie, gothic stories. The most famous of these was *Dracula* (1897), which introduced the world's most famous vampire. The story of good versus evil turned into an international bestseller that has remained popular into the present day. It's been said that Count Dracula has appeared in more movies than any other fictional character. Stoker's other popular works include *The Jewel of Seven Stars* (1904) and *The Lair of the White Worm* (1911).

Oscar Wilde (1854–1900)

Oscar Wilde produced some of the late nineteenth century's most brilliant plays. The tragedy of his career is that prejudice snuffed out his incandescent wit in its prime.

Oscar Wilde was born into a house where his creativity could reign free: his father was a famously eccentric surgeon, while his mother, "Speranza" Wilde, was a well-known socialite and writer of nationalist poetry. With his privileged background, Wilde was able to study at Oxford, where he became a disciple of Walter Pater and led the aesthetic movement, in which he advocated the idea of "art for art's sake." He was famous for his long hair, his eccentric dress, and his habit of carrying flowers everywhere. His idiosyncrasies were satirized in Gilbert and Sullivan's *Patience* (1881).

Wilde married Constance Lloyd in 1884 and the couple settled in London. He wrote poems and children's books for a few years, and then in 1891 he emerged as a literary star with *The Picture of Dorian Gray*. The novel is about the moral degeneration of a man who is kept young by a mystical painting that reflects his true age and corruption. Wilde followed this novel with a string of brilliantly witty plays, including *Lady Windermere's Fan* (1892), *Salomé* (1893), *An Ideal Husband* (1895), and *The Importance of Being Earnest* (1895). For a while, he was the toast of London.

Unfortunately, tragedy brought him down. Wilde was a homosexual, and he had carried on an affair with Lord Alfred Douglas for some time. Douglas's father, the marquis of Queensberry, accused Wilde of committing sodomy, a crime in Victorian England. Wilde sued the marquis for libel, but after a sensational trial Wilde was convicted and sentenced to two years of hard labor. His incarceration left him physically, financially, and spiritually ruined. He fled to Paris, where he died, broken and penniless, in 1900.

The Celtic Revival

The last decades of the nineteenth century saw a resurgence of interest in Celtic language and mythology as artists and writers began looking for inspiration within their own Irish heritage. This period of Ireland's creative renaissance is known as the Celtic Revival.

William Butler Yeats (1865–1939)

W. B. Yeats is widely considered to be one of the greatest poets of the twentieth century. He was born in Dublin in 1865 to an Anglo-Irish landowning family. His father, John Butler Yeats, was a well-known painter. Yeats spent much of his childhood in County Sligo, in West Ireland. He pursued painting as a young man, but he soon decided that his true passion was poetry.

The first inspirations for Yeats's poetry were the landscape, language, and mythology of Sligo. The folktales he heard from the local people led him to develop a fascination with Celtic stories and mysticism that influenced his work throughout his life. In the 1880s he became one of the leading voices promoting the study of Irish language and folklore. His poems, such as "The Wanderings of Oisin" (1889) and "The Lake Isle of Innisfree" (1893), communicated his love of Celtic myth to a wider audience.

FACT

In the 1890s Yeats was drawn into the Irish Nationalist movement, partly because he was in love with the beautiful and radically Nationalist Maud Gonne. Both Yeats and Gonne wound up marrying other people, but he continued to feature her in poems throughout his life.

Although he shunned violence, Yeats was passionately committed to the idea of an independent Irish state. The heroine of his play *Cathleen ni Houlihan* (1902) became a symbol of the Nationalist movement. One of his best-known poems, "Easter 1916," expressed his powerful conflicting emotions on the hope and violence embodied in the 1916 Easter Rebellion.

Yeats was a prolific and versatile writer throughout his career. His work in drama, folklore, and essays would each independently have made him a luminary of Irish literature. His true genius, however, came out in his poetry. In 1923, the year the Irish Free State was declared, Yeats won the Nobel Prize in literature "for his always inspired poetry, which in a highly artistic form gives expression to the spirit of a whole nation."

John Millington Synge (1871–1909)

J. M. Synge was working as a literary critic in Paris when, by chance, he ran into Yeats and asked him for advice on how he could start his own literary career. Yeats suggested he go to the Aran Islands and study the vigorous, poetic language spoken there. Synge followed this advice, and his experiences on the islands inspired him to create some of the most powerful plays ever performed in Ireland.

With Yeats's assistance, Synge produced *In the Shadow of the Glen* in 1903. He followed this with *Riders to the Sea* (1904), a one-act play that re-creates the starkly lyrical atmosphere of a Greek tragedy in the Irish countryside. His most famous play, *The Playboy of the Western World*, sparked riots at the Abbey Theatre in 1907. Some considered it obscene, while others felt it challenged romantic notions of the innocence of Irish common folk. Because of the controversy, the performance of his next play, *The Tinker's Wedding* (1907), was postponed until after his death.

Synge died of cancer in 1909. Yeats and Lady Gregory prepared his final, unfinished play, *Deirdre of the Sorrows*, for production at the Abbey Theatre in 1910. Its poetic language hints at the great things that Synge might have accomplished had tragedy not cut him down. He is remembered today for his unparalleled ability to bring the richness of Irish language and myth to the stage.

Transformation of the Modern Novel

James Joyce (1882–1941) revolutionized the novel, the short story, and modern literature as we know it. He was born in Dublin, the first of ten children in a Catholic family. His father was a civil servant whose poor financial judgment left the family impoverished for much of Joyce's youth. He attended Dublin's fine Jesuit schools, which gave him a firm grounding in theology and classical languages—subjects that repeatedly appeared in his later work. The story of his early life and his intellectual rebellion against Catholicism and Irish Nationalism are told in the largely autobiographical novel *A Portrait of the Artist as a Young Man* (1916), originally published in 1904 as *Stephen Hero*.

In 1902, at the age of twenty, Joyce left Dublin to spend the rest of his life in Paris, Trieste, Rome, and Zurich, with only occasional visits back home. Despite this self-imposed exile, Dublin was the setting for most of his writings. *The Dubliners* (1914) is a collection of short stories describing the paralyzing social mores of middle-class Catholic life. Its style is more accessible than most of Joyce's work. "The Dead," the final story in the collection, is frequently listed as one of the finest short stories ever written.

Ulysses (1922)

Joyce spent seven years working on *Ulysses*; once he finished writing it, he almost couldn't find anyone to publish it. Once it was published, Ireland and the United States immediately banned it as obscene, and most people who located copies found the writing nearly incomprehensible. Despite these obstacles, *Ulysses* has come to be generally recognized as the most influential English novel of the twentieth century.

E-SITE

Every year on June 16, the people of Dublin celebrate Bloomsday—the day on which, in 1904, the actions of *Ulysses* supposedly took place. The James Joyce Cultural Centre sponsors a re-enactment of the funeral and wake, a lunch at Davy Byrne's Pub, and a Guinness breakfast. There are various other literary activities and pub crawls throughout the week.

The novel was revolutionary in a number of ways. First, the structure was unique: Joyce re-created one full day in the life of his protagonist, Leopold Bloom, and modeled the actions of the story on those of Ulysses in the *Odyssey* (Ulysses is the Latin equivalent of the Greek name Odysseus). In recounting Bloom's day, Joyce mentions everything that happens—including thoughts, bodily functions, and sexual acts—providing a level of physical actuality never before achieved in literature. To provide psychological insight comparable to the physical detail, Joyce employed a then-revolutionary technique called stream of consciousness, in which the protagonist's thoughts are laid bare to the reader.

The most enjoyable part of *Ulysses* is the language itself, which is at times poetic, at times witty, and sometimes ridiculously erudite. It's been said that, to understand the novel fully, a reader must have a comprehensive understanding of Roman Catholic theology, church history, Judaism, Irish mythology and history, Dublin geography and slang, astronomy, Latin, Greek, Gaelic, and it wouldn't hurt to have a solid grounding in the last 3,000 years of Western cultural history. In other words, it's not an easy read, but for many people it's an immensely rewarding book.

Finnegan's Wake (1939)

From 1922 until 1939, Joyce worked on a vast, experimental novel that eventually became known as *Finnegan's Wake*. The novel, which recounts "the history of the world" through a family's dreams, employs its own "night language" of puns, foreign words, and literary allusions. It has no clear chronology or plot, it begins and ends on incomplete sentences that flow into each other, and some people aren't even sure it's in English. Many of Joyce's supporters thought he was wasting his time, although Samuel Beckett helped compile the final text when Joyce's eyesight was failing. Today, *Finnegan's Wake* is viewed as Joyce's most obscure and possibly most brilliant work.

Joyce didn't have an easy life. He met the love of his life, a Dublin chambermaid named Nora Barnacle, on June 16, 1904—which happens to be the date described in *Ulysses*—and the two ran away together to Trieste. Nora and their two children followed Joyce around Europe as he pursued low-paying teaching and clerical jobs to support his writing.

Brilliant Playwrights Abroad

Like Joyce, many of Ireland's most talented writers continued to leave Ireland. Government and Church censorship, combined with the economic limits of the Irish market, sent young intellectuals abroad. Two of Ireland's greatest playwrights achieved their success overseas: George Bernard Shaw in England and Samuel Beckett in France. Although they left their birthplace far behind, the Emerald Isle continued to influence their work throughout their careers.

George Bernard Shaw (1856–1950)

George Bernard Shaw was born in Dublin in 1856. The difficulties of his early life, including frequent poverty and an alcoholic father, probably helped create the social conscience that motivated much of his later work. In 1876 Shaw moved to London, where he continued his education and became involved in socialist circles. It was at this time that he began working as a drama critic and eventually began producing his own dramatic works.

Shaw wrote over fifty plays, including *Arms and the Man* (1894), *Man and Superman* (1903), *Pygmalion* (1913), and *Saint Joan* (1923). His most Irish-themed play was *John Bull's Other Island* (1904), which criticized the injustice of British policy toward Ireland. His plays use an ironic tone and witty dialogue to address contemporary moral problems. The major theme throughout his work is the challenge for individuals to maintain freedom and responsibility in the face of a conformist society. In 1925 Shaw received the Nobel Prize in literature "for his work which is marked by both idealism and humanity, its stimulating satire often being infused with a singular poetic beauty."

Shaw continued writing into his nineties. Several of his plays were made into movies, of which the most famous are *Ceasar and Cleopatra* (1945, with Claude Rains and Vivien Leigh) and *My Fair Lady* (1964, with Rex Harrison and Audrey Hepburn), which was an adaptation of *Pygmalion*. Throughout his career, Shaw was an outspoken advocate of social causes, notably socialism, pacifism, and vegetarianism.

Samuel Beckett (1906–89)

Beckett was born in Dublin to a middle-class Protestant family. After an education at Trinity College, he moved to Paris, where he befriended James Joyce and became involved in the Parisian literary scene. Beckett experimented with various styles during this period, producing poems, novels, and short stories that were popular in French critical circles. During World War II, Beckett stayed in France and was active in the Resistance.

In the postwar years, Beckett began to find true success by evolving his own style and writing primarily in French (he usually translated the English versions himself). He wrote a critically acclaimed trilogy of novels: *Molloy*, *Malone Dies*, and *The Unnameable*. His greatest successes were his plays, particularly *Waiting for Godot* and *Endgame*. These works are considered major advances in the literature of the absurd, a movement that seeks to uncover the irony of the human condition and the hopelessness of achieving any deeper understanding. Beckett's writing is characterized by pessimism, inventive word use, and a surreal tone.

FACT

Waiting for Godot tells the story of two tramps who are waiting to meet a mysterious figure named Godot (who may represent God). Each day Godot sends a boy who says Godot will appear, but he never arrives. Meanwhile, the tramps conduct an absurd dialogue about life. The play suggests that there is no greater truth, but life goes on anyway.

In 1969 Beckett received the Nobel Prize in literature "for his writing, which—in new forms for the novel and drama—in the destitution of modern man acquires its elevation" (in other words, for inventing absurdist drama). He produced a number of plays in the 1970s and 1980s, which were widely read but less original than his earlier works. He died in Paris in 1989.

The Irish Struggle in Literature

Joyce, Shaw, and Beckett managed to isolate themselves from Ireland's worst conflicts by leaving the country before the Anglo-Irish War and the Civil War. For those who remained in the country, however, Ireland's strife inspired a number of major literary works.

Sean O'Casey (1880–1964)

Sean O'Casey actively supported the Irish Nationalist movement as a member of both the Gaelic League and the Irish Citizen's Army. His experiences with the independence movement inspired his first play, *The Shadow of the Gunman*, which was produced by the Abbey Theatre in 1923. This was followed by *Juno and the Paycock* (1924), which many consider his masterpiece, and *The Plough and Stars* (1926), which sparked riots in Dublin for its allegedly anti-Irish stance. O'Casey's plays used vibrant language and elements of comedy and tragedy to depict the tensions in Irish society.

O'Casey broke with the Abbey Theatre in 1928, and many of his later plays were produced in London. These plays were increasingly concerned with expressing the author's socialist views. O'Casey also published a six-volume autobiography, beginning with *I Knock at the Door* in 1939.

Brendan Behan (1923–64)

Brendan Behan was born at the dawn of Irish independence to a family closely tied to the Irish Republican Army. Behan joined the IRA as a young man, and it swiftly led him into trouble. At the age of sixteen Behan was arrested for plotting to blow up an English battleship. He spent three years in the Borstal Reform School, which provided him with material for his most famous book, *Borstal Boy* (1958). Behan spent two more terms in prison for revolutionary activity, and he was eventually deported to France.

Behan poured the experiences of his troubled youth into passionate plays, such as *The Quare Fellow* (1956) and *The Hostage* (1958). He was internationally famous for his talents as a playwright, but he was equally famous for his alcoholic exploits, such as showing up roaring drunk to performances of his plays. Behan's shenanigans made him something of a media favorite, but they also brought him criticism for perpetuating the image of a wild, drunken Irishman. Sadly, he died at the age of forty-one from a combination of diabetes and alcoholism.

Seamus Heaney: Poet of the Troubles

The American poet Robert Lowell said that Seamus Heaney (1939–present) is the greatest Irish poet since Yeats. Heaney was the oldest of nine children in a Catholic farming family in County Derry, Northern Ireland. At St. Columb's College in Derry and Queens University in Belfast, Heaney received the grounding in Latin, Irish, and Anglo-Saxon that have enriched the language of his poetry. The themes of his poems arose from the tensions of the land in which he lived: Ulster's industrial present versus its rural past; English roots versus Gaelic; and the rising conflict between Northern Ireland's Catholics and Protestants.

Seamus Heaney is still extremely active as a poet and scholar. He is currently a professor at Harvard University, although he teaches only four months of the year. He spends the rest of the year writing, speaking around the world, or spending time with his family in County Wicklow.

Heaney has produced a number of vibrant poetry collections: *Death of a Naturalist* (1966), *North* (1975), *Station Island* (1984), and *Seeing Things* (1991). In addition, he has written plays, essays, and a bestselling translation of the Anglo-Saxon epic *Beowulf* (1999). Heaney received the 1995 Nobel Prize in literature "for works of lyrical beauty and ethical depth, which exalt everyday miracles and the living past." Ⓔ

Chapter 18

Ⓔ **Emigrants and Exports**

The Irish have made major contributions to world literature and music. Ireland's greatest contribution, however, has been the millions of people who left their island in the hope that they'd find a better life for themselves and their children. Those emigrants' descendants have had a tremendous impact on the politics and cultures of the countries they came to call home.

Irish-Americans in Politics

The Irish have had a great influence in American politics. The Scotch-Irish from Ulster who came to the American colonies in the seventeenth and eighteenth centuries brought with them a Scottish ethos of independence and civil liberty. In a sense, they achieved the freedom in America that their relatives in Scotland and Ireland were denied. When the colonies declared independence in 1776, nine of the men who signed the declaration were of Irish descent.

The Scotch-Irish were a firmly established part of U.S. society from the very beginning. It took many more years before Catholic Irish immigrants were able to gain acceptance, but eventually, they too became established Americans. Catholic Irish political power came first from Democratic political machines, such as the Tammany Hall machine in New York. As immigrants' descendants moved into the middle class in large numbers, Irish-American politicians were able to extend beyond their local political machines and take office on regional and even national scales.

American Presidents

No fewer than sixteen American presidents are of Irish descent:

1. Andrew Jackson, seventh president (1829–37)
2. James Knox Polk, eleventh president (1845–49)
3. James Buchanan, fifteenth president (1857–61)
4. Ulysses S. Grant, eighteenth president (1869–77)
5. Chester Alan Arthur, twenty-first president (1881–85)
6. Grover Cleveland, twenty-second and twenty-fourth president (1885–89, 1893–97)
7. William McKinley, twenty-fifth president (1897–1901)
8. Woodrow Wilson, twenty-eighth president (1913–21)
9. John Fitzgerald Kennedy, thirty-fifth president (1961–63)
10. Lyndon Baines Johnson, thirty-sixth president (1963–69)
11. Richard Milhous Nixon, thirty-seventh president (1969–74)
12. James Earl Carter, thirty-ninth president (1977–81)
13. Ronald Wilson Reagan, fortieth president (1981–89)

14. George Herbert Walker Bush, forty-first president (1989–93)
15. William Jefferson Clinton, forty-second president (1993–2001)
16. George W. Bush, forty-third president (2001–present)

QUESTION?

Why is JFK considered the first Irish-American President?
There were eight presidents before Kennedy of Scotch-Irish descent, but they didn't identify themselves as Irish. The Protestant Scotch-Irish tended to look down on the poorer Catholic Irish. Both the Irish and the Irish-American community considered Kennedy's election a major advance.

Most of these presidents came from Scotch-Irish rather than Catholic Irish families. The victory of Andrew Jackson in 1829 can be seen as a victory of Scotch-Irish values over the more aristocratic ones of the English-descended presidents who preceded him. Jackson's administration was known for favoring common citizens over wealthy landowners, a trait that can be traced to the Scotch-Irish value of individual freedom over hierarchy.

John F. Kennedy was the first Catholic Irish president. Kennedy's victory in 1960 was seen as the final sign of acceptance for the Irish-American community.

The Kennedys

The Kennedy family of Massachusetts is perhaps the greatest symbol of the rise of the Irish in American political life. Descended from County Wexford potato farmers who emigrated during the Great Famine, the Kennedys rose in the Democratic Party to take power in the U.S. Senate and presidency. Their story is one of greatness marked by tragedy.

"Honey Fitz" Fitzgerald (1863–1950)

John Fitzgerald Kennedy's political path was first cleared by his maternal grandfather, John "Honey Fitz" Fitzgerald. Fitzgerald was born in

1863 to an Irish immigrant family. The son of a storekeeper, he quickly rose through the political ranks in Boston to serve as a U.S. congressman and as mayor of Boston. He was a popular mayor, particularly with Boston's large Irish community, but his administration was widely accused of corruption. He ran in campaigns for both the U.S. Senate and the governorship of Massachusetts, but never won. In his later years, he concentrated on steering the political careers of his increasingly influential family.

When Joseph Kennedy, the son of an immigrant saloonkeeper, asked Fitzgerald's daughter Rose to marry him, Honey Fitz refused the match; he thought that the Kennedys were beneath the Fitzgeralds. Rose Fitzgerald married Joe Kennedy anyway in 1915, and Joe soon demonstrated that he didn't think the Kennedys were beneath anyone. In fact, it would be difficult to find a more ambitious character in all of American history.

Joe Kennedy, Sr. (1888–1969)

Joseph Kennedy pursued a wide range of business interests, including finance, shipping, and motion-picture distribution. Historians generally agree that he made a lot of money by importing alcohol during Prohibition. He invested this money very skillfully: he rode the stock market boom of the 1920s, pulled out just before the great crash of 1929, then reinvested his money when stocks were at all-time lows. This fortune proved most useful for his family's political advancement.

Like his father-in-law, Joseph loved politics. President Franklin D. Roosevelt appointed him the first chairman of the Security and Exchange Commission in 1934, reasoning that no one knew the tricks of financial manipulation better than Joseph Kennedy. In 1938 Joseph became the first Catholic Irish ambassador to Britain. He harbored presidential aspirations of his own, but his support for an isolationist policy during World War II hurt his political standing and cost him the ambassadorship. From that time on, he dedicated himself to the political careers of his sons—Joe, John (Jack), Bobby, and Ted.

The family's first hope was Joseph Kennedy, Jr., who was the oldest son. Joseph Jr. was tall, handsome, and brilliant; his father was determined to make him the first Irish-American president. Tragically,

Joseph Jr. died in a bombing raid over Germany during World War II. The family's eyes then turned to John Fitzgerald Kennedy, the second son.

ESSENTIAL

JFK certainly had the Irish gift of the gab. In his inaugural address, he said, "Ask not what your country can do for you, but what you can do for your country." His word choice wasn't always so good, though; in a 1963 speech in Berlin he said, "Ich bin ein Berliner," which literally means, "I am a doughnut."

John F. Kennedy (1917–63)

John Kennedy, like his father and brothers, went to Harvard. He first came to prominence as a PT boat captain in World War II. After Kennedy's boat was rammed and sunk by a Japanese destroyer, Kennedy organized his crew and led them to safety. His father's publicity machine turned Kennedy into a national hero. He used his fame and his father's money to win a seat in the U.S. House of Representatives after the war, and in 1953 he advanced to the Senate.

◀ John Fitzgerald Kennedy

Kennedy was a talented politician—charismatic, smart, and possessing an innate sense for how to use the media to his best advantage. He married the beautiful and sophisticated Jacqueline Bouvier in 1953.

In 1960 Kennedy ran for the U.S. presidency against the standing vice president, Richard Nixon. Kennedy still had to face the anti-Catholic prejudice that had sunk the campaign of Al Smith in 1928, but he had two big advantages: his father had lots of money, and John looked great on television. He won in a close election, and in 1961 took office as the first Roman Catholic president. He was also the youngest U.S. president ever.

Kennedy's administration was marked by bold initiatives. He launched the Peace Corps and the Apollo Program, with the mission of putting a man on the moon within a decade (which was successful). His administration also oversaw dramatic foreign policy events, such as the failed Bay of Pigs invasion and the Cuban Missile Crisis, in which Kennedy insisted that the Soviets remove their missiles from Cuba. After several tense days, the Soviets backed down. In 1963 Kennedy was talking about starting a national campaign to end poverty, but it was not to be. On November 22, 1963, an assassin's bullet ended Kennedy's life in a motorcade in Dallas.

Bobby (1925–68) and Ted (1932–present)

When JFK died, Kennedy family supporters turned to John's colleague and younger brother, Bobby. Robert "Bobby" Kennedy lacked his older brother's charisma, but he had at least as much passion. He had managed John's successful campaigns for the Senate and the presidency, and he served as U.S. attorney general in his brother's administration. In 1964, choosing not to continue with the Johnson administration, he ran for and won a Senate seat in New York state. He was considered a leading contender for the presidential race in 1968. Tragically, an assassin shot him in Los Angeles right after he had won the California primary.

With the three oldest Kennedy sons gone, eyes turned to the youngest son, Edward "Ted" Kennedy. Although he had earned a reputation as something of a playboy, Ted still managed to win his brother's old U.S. Senate seat in Massachusetts in 1962, at the age of thirty. Since that time he has been re-elected to six more terms, most recently in 2000.

Many expected Teddy to become the next Kennedy president, but an accident in 1969 effectively ruined his chances. He was involved in a car accident on Chappaquiddick Island, off the coast of

Massachusetts, in which a young woman named Mary Jo Kopechne drowned. Teddy left the scene and didn't call authorities until hours later. He managed to retain his seat in the Senate after the scandal, but lingering questions about the incident ruined his 1980 bid for the presidency.

FACT

Ted Kennedy has become known as one of the leading liberals in the Senate, focusing on issues such as health care and education. Unfortunately, in his younger days, he was known for his drinking and womanizing.

Irish-Canadian Prime Ministers

Irish immigrants played important roles in the political development of Canada as well. Canada was an important destination for emigrants, particularly those coming from the North. During the twentieth century, three of Canada's prime ministers were of Irish descent.

Louis St. Laurent (1882–1973)

Louis St. Laurent was the son of a French-Canadian father and an Irish-Canadian mother. This blend of cultures helped make him a strong voice for Canadian cultural unity in his later career. Laurent was a very successful lawyer in Quebec, using his bilingual skills to represent French-speaking clients in an English-speaking world. He had little involvement in politics until 1941, when the English king appointed him as his lieutenant in Quebec. He turned out to be a skillful politician and a reliable one in wartime. He was soon one of the more popular figures in the Liberal Party.

He became prime minister in 1948 and served until 1957, when the Liberals fell from power. His administration was known for its efforts to bring together the French- and English-speaking communities of Canada. He also oversaw, with Lester Pearson, Canadian arbitration in the Suez Canal crisis.

Lester Pearson (1897–1972)

Lester Pearson was the leader of the Liberal Party after St. Laurent, and he is generally considered to be one of Canada's greatest diplomats. Born in Toronto, he studied at both the University of Toronto and the University of Oxford. He joined the Foreign Service in 1928 and soon discovered that he had a talent for international diplomacy. Lester's skills were very much in demand during the years of World War II and its Cold War aftermath, in which Canada tried to pursue its own independent path while maintaining close ties with England and the United States.

Pearson attempted to head off violent conflicts through the intervention of international bodies. He was influential in the creation of the United Nations and the North Atlantic Treaty Organization (NATO), and he was president of the General Assembly of the United Nations when it put together the framework agreement to end the Korean War. For his international contributions, Pearson won the Nobel Peace Prize in 1957.

Pearson was equally ambitious on domestic issues, although his achievements on that front have been perhaps more controversial. During his term as prime minister (1963–68), he introduced several far-reaching changes in Canadian society: bilingualism, biculturism, Medicare, and modern Canadian Nationalism (i.e., maintaining policies independent from the United States and England). While he is credited with helping make Canada what it is today, some blame him for setting up some of the long-term cultural and financial problems that have beset Canada in recent decades.

Brian Mulroney (1939–present)

Brian Mulroney was born to Irish immigrants in the small Quebec town of Baie-Comeau. Mulroney was successful in both the law and in business, eventually becoming the president of the Iron Ore Company of Canada (an American-owned company). He had been active in politics since his student days, joining the Conservative Party in 1956. He first came to national prominence in the 1970s, when he headed a commission that exposed corruption and violence in the construction industry.

FACT

Brian Mulroney's 1985 meeting in Quebec City with Ronald Reagan, another famous Irish descendant, was termed the "Shamrock Summit" after the two of them were heard singing "When Irish Eyes Are Smiling." Many Canadian liberals have lamented that meeting as Mulroney's surrender to American corporate interests.

Mulroney served as prime minister from 1984 to 1993. His election was a historic landslide for the Conservative Party, although by the 1990s his perceived complicity with American business interests had made him a fairly unpopular character in Canada. Mulroney's greatest achievement (or greatest failing, depending on the viewpoint) was to usher in the North American Free Trade Agreement (NAFTA) that made North America a free-trade zone. Mulroney attempted to rectify the uncomfortable constitutional position of Quebec, but his efforts were ultimately unsuccessful.

Ned Kelly—Irish-Australian Outlaw

The Irish in Australia have made great contributions, much like their cousins in North America. The Irish-Australian heritage, however, is tinged by the slightly different way that many of them got there—as prisoners in English transport ships.

The most famous Irish-Australian outlaw was Edward "Ned" Kelly (1855–80). Ned's father was a "selector," a criminal who had been transported to Australia, served his time, and then was allowed to select a plot of land to farm. Ned came from a large family that occasionally supplemented its meager income with horse rustling and cattle stealing. The family legend is that the Kellys were constantly persecuted by the police because they were Irish Catholics in a land dominated by English Protestants. When Ned was in his early twenties and on the run from a horse-rustling charge, his mother was sentenced to three years hard labor on a fabricated charge of attempted murder of a policeman. Ned and his three followers, called the "Kelly gang," swore revenge.

Today, many Irish-Australians look back on convict ancestry with pride, because it means that their ancestors were willing to stand up to unjust English laws. In reality, the majority of transported convicts were common criminals, not revolutionaries, but contemporary folklore tends to put them all in the same boat.

The Kelly gang ambushed a group of policemen, killed three of them, and then disappeared into the bush (the vast Australian wilderness). The gang lived on the run for two years, robbing several banks in the process. The government offered increasingly large bounties for its capture, eventually reaching the astronomical sum of £8,000 each for Ned and his brother Dan, but no one turned them in. In the bush, the Kellys were treated as heroes for their bold defiance of the law.

Shoot-out at the Glenrowan Hotel

Eventually, however, a group of 200 police officers surrounded the gang at the Glenrowan Hotel. The final shoot-out has become the stuff of legend, much like the shoot-out at the OK Corral in the American West. The policemen fired on the hotel and set it on fire. Ned came out wearing a fantastic suit of thick iron armor. At first it repulsed all the bullets, but eventually someone shot him in the legs and he went down. His gang members were killed by gunfire, and Ned was hanged a few days later.

FACT

In Australia, to say that someone is "as game as Ned Kelly" means that the person is tough, resourceful, and maybe just a little wild. These frontiersman characteristics are still very much valued in Australia, as personified by the character of Crocodile Dundee.

Today Ned Kelly is Australia's most popular folk hero, with dozens of books and museum exhibits dedicated to his exploits. Many aspects of his story appeal to the popular imagination: his desperate attempt to help his mother, his conviction that an Irishman like himself couldn't get justice from the law, his almost miraculous ability to live off the land, and his final, ironclad defiance of unbeatable odds. To Australians of today, who actually have one of the lowest crime rates in the world, Ned Kelly represents a side of themselves that they've left behind but aren't ready to forget.

St. Patrick's Day

When Irish emigrants moved overseas, they brought over many elements of their culture with them. One of the most significant of these cultural exports is St. Patrick's Day, Ireland's national holiday. In fact, it is celebrated in more countries than any other national holiday. Moreover, St. Patrick's Day became much more popular in emigrant communities than it ever had been back home.

As St. Patrick's feast day in Ireland, it had been an important social and religious day for centuries, but the Irish didn't traditionally throw the giant parades and festivals that we associate with the holiday today. Those festivities originated in the large immigrant communities of New York, Chicago, and Boston. Irish immigrants used St. Patrick's Day to show their pride in their heritage. For the Irish political machines of late-nineteenth-century America, St. Patrick's Day parades were a demonstration of power.

The holiday caught on in the rest of American society and in Irish immigrant communities around the world. Today, a far greater number of people celebrate St. Patrick's Day outside of Ireland than in it. Interestingly, the popularity of the holiday in the United States has helped to make it a bigger holiday in Ireland. In 1995 the government of Ireland established an official St. Patrick's Festival with parades and concerts; prior to that, the celebrations were relatively quiet.

Holiday Traditions

A number of traditions have sprung up around the American celebration of St. Patrick's Day. Among them are: wearing green (or else you get pinched); eating corned beef and cabbage; recklessly displaying shamrocks and leprechauns; drinking green beer; dyeing faces, nails, and rivers green. In Chicago they've turned the Chicago River a lovely shade of Irish green every year since 1961. (The dye they use for this purpose starts out orange but turns green when it mixes with the river water.)

St. Patrick's Day is celebrated on March 17, the date on which Patrick supposedly died in 461 C.E. The first celebration of the holiday in the United States is thought to have taken place in Boston in 1737. Today, the largest St. Patrick's Day parade is in New York City, where more than 150,000 marchers proudly wear the green.

Irish Pubs Around the World

Another Irish contribution to world culture is the famed Irish pub. From Cape Town to Copenhagen, from Singapore to Seattle, Irish immigrants have introduced enthusiastic patrons to this Irish concept. Irish pubs are about having a good time, and that doesn't just include drinking (although a pint is generally involved). The traditional pub provides hearty food, possibly music or dancing, and always lots of good conversation.

There are literally thousands of Irish pubs around the world. You can generally identify an authentic one by the Guinness on tap, the friendly atmosphere, and the Irish-themed name. To make their identification clear, many international pubs have named themselves after that most Irish of symbols, the Shamrock:

- The Purple Shamrock, Boston, USA
- The Rockin' Shamrock, Cape Town, South Africa
- The Basque Shamrock, Bilbao, Spain
- Shamrock Bar, Saint Petersburg, Russia
- The Shamrock and Thistle, Toronto, Canada

Another popular theme is to name the pub after an Irish city. Many choose the most famous Irish city of all:

- The Dublin, Santiago, Chile
- The Dubliner, Reykjavik, Iceland
- The Auld Dubliner, Bologna, Italy

- The Dubliner Irish Pub, Toshima-ku, Japan
- The Dubliner, Washington, D.C., USA

Of course, many publicans have chosen to name their pubs after themselves, or at least after people who sound Irish. There certainly seem to be a lot of Murphys out there:

- Scruffy Murphy's Irish Pub, Heidelberg, Germany
- Muddy Murphy's Irish Pub, Singapore
- Irish Murphy's, Hobart, Australia
- J. J. Murphy's, London, England
- Fidel Murphy's, Grand Cayman

Because of the hard work and cultural diplomacy of thousands of Irish emigrants, millions of people around the world are able to enjoy Guinness in the environment in which it was meant to be enjoyed. *Sláinte!* ("To your health!")

Chapter 19

Family and Food

Studying history and artistic achievements is one way to get to know a culture. Another equally valid way is to gain an understanding of how people live, what they eat, and how they spend their time. The Irish have used the strengths of their island—the fresh food and water, the tranquility, and the strong family connections—to create one of the most enjoyable lifestyles in the world.

Irish Family Life

It's difficult to make general statements about the family life of any country. People's lives can be very different, depending on where they live or how much money they have. Even people living next door to each other can lead very different lives. That being said, there are a few traits that people have accepted as describing the traditional Irish family.

The Irish Family

The stereotypical Irish family is Roman Catholic. Catholic roots go very deep in Ireland—so deep that they were able to withstand hundreds of years of English opposition. Irish households have traditionally been full of Catholic art and objects, and most Irish children have been educated at Catholic schools. The influence of the Church has tended to make Ireland a conservative country; the government has generally sided with Church positions on issues like abortion, divorce, and contraception.

The stereotypical Irish Catholic family is large, with many children close in age. Late marriage and abstinence have decreased family size in the 150 years since the Great Famine, but the twentieth century saw enough large Irish Catholic families to keep the image alive. Partially responsible for this phenomenon is the Catholic prohibition of contraception.

ESSENTIAL

To get a good picture of Irish family life from the 1950s until today, read the novels of Maeve Binchy and Roddy Doyle. Binchy's *Circle of Friends* and Doyle's *The Commitments* and *The Snapper* have been made into popular movies.

A Typical Irish Lifestyle

The Irish have long been seen as a pastoral people with strong connections to their families and community. When most people worked in agriculture, their lives were very much tied to the land. They worked long hours, lived in the same houses that their parents had lived in, and rarely traveled more than 10 miles from home. This lifestyle offered few luxuries, but it fostered strong family and community networks. The Irish are famous for their devotion to family, between children and parents or among siblings.

Economic modernization has caused many Irish people to move from the country to pursue jobs in the cities. This has resulted in a quantitative increase in the quality of life for most people, but also a disruption in the traditional community networks. Many young people relish the chance to escape from the farm or small town and earn money in the city, and they willingly cast off what they see as the shackles of religion.

FACT

One recent book that has done its share to perpetuate stereotypes is Frank McCourt's *Angela's Ashes: A Memoir*, the author's account of growing up poor in Limerick. Although the bestselling book won the Pulitzer Prize and received rave reviews for its humor and pathos, many people in Limerick feel that it unfairly maligns their city.

Irish Food: Potatoes, Beef, and Potatoes

The Irish family has traditionally gathered around the table, sharing the food it had in rich times and in poor. For the most part, it has been pretty decent fare. Ireland's thriving agricultural industry provides high-quality meat, dairy products, and vegetables that go directly to local markets. The fresh and nutritious ingredients have allowed the Irish population to stay remarkably healthy, even in times of relative poverty.

Irish Specialties

Irish food has never been known for its diversity. The traditional diet, consisting of meat, vegetables, and lots and lots of potatoes, has long been considered one of the blandest in Europe. What it lacks in flair, though, it makes up in heartiness. Some of Ireland's hearty national and regional dishes include the following:

- Blaa ("blah")—sausage rolls, from Waterford
- Coddle—boiled sausages and bacon with potatoes, from Dublin

- Colcannon—a casserole of potatoes, onions, and cabbage
- Crubeen—pig's feet, from Cork
- Guinness stew—a stew made with mutton, potatoes, carrots, and Guinness beer
- Soda bread—a thick brown bread, tasty when fried

The Irish Breakfast

The Irish tend to eat light lunches, so they take breakfast seriously. Visitors to Ireland are frequently amazed by the robust Irish breakfast. This is no dainty continental breakfast of a croissant and jam, but an extravaganza of meat and eggs that will keep you full all day. There is variation from place to place, but the Irish breakfast generally includes the following:

- Eggs (usually fried)
- Sausages
- Bacon (sliced thick)
- Ham
- Black pudding (a blood sausage)
- White pudding (a lighter sausage)
- Fried tomatoes
- Toast and jam
- Tea

This combination is served in pubs and bed-and-breakfasts across the country. A similar variant, called an "Ulster Fry," is served in the North. Observant visitors will notice that the Irish don't actually eat like this every day; a bowl of cereal or some toast and tea are more common ways to start the day.

A Cup of Irish Tea

It's hard to overestimate the importance of tea in Irish culture. Tea is simultaneously a beverage, a medicine, and a social ritual. The Irish drink on average four cups of tea a day, amounting to 7 pounds of dried tea leaves over the course of a year—easily the highest rate of per-capita tea consumption in the world. No respectable household would be found without tea, and pubs are legally required to provide it. At breakfast, lunch, and teatime (approximately 4 P.M.), tea is the beverage of choice.

QUESTION?

What's the deal with Irish breakfast tea?
Irish breakfast tea, available from tea purveyors everywhere, is a blend of black teas from the Assam region of India. It contains dark brown leaves that brew a hearty, malty, deep red tea that takes milk and sugar very well—perfect for breakfast.

The Anglo-Irish aristocracy introduced tea to Ireland in the nineteenth century. As an import from India, it was too expensive for most Irish people at first, but lower prices and generally improving economic conditions allowed more and more people to try this new taste sensation. Soon the whole nation was hooked. (They pronounced the name of their new drink "tay," from the French pronunciation.)

A cup of tea is often referred to as a "cuppa"—everyone knows what kind of cup you're talking about. People throughout the country take a break in the midafternoon to enjoy a cup of tea and some light snacks such as cookies or finger sandwiches. The Irish drink tea with sugar and generous amounts of milk. Tea devotees extol the drink's powers to aid digestion, cure headaches, and provide a gentle pick-me-up.

Where Irish Tea Comes From

The Irish tend to prefer stronger tea than the English—they have a saying that a good cup of tea should be "strong enough for a mouse to trot on." They've gravitated toward East African suppliers, who provide more aromatic leaves. Irish tea was traditionally made using free leaves, but in recent decades consumers have grown more accepting of tea bags. The Irish maintain very high standards for their tea; consequently, the quality of tea in Ireland is generally much higher than in the United States.

The Irish initially relied entirely on U.K. importers for their tea supply, which became a problem during World War II, when Ireland chose not to ally itself with the United Kingdom. Consequently, the government of Ireland set up Tea Importers (Éire), Ltd., a conglomeration of companies that imported tea directly from the producing countries.

Irish tea consumption continued to increase in the postwar years. In 1973 Ireland had to disband Tea Importers because it violated antimonopoly statutes of the EU, so the business was taken up by the subsidiary companies that had made up the organization.

E-SITE

The most renowned tea store in Ireland is Barry's Tea in Cork; they've provided high-grade tea to the people of Munster for over a century. Today, the Barry's brand sells across the country. The most famous place to have a cuppa in Dublin is the original Bewley's Café on Grafton Street, which has brewed tea since the 1840s.

The Irish Pub

Pubs play a very important role in Irish life. American visitors tend to assume that pubs are the same thing as bars, but this isn't exactly true. Pubs do serve alcohol, but they also serve as restaurants, music stages, meeting places, and even as local cultural museums. Most pubs aren't all these things simultaneously, but instead specialize in one area.

One thing that often surprises visitors is the presence of children and families in Irish pubs. The drinking age in Ireland is eighteen, but it's legal for children under that age to enter with their families. The families are there for the music or the food. Irish pub food—called "pub grub"—is generally inexpensive and hearty. While almost any pub can be expected to provide sandwiches or maybe a baked potato, some pubs have become famous for their food; The Reginald in Waterford, The Stag's Head in Dublin, and Langton's in Kilkenny are good places to visit for culinary delights.

Pubs are the place to go for traditional music, or "trad," as the locals call it. Larger places might bring in professional bands, but the most common format is the session, in which local musicians come with what instruments they have and just get down to business. The musicians in a session are usually playing for beer only, so there generally isn't a cover charge. The pubs in Doolin are famous for their trad.

Why are Irish bars called "pubs"?
"Pub" is short for "public house." The person who runs a pub is called a "publican." All pubs offer beer, but the most important thing for a pub to provide is *cráic* ("crack")—that's Irish for a jolly good time.

The Irish Love for Beer

Ireland has one of the highest beer consumption rates in the world. The unique thing about Irish beer habits is that the most popular type of beer is stout, whereas all other European markets prefer lagers or ales. The most famous stout, of course, is Guinness.

Guinness

If you stop at a pub in Ireland and ask for a pint, the bartender will invariably bring you a Guinness. This unspoken understanding demonstrates the centrality of Guinness in Irish pub culture. Guinness stout is not only the national drink, it is also one of Ireland's leading exports; in recent years Guinness has sold close to 2 billion pints of stout per year in more than 150 different countries.

Arthur Guinness started the first Guinness brewery in 1759 with the help of a £100 inheritance from his godfather, the archbishop of Cashel. A man with vision, Guinness took out a 9,000-year lease on a run-down brewery on St. James Street in Dublin, right next to the Liffey River. This location was crucial, because it ensured a ready supply of pure Irish spring water. Guinness was a big fan of porter, as stout was called then, and he dedicated his new brewery to producing it. After some experimentation he found a taste that people loved, and the business has been growing ever since.

Like all beers, Guinness is made from barley, hops, yeast, and water (originally from the St. James wells in County Kildare). Guinness's distinctive flavor and dark color come from the practice of roasting the hops before brewing them. The beer isn't black, as many people think, but actually a deep ruby color—you can see the true color by holding your pint up to the light.

Guinness has given the world more than stout; it also produces the *Guinness Book of Records*. Guinness has published the book ever since 1955, after the managing director of Guinness got into an argument over which game bird was the fastest in Europe. He vowed to create a book that would settle pub arguments once and for all, and so the book of records was born.

A Proper Pint

A proper pint of Guinness should have a thick head of foam on top. To get this right, the bartender pours the draft into the pint, lets it sit for three or four minutes, then tops it off for serving. Traditionally, Guinness stout was served at room temperature. (Irish room temperature can be pretty cool, so that doesn't mean the beer was warm.) Some pubs in Ireland continue that practice. There used to be a big difference between the flavors of draft Guinness and bottled Guinness, but recent advances in packaging technology have produced cans that can pour a pint almost as good as you'd find in a pub in County Meath.

With Guinness stout's strong flavor and popularity, it was inevitable that people would think of innovative ways to serve it. There are now many mixed drinks involving Guinness. Here are some of the more popular variants:

- Black and Tan—Guinness and a lager or pale ale (traditionally Bass Ale)
- Black Velvet—Guinness and champagne
- Snakebite—Guinness and cider
- Purple Meany—Guinness and a bitter
- Drop of Diesel—a shot of Guinness in a pint of Smithwicks ale

The most popular pint, of course, is pure draught Guinness. There is considerable dispute in Ireland about where you can find the best pint. In

Dublin, the two leading contenders are the St. James Gate Brewery and Mulligan's, a nearby pub that, according to folklore, has a pipe connecting its basement to the brewery. Other Irish people claim that you'll find the best pint in little pubs out in the country that serve their beer at room temperature and never clean the tap.

E-SITE

The best place to learn more about Guinness is at the St. James Gate Brewery in Dublin, which both produces beer and offers a glimpse into the magic of making stout. A glass of stout is included in the tour. Guinness has developed an advanced marketing machine, so get ready for the hard sell.

Other Contenders

Guinness gets the lion's share of attention, but there are a number of other excellent Irish beers. Brewers in Cork make Murphy's and Beamish, stouts that appear similar to Guinness but have distinctly different flavors. In Cork and the rest of Munster, these local brews are often more popular than Guinness stout. You can occasionally find Murphy's in bars outside of Ireland.

Smithwicks ("Smiddicks") is the local brew in Kilkenny. Smithwicks is an amber ale with a slightly hoppy flavor. It's served throughout Ireland. In continental Europe, you might find it under the name "Kilkenny."

There are a number of other beers that have recently come on the market to take advantage of the international enthusiasm for Irish beer. Harp is a lager brewed by Guinness. Murphy's has started brewing an ale called Murphy's Irish Red. With the proliferation of Irish pubs around the world, expect more Irish beers to appear in the near future.

Whiskey—a More Potent Beverage

Queen Elizabeth I of England once remarked that her only true Irish friend was whiskey. The word "whiskey" comes from the Gaelic words *uisce beatha,* which mean "water of life." The origins of whiskey are lost in the mists of time; some historians think the distilling technology was developed in the Far East and brought to Scotland and Ireland by traveling Celts. By 1000 C.E. people in both Scotland and Ireland were fermenting grains, distilling the brew, and aging the final product in wooden barrels.

Modern Irish whiskey is similar to Scotch whisky, but it's distilled three times instead of two, it's slightly sweeter, has less peat flavor, and it's spelled with an "e"—Scotch is spelled "whisky." Although Scotch whisky enjoys a far larger market today, in the nineteenth century Irish whiskey was the more popular drink. It was the liquor of choice in Victorian England, but in the period from 1910 to 1945 the Irish whiskey industry hit on hard times when the combination of Irish independence, American Prohibition, trade disputes with England, and World War II effectively ruined the export market.

Reviving the Spirits of Irish Whiskey

Nevertheless, the domestic Irish market managed to keep a few distillers alive. The Bushmill's distillery in the North continued to produce Bushmill's malt whiskey, and the Midleton distillery near Cork produced the Jameson, Powers, and Midleton whiskies.

In recent years, Ireland's tourist boom has encouraged entrepreneurs to revive old Irish brands and distilleries. Today, there are dozens of Irish whiskey brands on the market, like Paddy, Kilbeggan, Locke's, Tullamore Dew, Redbreast, and Greenore.

E-SITE

To get the full story on Irish whiskey (and a free shot of the stuff) visit the Irish Whiskey Heritage Center in the old Jameson distillery in Dublin. To tour a currently functioning distillery, go to the Bushmill's distillery on the Antrim coast.

Irish Poteen

A discussion of Irish distilled beverages would not be complete without a mention of poteen, *poitín* (po-CHEEN) in Irish Gaelic, an extremely strong grain alcohol made in unlicensed stills in the country—like moonshine. It's said that farmers used to give *poitín* to cows in labor. Supposedly, you can still find it in remote rural areas, but we don't recommend that you drink it; the ethyl alcohol in bad batches can be poisonous.

Alcohol: A Mixed Blessing

For better or worse, alcohol is an important part of Irish life. Irish beer and whiskey provide jobs for thousands of people, they pump export money into the economy, and they help create the boisterous pub atmosphere that is such a big part of Irish life. The unfortunate side effect of this success is the high rate of alcoholism in the Irish population. Ireland has consistently had one of the highest alcohol consumption rates in Europe; in 2000, the average Irish person consumed 12.3 liters of pure alcohol. This tradition of excess has taken its toll in lost productivity, lives cut short, and a reputation for drunkenness that has been hard to shake.

The stereotype of the drunken Irishman has a complicated history. Some aspects of Irish culture have tended to promote alcohol consumption: the long-standing heritage in producing beer and whiskey, the desire to escape from continuing poverty and oppression, and the relatively benign view that the Catholic Church has tended to take on alcohol. But while the stereotype has probably been backed up by elements of truth, it is also true that it was often perpetuated by politicians who wanted to suppress Irish political power. Anti-Irish and anti-Catholic politicians in England and the United States frequently evoked the image of the drunken Irishman to stir up animosity against the Irish.

Irish blessings are legendary, as are Ireland's proverbs. Here is one we should all keep to heart: *An rud nach leigheasann im ná uisce beatha níl aon leigheas air.* This means, "What butter or whiskey does not cure, cannot be cured."

The Republic of Ireland has fought to bring down alcoholism and the stereotype that goes with it. Government actions have increased the penalties for drunk driving, limited the hours that pubs can be open, and mandated that pubs must serve nonalcoholic beverages. Public education campaigns have helped reduce some of the worst consequences of drinking, but the overall rate of consumption is still high. How Ireland will deal with this issue in the future remains to be seen.

Understanding the Irish

One of the most enjoyable aspects of visiting Ireland is getting a feel for how the Irish live. A quick way to get a glimpse of this lifestyle is to sample the pub culture, the food, and the drink that have been described in this chapter.

However, understanding how the Irish really live takes a bit more effort. The best way to do this is to meet real Irish families. The Irish are very friendly people, so this isn't hard to do. By having tea with the grandmother who runs a bed-and-breakfast, or starting up a chat about football at the local pub, you can begin to meet the real Irish. These can be the most rewarding experiences of any visit to Ireland.

Chapter 20

E **Geography and Climate**

Ireland's physical environment has always had a tremendous impact on the lives of its people. Its land, waters, and wildlife have determined what people eat and how they live. Its geographic location has played a large part in its political history, protecting it from some European armies and exposing it to others. In modern times, Ireland's great natural beauty has helped build a booming tourist industry.

Around the Island

Ireland is shaped kind of like a fallen soufflé, raised on the perimeter and fallen in the middle. The central part of Ireland is mostly flat, a base of prehistoric limestone covered with rich soil or raised bogs. The town of Birr is at the geographical center of the island; ancient writers called it *umbilicus hiberniae,* "the navel of Ireland."

Counties Louth, Monaghan, and Cavan occupy an area known as the Drumlin Belt. Drumlins are small, teardrop-shaped hills that were created by retreating glaciers during the last Ice Age, and this area is covered with them. The name *Monaghan* means "little hills" in Irish. The area is generally quite fertile.

The Southeast

The southeastern corner of Ireland is separated from the rest of the island by the Wicklow Mountains, which form a natural barrier from western attackers. The people who have lived here have historically had more to do with England and Europe than have people in the rest of Ireland. The Vikings settled here, especially in Waterford, Wexford, Wicklow, and Arklow. The southeast is known to have more sunny days than the rest of the island, and the local geography and sea currents have produced a string of calm, sandy beaches along the coast. These beaches attract tourists from Ireland and all over Europe.

The Southwest

The southwest of Ireland is one of the most beautiful parts of the island. The Kerry Peninsula juts out into the Atlantic, a landscape of rugged cliffs descending into crashing waves. The Gulf Stream warms the coast, making the area fertile to both plants and animals. Seabirds love the islands off the coast here; the Skellig Islands are home to many gannets, and the aptly named Puffin Island is home to thousands of puffins. Cork has long been the port from which people come and go to the European continent, and Kerry has been the traditional point of departure for the

Americas. The Dingle and Iveragh peninsulas are very isolated from the rest of Ireland; for this reason the Irish language has survived there.

E-SITE

If green mountains, pristine lakes, and grazing sheep are your idea of a good time, then the Ring of Kerry, a circuit of the Iveragh Peninsula, is one of Ireland's must-see destinations. The Ring can get crowded with tour buses, though; the nearby Dingle and Beara Peninsulas have equally stunning scenery and far fewer tourists.

The West

The west of Ireland, traditionally called Connacht, includes the Counties Mayo, Galway, Leitrim, Sligo, and Roscommon. The region is beautiful but quite rocky. The cliffs, although dramatic, don't offer many good places to launch or land boats. That's why people in the west have congregated around Galway Bay and the Shannon Estuary, which offer relatively safer waters. Though it's no farmer's paradise, even rocky Connacht can support quite a few people; before the Great Famine of the 1840s, Ireland's rocky west was feeding a good portion of Ireland's 8 million people with potatoes grown on hillsides.

The Connemara Mountains and the Aran Islands are stunningly beautiful and full of history; early Christians sought out these remote areas as safe havens. The Irish fled (or were banished) to these areas when the English took over, and the remoteness helped them preserve their culture and language. Connacht continues to be home to a number of Irish speakers. County Sligo was the favorite landscape of William Butler Yeats, who celebrated the region in his poems.

The Northwest

Up in the northwest corner is County Donegal, a remote area of mountains and beaches. The coastline is full of jagged cliffs, home to seabirds that enjoy fishing in the ocean there. Humans also fish; lobster is one of the most important catches in the area. The most famous product of Donegal is its tweed cloth, traditionally dyed brown with a fungus scraped off of local rocks.

Ireland's Neighbors

The fundamental geographical fact about Ireland is that it is an island; this fact has had tremendous impact on Ireland's history and character. No point on the island is more than 70 miles from the sea. For generations, the sea has represented food, danger, and hope for the Irish people. It has also meant isolation. Because of the difficulty of reaching them, islands tend to be more politically and culturally isolated than nations on larger landmasses. Ireland's position on the far western end of Europe has increased this isolation; contrast it with Sicily, an island of similar size but with a far more volatile history because of its location in the middle of the Mediterranean.

▲ Map of Western Europe

The northwestern tip of Ireland is very close to Scotland; from ancient times, the people in northern Ireland and western Scotland have spent a lot of time with one another. St. Columcille went to the island of Iona, a part of Scotland that is a short boat ride from Ireland; from there he spread Christianity among the Scottish people. Ulster has always had a sizable Presbyterian Scottish population, called the "Scotch-Irish" or "Scots-Irish."

England and Wales are slightly further away than Scotland, but they are still close. Ireland's proximity and geographical similarity to England made it an appetizing colony for Anglo-Normans. In more recent times, the Irish have found England a handy place to go for work, close enough that they can visit home regularly.

Ireland's other neighbors include France, Spain, and the Scandinavian countries. In the 1700s Wolfe Tone found France close enough to Ireland to make a military attack from there feasible. Spain is slightly farther than France, but not a bad boat trip; ancient Celts made the voyage more than 2,000 years ago, moving their culture from Spain to Ireland, and people have imported horses from Spain for hundreds of years. The Vikings from Norway and Denmark attacked both British Isles, which were conveniently close and offered lots of appetizing shoreline.

ESSENTIAL

Ireland's isolation meant that Celtic culture could survive there after it was wiped out almost everywhere else. Ireland was a safe haven for Christian scholarship during the early Middle Ages, when the rest of Europe was a mess of barbarians and invasions. Even during World War II, Ireland used its physical isolation to maintain its political neutrality.

Pack Your Raincoat: Irish Climate

Americans are often surprised at how far north Ireland is—it's on the same latitude as Newfoundland. In the summer, daylight can last for eighteen hours; in the winter, nights are long and days are very short.

But even though Ireland lies far to the north, its climate is quite mild.

The Gulf Stream current in the Atlantic moderates the weather, preventing extremes of either heat or cold. It seldom freezes in winter and snows very little. Summer temperatures are pleasantly warm but very rarely hot. Within this moderate range, though, temperatures can be unpredictable; sometimes it is terribly cold in July or quite warm in January.

What is predictable is rain. Ireland gets a lot of rain. Some regions, such as County Kerry in the southwest, enjoy up to 270 rainy days a year. The prevailing winds come from the southwest, picking up rain clouds in the Atlantic and then dumping them on the island. All this rain makes Ireland a paradise for green growing things—hence its nickname, the Emerald Isle.

Terrain: Lakes and Forests

Ireland's terrain is one of the reasons it's such a pleasure to visit. Although it has few dramatic features, like large mountains or giant lakes, it has an attractive diversity of landscapes that are accessible on a human scale. It's not the place for rugged hiking or wilderness expeditions, but it can't be beat for pleasant strolls in the countryside.

A Watery Wonderland

Ireland is full of picturesque lakes, gouged out by glaciers during the last Ice Age. The lakes near Killarney have stunned visitors for years. Lough Neagh in Northern Ireland is Ireland's largest lake.

Ireland is also full of rivers, which have allowed people to penetrate Ireland's interior either to settle it or to attack it. The Shannon is the longest river; it runs from County Cavan to the Shannon Estuary between Counties Clare and Limerick, traveling more than 230 miles across the middle of the island.

Forests and Farms

In prehistoric times, Ireland was covered with forests. Most of these trees were oaks, mixed with birch and pine on the hills and with elm, alder, ash, and hawthorn in the lower areas. Other plants grew under the trees. The forest was home to a large variety of animal species.

Farmers started cutting down trees about 6,000 years ago, but deforestation didn't become rampant until the 1500s. At that time the English occupiers cut down most of Ireland's oak to use in shipbuilding and barrel making. By the eighteenth century, Ireland had very little forest left and had to import most of its wood. In the twentieth century, Irish people began planting tree farms, and now about 5 percent of the country is covered with trees again. Most of that is commercially grown pine, but some people are working on planting oaks and other native trees again.

The forests have been replaced with natural bogs and man-made agricultural fields. Ireland has long been a great place to farm; even the most marginal land on hillsides can support bumper crops of potatoes, though it's not good for much else. The richest soil is in central and eastern Ireland, east of the Shannon River. The west is rockier and not especially good for agriculture; that's why Oliver Cromwell banished rebellious Irish out there, keeping the better land for his own supporters (See Chapter 7).

QUESTION?

Were limericks invented in Limerick?
No one knows where they're from. The people of Limerick are known for their ribald humor and it's thought that the town was mentioned in many early poems of this form, and so the name stuck.

Bog, Burren, and the Giant's Causeway

As if general natural beauty weren't enough, Ireland also is home to some really unusual places and environmental conditions. The bogs have long defined Irish life as a source of fuel and building material, as well as an obstacle to quick overland transportation. The Burren and the Giant's Causeway are geological marvels.

A Boggy Land

The bogs are lush wetlands where plants grow thickly on top of shallow water (the ground is mushy, but you can walk on it). When the plants died, there wasn't enough oxygen in the water for them to rot quickly, so over the years a dense layer of plant matter accumulated to form peat. These bogs can be 20 to 40 feet thick.

For centuries the Irish people have used peat from the bogs to fuel their fires. They would cut chunks of peat every spring and set them out to dry in the sun; then they would burn this stuff, also called sod or turf, in their fireplaces. Few families still burn peat these days, but a substantial portion of Ireland's electricity (10 percent in the year 2000) comes from peat-burning power plants.

Bogs are so oxygen-poor that things buried in them often don't rot. Archaeologists have found tools, weapons, jewelry, and even well-preserved human bodies. The real treat, though, is bog butter; people buried huge clumps of butter in the cool peat to keep them fresh, but forgot to dig them up. Today, museums across the midlands proudly display these ancient chunks of petrified dairy fat.

Bogs support their own unique ecosystems, with spectacular flowers and plants that have evolved to thrive in the unusual environment. Carnivorous plants that eat insects thrive in bogs. They are also an important habitat for birds.

Bogs used to cover one-seventh of Ireland's landscape, but they have been depleted over the years. In the twentieth century, the Irish Peat Board excavated thousands of acres of bog to sell to power companies and other businesses that used the peat—they turned it into briquettes for burning and sold it to garden companies as compost. Some people fear that the bogs could disappear completely in the near future. Now the Irish Wildlife Service and the Peat Board are working together to preserve Ireland's remaining bogs, which they now consider a national treasure.

The Burren

The Burren in County Clare is barren and bleak. It's a startling place, a giant field of limestone slabs that look like a slightly greener version of the moon's surface. The slabs are dotted with big limestone boulders. Belowground they are full of caves hollowed out by millions of years of running water; some people make a fine hobby out of mapping this cave system.

Ireland has lots of limestone under its rich soil and greenery, but the Burren is the only place where most of it is exposed, because glaciers from the last Ice Age scraped away the topsoil about 15,000 years ago. The surface of the limestone is quite dry; all water that falls on it quickly drips down to the network of underground streams. There are a few lakes in the Burren, but they are prone to disappearing suddenly when the water table drops.

Though it looks bleak, the Burren supports an astonishing array of plant life. Beautiful flowering plants, such as foxgloves, rock roses, and a number of orchids, thrive on the limestone. Grass grows there, too, in the hollows of the rocks; the limestone stores heat, which allows the grass to grow all year round. A number of wild goats live off this grass. Sometimes farmers even move their cattle to the Burren to graze.

People have lived in the area of the Burren for millenniums, long before the Celts arrived. There are some seventy ancient tombs there, such as the Poulnabrone dolmen, constructed about 4,500 years ago, and the Gleninsheen wedge tomb, where a wonderful gold collar dating from about 700 B.C.E. was found.

E-SITE

The Burren Way is a walking path that runs 22 miles from Ballyvaughan to Ballinalacken. The nearby Cliffs of Moher are a spectacular sight and can also be visited on foot; this is a great place to watch puffins or propose marriage. One of the best caves to visit is Aillwee Cave, which boasts dramatic stalactites and the remains of ancient cave bears.

Giant's Causeway

The Giant's Causeway, on the coast of northern County Antrim, is one of the more stupendous sights in the world. It is a collection of bizarre rock formations set between the sea and the towering cliffs. Most of them are hexagonal columns that stand straight up from the ground. The flat tops of the columns look like stepping stones, and visitors can actually walk on them. Some of the odder formations have names such as Giant's Eyes (circular bubbles of basalt rock) and the Giant's Organ (columns of rock that look like the pipes of an organ). Others include the King and His Nobles, the Chimney Tops, the Honeycomb, the Giant's Loom, and the Wishing Chair.

The name "Giant's Causeway" comes from a legend about Finn MacCool, who supposedly built it. (Finn was sometimes spoken of as a giant.) In this story, he was spectacularly huge, and he had fallen in love with Una, a large and luscious lady on Staffa Island, off the Scottish Coast (which is across from this part of Ireland and happens to have the same bizarre, honeycomb-shaped rock formations as the Giant's Causeway). Finn built the causeway as a bridge between the two islands so he could take Una home with him. Everything was going swimmingly until Benandonner, an even more spectacularly large Scottish giant, decided to come after them and take Una back to be his girlfriend.

E-SITE

The Giant's Causeway has been called the Eighth Wonder of the World. It was declared a World Heritage Site in 1987. Travelers have sought it out for centuries; Samuel Johnson, William Thackeray, and Sir Walter Scott all journeyed to see it. Today it is Northern Ireland's most popular tourist attraction.

Finn was tough, but when he saw Benandonner's immense bulk, he realized that the Scot was just too big to fight. Fortunately, Finn was also clever—with Una's help, he disguised himself as an immense Irish infant. When Benandonner saw how big Irish babies were, he got scared of facing a full-grown one, and he ran back to Scotland, destroying the causeway in the process. That's why all we have left today are the remnants on the North Antrim Coast and on Staffa Island.

Geologists, however, believe that volcanic eruptions and the rapid cooling of theoleiitic basalt lava 60 million years ago resulted in the unusual polygonal shapes. Retreating glaciers exposed the basalt columns 15,000 years ago, and the Giant's Causeway was born.

Animal Life

Since the end of the last Ice Age, Ireland has been home to a huge variety of animal life. Like humans, animals have found Ireland's climate hospitable. Humans have, in turn, benefited from the plentiful fauna—in ancient times they could always find something to eat, and now fishing, hunting, and bird watching are popular activities with tourists and locals alike.

In the Sea

The oceans around Ireland are full of seals and dolphins, some of which enjoy greeting human visitors. The rivers teem with salmon and trout, which makes Ireland most popular with fishermen. Mackerel and pollock are plentiful in the nearby ocean. Galway Bay is famous for its oysters.

FACT

The most popular inhabitant of Dingle Town is a fun guy with an amazing appetite for fish—Fungi the dolphin! Fungi and his mother swam into Dingle Bay several years ago and became an immediate hit with the locals. Fungi's mom died a few years back, but her son stuck around. Fungi seems to enjoy human company; he's famous for playing with swimmers and scuba divers.

Bird watchers love western Ireland because its cliffs and islands are a favorite breeding location for seabirds. Puffins, cormorants, herons, and other birds all lay their eggs there; their colonies cover the cliff sides in the springtime. Ireland is also a stopover on the migration routes of many

Arctic and African birds. One of these African visitors is the corncrake, which comes to Ireland to breed in April. It is terribly endangered because its nesting areas have all become farmland, but people are now trying to preserve it.

On the Land

Ireland has lots of foxes and badgers. Rabbits are plentiful, too; the Normans introduced them 900 years ago for food, and they have thrived. There are native red deer in hilly areas, especially Killarney National Park and the Wicklow Mountains.

Ireland is famous for its horses. Horses have lived there for about 4,000 years, and they seem to find the environment quite congenial; some people claim that the limestone underneath Irish soil makes the grass there especially good for growing strong horse bones. Irish racehorses and show horses are known for their strength and beauty. In the eighteenth and nineteenth centuries, the monarchs of Europe sought their horses in Ireland; Napoleon supposedly got his horse Marengo from the Emerald Isle. The Irish people take advantage of their terrain to create unique horse races, galloping their steeds on the beach or through the rough countryside.

E-SITE

The Irish National Stud in Kildare is the nation's pre-eminent site for horse breeding. The accompanying museum explains the rich heritage of Irish horse racing. There are exceptionally beautiful horses to be seen here, and the surrounding green hills make fantastic horse pasture.

Smaller but sturdier ponies also thrive in Ireland. Connemara ponies live in Connemara in the west, where they grow small but rugged, eating the local sea grass. The rare Kerry Bog pony lives in County Kerry. These ponies probably developed from ponies brought over from Spain in the 1600s. Kerry Bog ponies are tough and strong, good at hauling loads of turf or seaweed. There used to be large herds of them in Kerry, but their numbers dwindled in the nineteenth century. Enthusiasts are now breeding them again.

Environmental Organizations and National Parks

Like many developed countries, Ireland has recently become interested in preserving its natural environment and saving endangered species. A governmental organization called Dúchas monitors national parks and gardens. The Irish Wildlife Trust oversees wilderness areas. The National Trust, called An Taisce in Ireland, preserves important natural sites and historical structures. These organizations are all working to designate and protect areas of natural and cultural significance, and to make them accessible to visitors.

Ireland also boasts five national parks:

- The Burren
- Connemara
- Glenveagh
- Killarney
- Wicklow Mountains

In addition, there are several forest parks, an area of blanket bog in County Mayo, and a number of National Nature Reserves.

A Land Worth Protecting

The Irish interest in protecting the beauty of their natural landscape will benefit all who are interested in Ireland. Ireland's varied and picturesque terrain makes it one of the most charming countries in the world to visit. The appeal of the landscape, however, is more than just visual. Ireland's geography—its location, climate, and natural resources—has played a crucial role in the political and cultural development of the Irish people. To understand Irish history and heritage, it's important to appreciate the land itself.

Chapter 21

Ⓔ Ireland Today and Tomorrow

Many people are pleasantly shocked when they visit Ireland these days. The festering conflict in Northern Ireland, although far from resolved, is beginning, however tentatively, to show signs of healing. The status of human rights and the position of women in Irish society have taken major steps forward.

1972 Ireland agrees to join the EEC

1983 Amendment to Constitution forbids abortion

1985 Anglo-Irish Agreement

1986 Referendum to allow divorce fails

1990 Mary Robinson becomes the first female president of Ireland

1992 Case X arouses national controversy over abortion

1993 Homosexuality and contraceptives declared legal

1998 Good Friday Agreement (Accords)

The Celtic Tiger

Historically, Ireland has been poor. In the Middle Ages, visitors were often shocked at the almost Stone Age poverty of many Irish farmers. In Victorian times, English visitors were appalled to learn that conditions had not improved much since medieval days. Even in the 1950s, the per-capita income of rural Irish citizens was less than one-third of the average for Europe. To many observers, it seemed that poverty was Ireland's natural state.

If those observers could have jumped ahead to the year 2003, they would have been stunned by the transformation. From the 1960s to the 1980s, Ireland experienced a series of economic growth spurts, which kicked into high gear in the mid-1990s. After several consecutive years of leading Europe in economic growth, Ireland now has one of the better standards of living in the world. This extraordinary development has earned Ireland the name "Celtic Tiger."

How Did All This Come About?

As with all macroeconomic questions, the answer is multifaceted and ambiguous, but a few key factors stand out. The first is Irish participation in the European Economic Community (EEC) and its successor organization, the European Union (EU). Since Ireland joined the EEC in 1972, it has been the single largest net recipient of EEC and EU funds— over £20 billion to date. The EU follows a policy of supporting less prosperous member nations to help them reach the economic levels of wealthier members. Ireland used this money to build roads, update utilities, build up a tourism infrastructure, and subsidize agriculture. Ireland is small and the money was generally well spent, so the investments have made a noticeable impact on many people's lives.

International business investment was the next major reason for Ireland's success. The Irish government has gone out of its way to lure American and European businesses with tax breaks and incentive packages. The Republic of Ireland (which excludes Northern Ireland) is now an extremely safe place with very little crime, essentially no chance of war, and a stable government. The Republic has few large businesses of its own, so it is unlikely to initiate costly tariffs to protect native industry. Finally, the Republic of Ireland is an excellent place to locate an operation that does business in both Europe and North America, both because of its physical location and because it has a large percentage of bilingual English speakers.

QUESTION?

Will the Celtic Tiger continue to roar?
No one can say for sure. Many of Ireland's economic fundamentals are sound: an educated and industrious work force, some solid industries, and booming tourism. On the other hand, as Ireland's domestic economy improves, EU subsidies and foreign investments may dry up. Current prospects, however, appear positive.

This last point demonstrates the Republic of Ireland's third big advantage—its people. The Republic of Ireland has a very strong education system that has produced one of the most educated work forces in the world. Whereas in the past the Irish were known for their laid-back—if not lackadaisical—approach to enterprise, the current generation of workers is widely recognized for its energy and ambition. The traditional English stereotype of the feckless Irishman has fallen to pieces on the ambition of the Republic of Ireland's charging young work force.

Ireland and the European Union

Participation in the EU has had extraordinary consequences for the Republic of Ireland. It led to the economic boom that the Irish are enjoying today, but those economic changes haven't made everyone happy. EU membership opens up to Irish businesses the giant market of European consumers, but it also means that the Republic of Ireland's weaker industries are now exposed to international competition. Traditional dairy farms, for example, simply can't compete with industrialized factory farms. Europe and the Republic of Ireland have so far supported these farmers with subsidies, but there is substantial pressure for the Irish agricultural industry to modernize itself to compete on the free market.

Another major impact of Europe has been on social issues. Traditionally, the Republic of Ireland has been a very conservative country, with close ties to the Catholic Church. Prevailing attitudes on the Continent have taken a much more liberal direction on issues like women's rights, abortion, and divorce. Although the Irish government has dragged its heels, international pressure and the will of the Irish people have forced it to liberalize many laws.

One of the more controversial issues for the Republic of Ireland is how its traditional stance of neutrality figures into EU membership. While the EU is not primarily a military organization, it does require a form of military alliance from its members. Concerns over possible future military entanglements led a majority of Irish voters to reject the EU Nice Treaty in 2001 (the Treaty opens EU membership to ten Eastern European countries that are possibly less stable than the current Western European members). After the Republic of Ireland's politicians spent a year promoting the treaty and wrangled some legal concessions out of EU bureaucrats, voters passed the treaty in a second referendum in 2002.

The Republic of Ireland is still an active member of the United Nations. Irish peacekeeping troops have been well received around the world because of their clear history of neutrality. In recent years, Ireland has been known in the UN as an outspoken proponent of human rights and the empowerment of small countries.

Modern Politics

The last thirty years have been a tumultuous time for Irish politics. A series of governments in the 1970s and 1980s fell because they couldn't end the violence in the North or fix the Republic of Ireland's persistent unemployment. In addition, thorny social problems and an abundance of scandals made a rocky path for Irish politicians. Fortunately, matters seem to have improved in the 1990s.

Dealing with the Situation in the North

No political issue in Ireland has aroused as much emotion as the question of the North. The Fianna Fáil Party, Ireland's dominant political party throughout the century, was founded on the premise that Ireland should never have been divided. After the issue nearly tore the country apart in the 1920s, politicians placed it on the backburner as a continuing source of grievance. De Valera's constitution of 1937 even laid claim to the territory as part of the Republic. In the following three decades, however, most people accepted that the North belongs to the United Kingdom.

FACT

Ireland faces a human rights challenge with the Travellers. Also known as Tinkers, this gypsylike community travels around in caravans and rarely puts down roots. The people suffer severe discrimination in many Irish communities, who fear that the Travellers bring crime. The government has tried to ease the situation, but it's difficult to provide social services to a transient community.

When the Troubles erupted in the North, many people in the Republic had deeply conflicting feelings. On the one hand, they wanted to side with their Catholic brethren in Ulster, but on the other, they didn't want to disrupt their own country or their peaceful relationship with the United Kingdom. A crisis broke out in 1971 when two Cabinet ministers, including the future Taoiseach Charles Haughey, were implicated in a scheme to smuggle weapons to Northern Catholics. The ministers resigned, but the question remained of how far the Republic should involve itself in the crisis.

In the end, the Republic wound up siding with Britain—both nations agreed that they would rather see an end to the violence than press their respective territorial claims. In 1985, they signed the Anglo-Irish Agreement, a framework for a peace settlement. Unfortunately, combatants in the North refused to give up the fight.

Irish leaders continued to try to end the violence. In 1998 Bertie Ahern, the leader of Fianna Fáil and the Irish Taoiseach, took part in the Good Friday Peace Talks that finally brought a lasting peace agreement. Ahern brought back a referendum for the Irish people to approve the agreement, specifically the Republic of Ireland's rejection of its historical claim to Northern Ireland. The referendum passed by a wide margin. The question of the North is by no means answered for good, but for the first time in many years people believe that it's moving in the right direction.

The Economy

The current Fianna Fáil government of Bertie Ahern has benefited from the economic good times. Not all Irish are convinced that economic prosperity will stay for the long term. Some naysayers point out that boom times tend to end with busts. Others predict that the recent wave of foreign investment, spurred by tax incentives and traditionally low labor costs, will dry up as soon as conditions aren't so favorable. For the time being, the Irish are keeping their fingers crossed.

A Wave of Scandals

In recent decades, a series of political scandals has significantly reduced the faith of the Irish in their leaders. Many of these scandals took place during the administration of Charlie Haughey, son-in-law to the legendary Fianna Fáil leader Sean Lemass, who had dominated Irish politics in the 1950s. Haughey had already been implicated in a smuggling scandal in 1971, but he somehow managed to clear his name and rose up to lead Fianna Fáil from 1979 to 1992, serving as Taoiseach for several of those years.

The voters liked Haughey, but a shadow of corruption always seemed to follow his administration. The police force had a series of scandals under the Haughey regime. Several government departments experienced financial scandals, which somehow never implicated Haughey himself. The worst crisis came when it was discovered that Haughey's supporters had been wire-tapping journalists hostile to his administration; it was an Irish form of Watergate. Somehow, Haughey's popularity with the Fianna Fáil faithful kept him in charge of the party until 1992, when a biting investigation into corruption in the beef industry finally did him in.

Shadows of corruption still haunt the Irish political system, but there have been relatively few major crises in the last decade. It seems that current politicians are either more honest or more discreet.

Politics Today

The Irish political structure continues to be something of an anomaly, since the two dominant parties are divided less by ideology than by historical associations. Fianna Fáil, the party founded by Éamon de Valera and the forces who opposed the Anglo-Irish Treaty, has been the dominant party throughout the century. Fine Gael, the organization that emerged from the Free State politicians who supported the treaty, has managed to take control of the government on a number of occasions with the help of third parties. The major political parties in Ireland today are:

- Fianna Fáil—the original anti-treaty party
- Fine Gael—the original pro-treaty party
- Labour—a liberal workers' party
- Progressive Democrats—an offshoot of Fianna Fáil that is economically conservative and socially liberal; it has allied with Fine Gael at times
- Democratic Left—the modern incarnation of the original Sinn Féin; leftist but no longer socialist
- Greens—an environmental party

To Europeans, who are used to wide ideological divisions in politics, Fine Gael and Fianna Fáil appear almost identical. Roughly speaking, Fianna Fáil appeals more to farmers and laborers, and it is more socially conservative and less economically conservative than Fine Gael. Fine Gael is identified with the middle class and has more ties to business.

The Liberalization of Ireland

Throughout the twentieth century, Ireland was known for its conservative social policies. When the rest of Europe was adopting liberal measures, Ireland held a firm stance against contraception, abortion, and divorce. These stances were inextricably linked to the close connection between the Roman Catholic Church and the Irish government. The early leaders of the Irish Free State wanted it that way; they consciously sought connections with the Catholic hierarchy in order to help establish the legitimacy of their government with the Irish people.

Ireland held firm to its traditional values for most of the century, but the winds of change blew in with the 1960s. When Ireland began to establish closer ties with the EEC and EU, many Irish people began to think their laws should be more in line with the general trends of European progressive values. The rise of feminist thought provided counterpoints to many of the patriarchal values of the Irish government. Some Irish also believed that a more distinct line between the government and the Catholic Church would help ease tensions between the Republic and Northern Ireland.

Contraception

Catholics are taught that sexual intercourse should take place only for the purpose of procreation; the use of contraceptives to prevent conception is an immoral act. For decades, the government of Ireland made it illegal to import or sell contraceptives. In 1966, however, the United Nations declared it a basic human right for an individual to control his or her own fertility. Although the government resisted this idea, many Irish people—particularly women—agreed.

FACT

One of the major reasons for the liberalization of contraception laws was the onset of AIDS in the 1980s. When it became clear that condoms could save people's lives, many conservatives withdrew their opposition to allowing the sale of contraceptives.

There were numerous cases of Irish families who had been reduced to poverty by having more children than they could support, or of women whose health was wrecked by having ten or even twenty children. Public opinion decided that if family planning could improve people's lives, then it wasn't immoral. In the late 1960s doctors began prescribing birth control pills to married women, ostensibly for health reasons. In the early 1970s it became legal for married couples to buy condoms, provided they had a prescription. Over the next two decades the laws were relaxed to the point where people can now purchase condoms in vending machines.

Abortion

The struggle over abortion has been one of the most acrimonious issues in contemporary Irish politics. Abortion has never been legal in Ireland (except in cases where the mother's life is at risk), and that does not appear likely to change in the near future. The controversy has been over whether women should be allowed to travel abroad for abortions, and whether they should be able receive information about it from medical professionals. Although it is difficult to get exact statistics, it is thought that a few thousand women every year travel to England to get an abortion. For the most part, the Irish government has been willing to ignore this practice.

In 1992, however, a case exploded that could not be ignored. A fourteen-year-old girl referred to as "X" by the media was raped by a family acquaintance and became pregnant. Her parents planned to take her to England for an abortion, but they wanted to bring back fetal tissue to use in the prosecution of their daughter's assailant. When they asked the police about this, the police turned the issue over to the district attorney's office, which declared that the girl could not leave the country specifically to receive an abortion. The parents sued for the right to take her abroad.

The conflict created a national scandal. Although most Irish people opposed abortion in most situations, they generally supported the girl's right to end a pregnancy that seemed so wrong. European Union officials complained that a free government did not have the right to inhibit its citizens' travel in that way. Eventually, government officials allowed her to leave under the pretext that the girl was suicidal, thereby allowing the traditional exception concerning the life of the mother.

The issue wasn't over. In 1993, conservative leaders proposed a constitutional change that would have made it illegal for women to travel abroad for abortions. The referendum failed, but it's interesting to note that 40 percent of voters supported the amendment. For the time being, the situation is much like it was before Case X, with thousands of women traveling to England for secret abortions.

Divorce

Divorce has been another political hotspot in recent years. The Catholic Church opposes divorce on the grounds that marriage is a lifelong sacrament. While the Church does allow annulments—an official declaration that the marriage never took place—the policy has been unwieldy in practice and does not resolve the tricky legal disputes that divorces create. The legal complications have been one of the main reasons why Ireland has opposed divorce; in a country where the family farm is paramount and the husband owns all property by default, the government has been reluctant to tackle the issue of community property.

Over the last few decades, however, it became clear that Ireland had thousands of broken marriages, just like every other country in Europe. It seemed to many people that Ireland was dodging the problem by declaring that it didn't exist. In 1986 the country held a referendum to make divorce legal, but it failed by a fairly substantial vote. In 1996, pressured by EU policies on divorce and property rights, Ireland held a second referendum, which passed by a tiny margin. Divorce is now legal, but there are still many people who view it as the wrong decision.

FACT

Homosexuality was illegal in Ireland until 1993. There were gay people in Ireland before that, but they had to be very discreet. Nowadays there are gay pubs and nightclubs in the big cities, and Dublin has a thriving gay nightlife. However, many rural areas have retained conservative views on homosexuality.

Women in Charge

One remarkable feature of modern Irish politics has been the advance of women to high offices. The seventh and eighth presidents of Ireland have been women. While this role has primarily been a figurehead office for most of its existence, Mary Robinson and Mary McAleese have redefined the position into a platform of international significance.

Mary Robinson

Mary Robinson was born in Ballina, County Mayo, in 1944. She earned law degrees from Trinity College and Harvard University, and in 1969 she became Trinity College's youngest law professor ever. She became involved in Irish politics early, representing the Labour Party in the Irish Upper House of Parliament from 1969 to 1989. In 1988 she and her husband, Nicholas, founded the Irish Centre for European Law.

Robinson served as president of Ireland from 1990 to 1997. She pursued economic, political, and cultural ties with other nations, continuing Ireland's tradition of active involvement in the European Union. But Robinson didn't only seek to advance Ireland's ties to its wealthy neighbors; she also used the post to advocate the rights of poor countries throughout the world. Citing Ireland's experiences in the Great Famine, she argued for the responsibilities of industrialized nations to help developing nations.

Robinson brought this sense of international responsibility to the United Nations, where she served as high commissioner for human rights from June 1997 to September 2002. Only the second person to serve in the role, Robinson used the relatively unknown position to take strong stances on human rights issues around the world. She traveled to dozens of nations during her term, often creating controversy. Her condemnation of human rights abuses in China and Chechnya aroused defensive reactions from the Chinese and Russian leaders. She created more surprise by criticizing NATO bombing in Serbia and U.S. bombing campaigns in Afghanistan.

Robinson has won a number of prizes in recognition of her efforts, including the Fulbright Prize for International Understanding and the Indira Gandhi Peace Prize.

ESSENTIAL

Mary Robinson has fought hard to protect marginalized groups. As the UN human rights commissioner, she said, "My mandate requires that I be a voice for those who don't have a voice . . . desperate people with no sense that the world cares enough . . . we have to show 'yes we do,' we take seriously the trauma of individual families."

Mary McAleese

Mary McAleese was born in 1951 to a Catholic family in Belfast. She became aware of Northern Ireland's problems at an early age, when her father's shop was fired on in sectarian violence. Her early career was similar in some ways to Mary Robinson's; she earned a law degree at Queens University and became a law professor at Trinity College. McAleese has served on several legal committees in Ireland, and in 1987 she became pro-vice chancellor of Queens University, the first woman to hold that role. She has also been an active broadcaster with Radio Telefís Éireann.

McAleese took office as the eighth president of Ireland in November 1997, the first person from Northern Ireland to serve in this role. "Building Bridges" has been the theme of her presidency—she has sought to promote social inclusion, equality, and reconciliation throughout Ireland's population. Many people hope that her inclusive philosophy will help build a stronger relationship between the North and the South.

FACT

One reason that Mary Robinson and Mary McAleese have been so popular is that they have been able to balance high-profile careers with the demands of their families—both presidents are married and have three children.

The Changing Face of Ireland

The face of Ireland is changing. The charming but patronizing images of the past—the simple farmer, the friendly drunk—have given way to the real faces of Seamus Heaney, U2's Bono, and Mary Robinson. Europe's perennially poor cousin has become the Celtic Tiger.

In the midst of all this change, however, Ireland has not forgotten its past. The Irish people look to their past for education and inspiration. It isn't difficult, because the past is all around them: Stone Age tombs exist alongside monastic round towers; modern-day bards perform Celtic tunes in Anglo-Irish mansions. The many elements of Ireland's rich heritage blend with its present to make Ireland a beautiful and fascinating place. (E)

Chapter 22

Guide for Descendants of Irish Emigrants

The world is full of descendants of Irish emigrants. In the United States alone, some 42 million people are descended from Irish Catholic or Protestant immigrants. Most of these descendants know little more about their Irish roots than the names of their family and the county they came from. But more and more people are taking an interest in learning about Irish heritage, tracing their family histories, and even reaffirming ties to relatives back in the old country.

It's All in the Name

There are a number of family names that are widely known to be Irish. Some of them are very old indeed, dating back to the Celtic peoples who controlled the island many centuries ago. Other names were added later, as waves of invaders gradually merged with the Irish population. Thus, Irish surnames include Old Gaelic (O'Brien, O'Neill), Norman (FitzGerald, Butler), Scots (Hamilton), as well as a plethora of English names (White, Williamson).

FACT

The Irish didn't really use family names until the tenth century, when Brian Boru supposedly introduced the practice. Instead, they identified themselves as the son or descendant of a father or earlier ancestor. This practice was continued in the many *O*'s and *Mc*s that precede Irish names.

About 10 percent of Irish surnames come from the Anglo-Normans of the twelfth and thirteenth centuries—the French, English, Welsh, and Flemish. A large proportion of surnames in the North come from Scotland, due to the Ulster Plantation in the 1600s. Furthermore, the English government Anglicized many old Irish surnames.

O'Somebody

The prefix *O'* means "descended from." Thus, someone named O'Grady is descended from an ancestor named Grady. Names beginning with this prefix are a dead giveaway that someone is of Irish descent. Sometimes the *O'* gets dropped; if you want to look up a surname, check listings both with and without it—for example, when looking up the name "O'Reilly," also check for "Reilly."

O'Brien is an illustrious name; this name supposedly comes in a direct line from Brian Boru, the great king of the eleventh century. Not all O'Briens are descendants of Brian Boru; some versions of the name are a corruption of "O'Byrne" or derive from the Norman surname Bryan. Many O'Briens come from County Clare or the town of Killaloe, where Brian Boru had a palace.

E-SITE

In Clarecastle, you can visit the ghost of Maire Rua O'Brien, widow of the seventeenth-century rebel soldier Conor O'Brien. She had a black stallion that helped her get rid of unwelcome suitors; they would ride the horse at a gallop to the edge of the Cliffs of Moher, the horse would stop suddenly, and the suitor would keep on going straight down.

The name **O'Connor** also has a long history; it's a very old Gaelic surname. The O'Connors descended from King Conchobar of Connacht, who died in the tenth century. Roderick O'Connor was the last high king of Ireland. O'Connors became lords of Counties Mayo and Clare (in the Burren, they built Ballinalacken Castle).

The O'Connors from County Offaly trace their descent to a king of Ireland from the second century C.E.; they fought hard against English rule in the 1500s and as a result were more or less destroyed as a wealthy dynasty, although the name did survive. O'Connors were a dominant family in County Sligo from the fourteenth to the seventeenth century, but lost all of their possessions after Cromwell.

The **O'Donnells** were prominent in County Donegal in the fourteenth century. One of their members, Red Hugh O'Donnell, was famous for his bravery fighting the English under Queen Elizabeth I. After Cromwell, the O'Donnells spread through Counties Mayo and Leitrim, and there are still many of them there, as well as in west Donegal. Many O'Donnells emigrated to the United States and Australia.

The **O'Malleys** were a famous seafaring family who controlled most of the west coast of Ireland from their base at Clew Bay in County Mayo. The name is still common in County Mayo. It was sometimes Anglicized to "Melia."

FACT

One of the most famous O'Malleys was Grace O'Malley, who became an excellent sailor and a "Pirate Queen" in the 1500s. She fought a sea battle against the Turks one day after giving birth to her son. She also visited Queen Elizabeth to ask for clemency for all of her family's piracy; O'Malley must have impressed the queen, because she got what she asked for.

O'Neill is one of the most common surnames in Ireland; it's among the ten most common names in Counties Antrim, Derry, and Tyrone. The O'Neills are descended from medieval kings of Ulster, who ruled the northern province for four centuries before being put down by the English. They controlled a number of other clans, but had the hardest time keeping their own rival factions of O'Neills living harmoniously. Hugh O'Neill was their last chief; in 1603, the English general Mountjoy destroyed the O'Neills coronation chair at Tullaghoge. Many O'Neills fled to Europe, especially Spain, where they flourished as statesmen and soldiers.

◀ The O'Neill family coat of arms

O'Reilly is another very common name, especially in the north; it's the most common name in Counties Cavan and Longford. In Irish it means "descendant of Raghallach" (one of the kings of Connacht). The O'Reillys were a warlike group known for their skill with cavalry. They were also successful medieval traders and produced a number of archbishops and bishops. They traced their descent to the fourth-century king Uí Briúin Breifne. They lost most of their property under Cromwell.

The name **O'Rourke** comes from "O'Ruairc," which means "descendant of Ruarc;" the name Ruarc comes from the Norse word *hrothekr,* or "famous king." Variants on the name include O'Rorke, Rourke, Roark, and Rooke. They trace their ancestry to Brian, the fourth-century king of Connacht; the Ruarc name comes from a tenth-century king of Breifne. The O'Rourkes fought the O'Connors for control of Connacht until the twelfth century, when the O'Connors won. The O'Rourkes also fought with the O'Reillys. Their stronghold was in County Leitrim. Many O'Rourkes went to Europe after Cromwell confiscated their property, where they thrived in church and state; many of their descendants became important people in Poland and Russia.

MacSomeone

The prefix *Mac* or *Mc* means "son of." People usually associate *Mac* names with Scotland, but there are many in Ireland, too. The *Mac* generally precedes the name of the person's clan, which was one of the primary social units for the Celtic populations in both Scotland and Ireland. These surnames, like *O'* surnames, sometimes drop their prefix. So if, for example, your name is McMahon, you might have to research it under Mahon.

The name **McBride** and its relative **Kilbride** come from Gaelic words meaning "devotee of the cult of St. Brigid." Brigid was one of Ireland's three patron saints, and her shrine was located at Kildare; there was a shrine to a different St. Brigid in Donegal, and many followers of the cult associated with it took the name McBride for themselves and their children. McBrides were very common in County Down in the 1600s. The St. Brigid cult was also popular in Scotland, which was the origin of many of the Kilbrides and the Bridges, some of whom moved to Ireland.

McCarthy is among the ten most common Irish surnames; the majority of them live in County Cork. The McCarthys trace their ancestry to the third-century king of Munster, Oilioll Olum, and his son Eoghan, founder of the Eóghanacht. The name comes from an eleventh-century ruler called Cárthach (which means "the loving one"); his descendants took the name McCárthach. McCarthys moved into Kerry, west Cork, and in the barony of Muskerry, where the McCarthys lived in Blarney Castle.

Irish women have their own family name system; Irish puts a *Ní* in front of an unmarried woman's surname, and an *Uú* in front of the surname of a married woman. Girls were often named Mary (or Maura), or after a female saint. Colleen isn't actually a common name for women; it's the Anglicized version of the Irish word for girl, *cailín*.

The name **MacGuiness** and variants originated in Ulster, where it is traced back to a fifth-century chief named Saran. In the twelfth century, the MacGuinesses controlled most of County Down. Many of them converted to Protestantism before the plantation. In the late sixteenth century, though, the head of the family joined the O'Neills in their rebellion against the British, and the MacGuinesses found themselves dispossessed. Many of them fled to Europe, where they assisted France, Spain, and Austria in their fights against the British.

McKenna is a common name in County Monaghan. It comes from a County Meath family called Mac Cionaith, who moved to Ulster to serve as soldiers. The McKennas were dispossessed after Cromwell, and many of them moved to Counties Derry and Down. Some McKennas changed their name to McKinney, though most Ulster McKinneys are descended from Scots with that name.

The **McMahons** (and MacMahons and Mahons) trace their ancestry to a grandson of Brian Boru, Mahon ("son of a bear") O'Brien. The McMahons controlled the baronies of Moyarta and Clonderlaw in southwest County Clare; McMahon is now the most common surname in County Clare. Also, MacMahon is one of the top five names in County Monaghan.

FACT

The three most common surnames in Ireland are Murphy, Kelly, and O'Sullivan. Murphy is the most common; Murphys are sometimes called "Spud Murphy," because they are "as common as potatoes."

Other Common Names

Many names often appear in two different forms, both with and without an *O'* or *Mac*. For example, both Kelly and Sullivan appear as O'Kelly and O'Sullivan.

Cunningham is a surname with multiple roots. Some Cunninghams are descended from the Old Irish Munster family O'Cuinneagain; some are descended from the MacCuinneagains of Connacht. Other Cunninghams come from Scottish families who settled Ireland during the plantation and intermingled with Irish people. Other forms of the name include **Coonaghan, McCuinnagan, Kinigan,** and **Kinahan.**

The name **FitzGerald** comes from Maurice Fitz Gerald, who invaded Ireland with the Normans in 1169; he was the grandson of one of the Normans who invaded England with William the Conquerer in 1066. Maurice's many sons left descendants in Counties Kilkenny, Kildare, and Kerry. His great-great-grandson Maurice was the ancestor of the FitzMaurices and Pierses in County Kerry. By 1600, FitzGeralds were prominent landowners in Counties Waterford, Limerick, Cork, and Kerry; many people in those counties still have the name.

The **Gallaghers** and O'Gallaghers were common in County Donegal. Although the family wasn't always prosperous, it often intermarried with and fought alongside the powerful O'Donnell family. The O'Gallaghers also produced a number of bishops. The name Gallagher is now common in Counties Donegal, Sligo, and Mayo and in Dublin, where it almost never uses the form O'Gallagher. It's also common in Liverpool, Manchester, and Leeds, where it is pronounced "Galloch-er," and in Scotland, where it is often spelled Gallchair.

Hamilton is a surname that comes almost entirely from Scots who settled Ireland during the plantation; many of them went to Counties

Monaghan, Cavan, Armagh, and Tyrone. The Hamiltons in Scotland descended from Walter Fitz Gilbert of Hambleton, who was granted land in Scotland by Robert the Bruce in the thirteenth century. Most Ulster Hamiltons are Protestant, though there are a few Catholics who descended from Sir George Hamilton.

Most people with the name **Joyce** are descended from the Joyce clan of Connemara in Galway. They were a prominent Gaelic family, and their territory was called Joyces' County. There are also a number of Joyces in Counties Cork, Kilkenny, and Wexford.

ESSENTIAL

There are several first names associated with the Irish. Patrick, shortened to Paddy, and Michael, shortened to Mick, are well known. The name Seamus (SHAY-mus) is Irish for James. First-born sons were traditionally named after their fathers.

Kelly is an extremely common Irish surname; there are more than 50,000 Kellys in Ireland and many more all over the world. The name means "descendant of Ceallach," which was a very common name and thus has resulted in families of Kellys and O'Kellys appearing independently in several places. There are Kellys in Counties Galway, Roscommon, Meath, North Wicklow, Antrim, Down, and Laois, as well as just about everywhere else. The most prominent Kelly clan was the Kellys of Uí Maine in Roscommon and Galway. The O'Kellys were one of the most powerful Old Irish families in Connacht up until the seventeenth century.

Maguire has been a common name in Fermanagh for more than 1,000 years. The name derives from the Gaelic Mag Uidhir, which means "son of the pale one." Maguires were chiefs of the region near Lisnaskea between 1200 and 1600. Their power was broken by Cromwell and King William, and many Maguires moved to France and Austria with the Wild Geese (the colloquial name for the Irishmen who emigrated from Ireland in the seventeenth and eighteenth centuries. Conor Maguire was executed for taking part in the massacre of 1641.

Murphy is the most common surname in Ireland. Like Kelly, the name has multiple origins, so the Murphys don't constitute one clan with a single shared ancestor. The name comes from the personal name

Murchadh, which means "sea warrior"; evidently, this was a very common occupation in Ireland. Murphy often had an *O'* or *Mac* added to it. There were clans of Murphys in Counties Cork, Wexford, Sligo, Roscommon, and Armagh. The Wexford Murphys were the most prominent, but the Cork Murphys were the most numerous. MacMurphys are found mostly in Ulster. Murphys spread out of their counties of origin and are now common all over Ireland.

The name **Nixon** is common in Ulster, especially in Counties Cavan and Fermanagh, and in County Wicklow. The Nixons in Scotland were part of a group of riding clans that included the **Armstrongs, Elliotts, and Croziers.** They moved to Ulster in the early 1600s to escape persecution under James VI. Richard Nixon, president of the United States from 1969 to 1975, is perhaps the most famous Nixon.

The **Ryans** are one of the oldest families of the Tipperary region. They seem to have descended from ancient Leinster chiefs who expanded into Munster. They also went by the name O'Mulryan.

FACT

One of the most famous Ryans is the outlaw Ned of the Hill, known for his deeds after the Treaty of Limerick. The Irish rock group the Pogues wrote a song about him.

Sullivan, or O'Sullivan, is another extremely common Irish surname. The name comes from the Gaelic Ó Suileabháin, which might mean "black-eyed," "hawk-eyed," or "one-eyed"—no one knows for sure. It is the most common surname in Munster, especially concentrated in Counties Cork and Kerry. The O'Sullivans were one of the most powerful families of the Eóghanacht in Munster. Most Irish Sullivans today have returned to the older form of O'Sullivan.

How to Trace Your Roots

Many people are deeply curious about their family backgrounds. They want to know who their ancestors were, whether they did anything famous or infamous, and whether they were noble or peasant. Researching genealogy has long been a popular pastime. It's easier than ever to find ancestors now that the Internet and e-mail have made it possible to find documents or contact relatives with a click of a button.

Drawing a Family Tree

The first thing to do is assemble as much information about your ancestors as possible. You want to know names, places and dates of birth, marriage or death, occupation, and the names of other family members, if possible.

Start with your own parents and their parents; the easiest way to get this information is to ask the people themselves. Then look at any documents you have, such as birth, death, and marriage certificates; family Bibles; obituaries; or anything else that seems useful.

Record all this information in a pedigree chart or family group record (you can download these from the Internet). This will make it obvious what information you have and what you still need. If you want to fill in the gaps, then choose the ancestors whose research you want to complete and start working backward in time. It's always easier to research more recent events, if only because there might be more people alive who still remember them.

You should also see if someone else has already researched your family's history. There is a ton of genealogical information already assembled, available online or in libraries. Perhaps one of your relatives put together a family tree some years ago, or maybe there is a published family history online. That can be very helpful, even if it doesn't include all the information you want. It can also help you determine whether you are looking at the right group of people; many Irish surnames are very common, but not all of the people who share a name are related to one another.

If you want to find more documents, you can search for them in libraries, government offices, or through genealogical services on the Internet. Every bit of information you find can help you complete the bigger picture.

Perhaps the easiest way to find one's ancestors is to hire a professional genealogist; there are many in Ireland. Genealogists can research the history of a surname, locate the counties where it is common, and do other research. They can also help you with your own search by assessing your information to see if it is adequate and suggesting places to look for more information.

The Church of Jesus Christ of the Latter-Day Saints has an excellent body of genealogical information; the religion requires members to research their own ancestors and retrospectively baptize them as Mormons. The Mormons encourage other people to use these resources to research their own family histories. You can begin investigating at ✎ *www.familysearch.org*.

Nobles in the Closet?

Wouldn't it be great to discover that you have noble ancestors who were chiefs or even kings of Ireland? Lots of people think so. Unfortunately, it can be very difficult to ascertain whether an ancestor was noble or not.

The Old Irish chiefs lost most of their political and economic power when the Normans arrived. Some of them kept their names, passing them down through the generations; they were called chiefs of the name because they had no property or power, only a noble name. The Irish Genealogical Office will give courtesy recognition to anyone who can prove satisfactorily that they are descended from a chief of the name, but almost no one has managed to prove such a claim since the practice began in 1944.

Sure you have noble Irish ancestors but can't prove it? You can still register a coat of arms with the Chief Herald of Ireland. This privilege is available to all citizens and residents of Ireland as well as to anyone with any significant links to Ireland.

Visiting the Relatives

One of the most rewarding kinds of travel abroad can be a visit to long-lost distant relatives in far-off lands. It can also be a major disappointment, depending on how things go. Many Irish people would be delighted to meet their American cousins, but others would prefer to be left alone.

If you do want to meet Irish relatives in person, first make contact from a polite distance. Send a letter or an e-mail, introducing yourself and explaining your relationship to them. Send a photograph of yourself and maybe a family tree. Let them reply, and try to build up a relationship gradually.

If you decide to travel overseas to meet the relatives in person, don't assume too much. Be prepared to stay in hotels and entertain yourself the entire trip if necessary; remember that they have lives of their own and simply might not have the time or resources to devote themselves entirely to you. Bring them gifts; it's polite and can ease the introductions.

At the same time, it's also quite possible that a huge crowd of cousins will overwhelm you with hospitality, entertainment, and food and drink. You might be introduced to hundreds of people who are evidently cousins, many of whom will gladly take you in hand and program every minute of your stay. That can be incredibly fun, but can also be stressful.

The most important thing to do is relax and go with the flow. Be prepared to put yourself in the hands of your hosts and let them dictate how you spend your time, but also let them know if you want to do something in particular. Having local contacts is incredibly valuable and can make your stay in a country much more rewarding than traveling on your own or with a tour group. But you know how it is with family—you love them and they drive you crazy, even if you've only just met.

If you visit Irish relatives, bring lots of photographs from home. They'll want to see your house and family, car, and pets. They'll also appreciate older pictures of your (and possibly their) ancestors.

Irish heritage can be a wonderful thing. Descendants of Irish emigrants can assure themselves that their ancestors came from a beautiful land with a vibrant culture and strong people. If your ancestors left their homeland under dire circumstances, you can assure yourself that they were tough enough to survive and carry on their names. You can take pride in that.

Appendices

Appendix A

A Primer of
the Irish Language

Appendix B

Irish Proverbs
and Blessings

Appendix C

Books and Movies
about Ireland

A Primer of the Irish Language

Irish Pronunciation

Irish has three main dialects, Connacht, Munster, and Ulster; each of these has its own pronunciation quirks. Schools teach a standardized form of Irish that combines features of these three dialects.

Vowels

Irish marks long vowels with an accent; short vowels have no accent. Here are the main vowel sounds:

- *a* as in "bat"
- *á* as "aw"
- *e* as in "pet"
- *é* as in "grey"
- *i* as in "hit"
- *í* as in "fee"
- *o* as in "son"
- *ó* as in "glow"
- *u* as in "took"
- *ú* as in "rule"

Diphthongs and Triphthongs

Diphthongs are two vowels stuck together, and triphthongs are three vowels put together. You use them all the time in English without even thinking about it. Here are some common Irish diphthongs and triphthongs:

- *ia* as "ee-a"
- *ua* as "oo-a"
- *eu* as "ai" as in "air"
- *ae* as in "cat"
- *ao* as "oo"
- *éo* as "yo"
- *iu* as "yew"
- *ái* as "awee" or "oy"
- *éi* as "ayee"
- *ói* as "oh-ee"
- *úi* as "oo-ee"
- *eá* as "ah"
- *ío* as "ee"
- *ai* and *ea* as "ah"
- *ei* as "eh"
- *oi* as "uh-ee"
- *io* and *ui* as "ih," as in "ill"
- *eo* as "uh"
- *aí* as "ee"
- *aoi* as "ee"
- *eoi* as "oh-ih"
- *eái* as "ah-ih"
- *iai* as "ee-ah-ee"
- *uai* as "oo-ih"
- *iui* as "ew-ih"

Consonants

Irish has many clusters of consonants that have their own idiosyncratic pronunciations:

- *bh* as "v"
- *bhf* as "w"
- *c* as "k"
- *ch* as a guttural sound, like the "ch" in "Loch Ness"
- *d* as "d" when followed by a broad vowel, and as "j" when followed by a slender vowel
- *dh* as "g" when followed by a broad vowel, as "y" when followed by a slender vowel
- *mh* as "w"
- *s* as "s" before a broad vowel, as "sh" before a slender vowel or at the end of the word
- *t* as "t" before a broad vowel, as "ch" before a slender vowel
- *th* as the "h" in "house"; at the end of a word, either silent or pronounced as the "t" in "hat"

Basic Words and Phrases

Here are a few common greetings and pleasantries:

- Please: *Le do thoil* (le do hall)
- Thank you: *Go raibh maith agat* (go rev mut agut)
- You're welcome: *Tá fáilte romhat* (taw foil-cha row-ath) or just *fáilte*
- Hello (to one person): *Dia duit* (dee-a gwit)
- Hello (to several people): *Dia daoibh* (dee-a gweev)
- Hello (in response to greeting): *Dia's Muire duit* (dee-as mwir-a gwit)
- Goodbye (to a person leaving): *Slán leat* (slawn lath)
- Goodbye (to a person staying behind): *Slán agat* (slawn agut)
- Goodnight: *Oíche mhaith* (ee-ha ho)
- Cheers (literally "health"): *Sláinte* (slan-chuh)

Irish Proverbs and Blessings

The Irish have long been known for their wit and wisdom. They have codified much of this in pithy sayings that are as associated with Irish culture as green and shamrocks. Here are a few of the better-known ones, and some we thought were funny.

Irish Proverbs

An Irishman is never drunk as long as he can hold on to one blade of grass and not fall off the face of the Earth.

A boy's best friend is his mother and there's no spancel stronger than her apron string. (A spancel is a rope used to tie up a sheep or other animal.)

A trout in the pot is better than a salmon in the sea.

If the knitter is weary the baby will have no new bonnet.

It's no use carrying an umbrella if your shoes are leaking.

If you lie down with dogs you'll rise with fleas.

Drink is the curse of the land.
It makes you fight with your neighbor.
It makes you shoot at your landlord—
and it makes you miss him!

Irish Blessings

May the road rise to meet you.
May the wind be always at your back.
May the sun shine warm upon your face.
And rains fall soft upon your fields.
And until we meet again,
May God hold you in the hollow of His hand.

Leave the table hungry.
Leave the bed sleepy.
Leave the table thirsty.

Here's to a long life and a merry one.
A quick death and an easy one.
A pretty girl and an honest one.
A cold beer and another one!

May those who love us love us.
And those that don't love us,
May God turn their hearts.
And if He doesn't turn their hearts,
May he turn their ankles,
So we'll know them by their limping!

Health and a long life to you.
Land without rent to you.
A child every year to you.
And if you can't go to heaven,
May you at least die in Ireland.

Books and Movies about Ireland

Ireland has generated a profusion of literary and cinematic works. These lists aren't definitive by any means, but might give you a starting point for further exploration.

Books

Angela's Ashes (1999), by Frank McCourt: A Pulitzer Prize–winning, bestselling account of the author's depressing childhood in Brooklyn and Limerick; followed by a sequel, *'Tis* (2000), which describes the author's life after he returned to the United States as a young man.

How the Irish Saved Civilization (1997), by Thomas Cahill: An entertaining history of how Irish monks preserved classical learning.

The Táin (2002), translated by Thomas Kinsella: A powerful new translation of the epic poem of Cuchulain, the Táin Bó Cuailnge.

Modern Ireland: 1600–1972 (1986), by R. F. Foster: A comprehensive but readable account of modern Irish times.

Portrait of the Artist as a Young Man (1916), by James Joyce: Joyce's classic autobiographical novel gives a taste of Ireland at the turn of the century.

Seeing Things (1993), by Seamus Heaney: Some of the best poetry written in Ireland today.

The Snapper (1992), by Roddy Doyle: A humorous and poignant story about how a Dublin family deals with an unplanned pregnancy.

Films

The Commitments (1991): An entertaining story about a group of poor young North Dubliners who form a blues band; includes some fabulous covers of blues classics.

The Secret of Roan Inish (1994): A fairy tale about a girl who seeks out her brother, captured by seals who are mysteriously related to them, and about reclaiming the traditional Irish lifestyle.

The Quiet Man (1952): A lovely, fanciful romance starring John Wayne as a disillusioned Irish-American boxer who returns to his picturesque birthplace to woo the fiery Maureen O'Hara.

Ryan's Daughter (1970): A dark love story set during World War I; the beautiful scenery of the Dingle Peninsula is the best part.

Michael Collins (1996): A big-budget depiction of the Irish Civil War under the leadership of Michael Collins and his friend-turned-rival Éamon de Valera.

The Field (1990): A disturbing tale about land and family in Western Ireland.

The Crying Game (1992): A startling juxtaposition of terrorism, racism, and gender ambiguity.

Circle of Friends (1995): A coming-of-age tale based on a novel by Maeve Binchy, describing a group of young friends at university in Dublin in the 1950s.

Index

A

Act of Supremacy, 84
Act of Union, 103, 104
Adams, Gerry, 210, 212–13, 215
Ahern, Bertie, 275, 276
Ailill, King, 34, 36
Airgedlámh, Nuadhu, 26, 31, 32
Alexander VIII, Pope, 91
Allen, William, 175
Amhairghin, 33
Angela's Ashes: A Memoir, 247
Angels with Dirty Faces, 168
Anglican Church, 96, 112
Anglo-Irish Agreement, 190–91, 193, 211, 275
Anglo-Irish War, 185–86
Antoinette, Marie, 100
Antrim, 266, 267
Aran Islands, 16, 124, 259
Ardmore, 56
Arklow, 258
Armagh, 75, 76, 116
Arms and the Man, 226
Artwork, 20–22, 179
Asceticism, 58–60
Asquith, Herbert Henry, 180–81, 182, 184
Attlee, Clement, 198
Australia, 161, 169, 170, 207, 239–41

B

Babd, 27–28, 32, 37
Ballinalacken, 265
Ballyvaughan, 265
Barnacle, Nora, 225
Battle of Aughrim, 91, 215
Battle of Belach Lechta, 75
Battle of Contarf, 76
Battle of the Boyne, 91, 215
Battle of the Diamond, 102
Beckett, Samuel, 218, 225, 226, 227
Behan, Brendan, 228–29
Belfast, 176, 196–97, 203–4, 207–8, 210, 229
Beltane, 29

Beowulf, 70, 229
Berkeley, George, 98
Beside the Fire, 138
Beverages, 248–55
Bible, 62, 63
Binchy, Maeve, 246
Birr, 258
Blair, Tony, 213
Blessings, 298
Bloody Sunday, 206–7
Boleyn, Anne, 84
Bolingbroke, Henry, 83
Book of Armagh, 65, 75
Book of Dimma, 65
Book of Durrow, 65
Book of Invasions, 30
Book of Kells, 65–66, 98
Book of Leinster, 33–34
Book of the Dun Cow, 56
Books, about Ireland, 299
Books, copying, 63–66
Borstal Boy, 228
Boru, King Brian, 284
Bouvier, Jacqueline, 235
Boycott, Captain, 177
Boyne River, 6, 8, 28, 41
Bran, King, 29
Braveheart, 81
Brehon laws, 18–19
Bres, King, 31–32
Bretons, 13, 15
Brian Boru, King, *xii*, 46, 75, 77, 127
Britain, 44, 45, 161–62, 169–70, 261
British Parliament, 84, 103, 105, 143
Bronze Age, 8–9, 17
Bruce, Edward, 82
Brunhild, Queen, 54
Burren, 263, 265
Butler family, 83, 84, 88

C

Caesar, Julius, 20, 22, 23, 26
Cagney, James, 168

Camogie, 133
Canada, 161, 163, 237–39
Casement, Roger, 182
Cashel, 63, 68, 69, 75
Cathbad, 20, 37, 38
Cathleen ni Houlihan, 222
Catholic Association, 100–103
Catholic Church, 44, 50, 84, 89, 109–21, 276–82
Catholic Emancipation Act, 105
Catholic Relief Act, 100, 101
Catholicism, 89, 95, 109–21, 277–78
Catholics, 95–97, 101–7, 109–21, 202–15
Cavan, 258, 262
Ceasar and Cleopatra, 226
Celtic arts, 20–22, 179
Celtic festivals, 29
Celtic gods/goddesses, 26–28
Celtic Ireland, 15–18
Celtic languages, 13–15, 70
Celtic music, 126–27
Celtic mythology, 25–41
Celtic revival, 138, 179–80, 221–22
Celtic Tiger, 272, 273, 282
Celtic Twilight, The, 138
Celts, *xii*, 10–23
Cennétig, King, 75
Cétchatchach, Conn, 68
Chamberlain, Arthur Neville, 195
Charity, 155–56
Charles I, King, 87, 114–15
Charles II, King, 88, 89–90, 91
Christian stories, 141–42
Christianity, *xii*, 12, 43–56, 112
Church of England, 112
Church of Ireland, 46, 96, 116
Churchill, Winston, 187
Circle of Friends, 246
Civil war, 87, 115, 187–89
Clare, 262, 265
Class system, 19
Cliffs of Moher, 265, 285
Climate, 2, 261–62

Clinton, Bill, 212, 213
Coat of arms, 286, 293
Collins, Michael, 185–88, 191, 203
Commentaries, 23
Commitments, The, 246
Conchobar, King, 20, 35, 38, 285
Confession, 45, 47
Conlon, Gerry, 209
Conlon, Giuseppe, 209
Connacht, *xi*, 15, 31–32, 34–36, 68, 80, 89, 124, 126, 137, 259
Connemara, 138, 259, 268
Conservatives, 120–21, 171, 179–80, 238, 277–78
Constantine, Roman Emperor, 44
Constitution, 194–95
Contraception, 120, 278
Convention Act, 101
Cork, 88, 148, 250, 253, 258
Coroticus, British King, 48
Corrigan-Maguire, Mairead, 213
Cosgrave, William T., 191
Costello, John, 197, 198
Crimthann, 51–52
Croagh Patrick, 48, 49, 117, 118
Croker, Thomas, 137, 167
Cromwell, Henry, 89–90
Cromwell, Oliver, *xii*, 87–89, 115, 142, 143
Cuchulain, 16, 20, 34–38, 134, 141
Cullen, Father Paul, 116
Cultural preservation, *xii*, 123–34, 179
Cumann na nGaedheal, 191, 194
Cumhaill, Fionn mac, 38–41
Curtin, Jeremiah, 137

D

Daghdha, 26, 27, 28, 31, 32
Dáil Éireann, 187, 190
Dál Cais family, 75–76
Dancing, 128–30
"Danny Boy," 127
Day-Lewis, Daniel, 209

de Clare, Richard FitzGilbert, 77, 80, 81, 148
de Lacy, Hugh, 81
de Valera, Éamon, 39, 119, 185, 187–88, 191–93, 195–97, 275, 277
"Dead, The," 224
Death of a Naturalist, 229
Declaration of Rights, 90–91
Defenders, the, 102
Deirdre of the Sorrows, 223
Delbáeth, King, 31
Derry, 204, 206, 229
Desmond, Earl of, 83, 85
Dian Cécht, 26, 31
Dingle Peninsula, 154, 259, 267
Dirty Protest, 209–10
Disease, 149–50, 154, 163
Divorce, 19, 280
Donatus, 62
Donegal, 126, 259
Doolin, 250
Douglas, Lord Alfred, 221
Doyle, Roddy, 246
Dracula, 220
Drake, Sir Francis, 146
"Drapier's Letters," 219
Drogheda, 88, 90, 196
Druids, 20, 39, 50
Dublin, *xii*, 72–74, 97–98, 179, 183–84, 196, 207, 250–54
Dublin Society, 97
Dubliners, The, 224
Dundalk, 196

E

Easter Rebellion, 119, 183–84, 192, 222
Economic War, 194, 195
Economy, 146–47, 151–56, 193–95, 198–99, 272–76
Education. *See* Schools
Edward VIII, King, 195
Eirc, Eochaidh mac, 30
Éire, *xi*, 195. *See also* Ireland

Elizabeth I, Queen, 85, 98, 112
Emain Macha, 76
Emigration, 156, 157, 159–72, 198, 231–41
Endgame, 227
England, 44, 45, 161–62, 169–70, 261
English Civil War, 87, 115
Eóghanacht, 68–69, 75, 288, 291
Étain, Cairbre mac, 32
Europe, 199, 260–61, 272–74, 278, 281
European Economic Community (EEC), 199, 272, 278
European Union (EU), 272–74, 278, 281
Eusebius, 63

F

Fairies, 4, 131–32, 137–38
Fairy Legends and Traditions of the South of Ireland, 137
Family histories, 283, 291–93
Family life, 124, 245–47, 256
Family names, 284–91
Famine, *xii*, 145–58, 160
Farming, 3–4, 124, 146–47, 156, 262–63
Fenian Movement, 158, 174
Festivals, 29, 129
Fiachna, Daire mac, 34
Fianna Fáil, 39–40, 191–94, 197–98, 200, 274–77
Films, 299
Fine Gael, 194, 197, 198, 277
Finnegan's Wake, 40, 225
Fir Bolg, 30, 32
FitzGerald family, 83–84
Fitzgerald, Garrett, 211
FitzGerald, Garrett Og, 83–84
Fitzgerald, John "Honey Fitz," 233–34
FitzGerald, Maurice, 289
FitzGilbert, Walter, 290
Flag colors, 190, 200
Flags and Emblems Act, 200
Folkloric revival, 136–38
Folktales, 137–40
Folktales of Ireland, 140

Fomorians, 30, 31, 32
Food, 247–48
Free State government, 190–91, 277
French Revolution, 100

G

Gaelic Athletic Association (GAA),
    133, 180
Gaelic languages, 13–14, 124–25
Gaelic League, 179, 192, 195
Galway, 126, 136, 148, 218, 259
Gandon, James, 98
Genealogy, 283, 291–93
Geography, 257–64
George, David Lloyd, 184, 186–87
George, Terry, 210
Giant's Causeway, 263, 266–67
Gibson, Mel, 81
Gladstone, William, 175–77, 178, 179
Glorious Revolution, 90–91
Godfather, The, 168
Gods/Goddesses, 26–28
Golden Age, 57–66
Gone with the Wind, 17
Gonne, Maud, 222
Good Friday Agreement, 119, 213–14, 275
Government aid, 151–56
Grattan, Henry, 99–100
Great Famine, xii, 145–58, 160
Gregory, Lady Augusta, 138, 140, 179,
    218, 223
Griffith, Arthur, 180, 186
Grimm's Fairy Tales, 137
Grosse Île, 163, 164
Guinness, Arthur, 251
Guinness Book of Records, 252
Guinness stout, 77, 251–53
Gulliver's Travels, 219, 220

H

Hadrian, 22–23
Hagiography, 52
Hamilton, Sir George, 290

Harrison, Rex, 226
Haughey, Charles, 275, 276
Heaney, Seamus, 144, 200, 218, 229, 282
Hedge schools, 125–26
Henry II, King, 80
Henry VIII, King, 83–84, 112
Hepburn, Audrey, 226
Herodotus, 20
Hisperica famina, 62
Hitler, Adolph, 197
Holidays, 29, 49, 129, 132, 133, 211,
    241–42
Home Rule Bill, 175–79, 181–83, 208,
    214
Hoover, Herbert, 169
Hostage, The, 228
Hume, John, 212, 213
Hyde, Douglas, 138, 179, 195

I

I Knock at the Door, 228
Ideal Husband, An, 221
Imbolc, 29, 51
Immigration. See Emigration
Importance of Being Earnest, The, 221
In the Name of the Father, 209
In the Shadow of the Glen, 223
Independence, xii, 100, 157–58, 173–88
Iona, 52–53, 261
IRA. See Irish Republican Army (IRA)
Ireland
    history of, xi–xii, 1–23
    independence of, xii, 100, 157–58,
        173–88
    liberalization of, 277–80
    population decline, 156, 159–60, 171, 198
    population growth, 101, 107, 147, 152, 199
    provinces of, xi, 15
    today, 271–82
    visiting, x, 271, 293–94
Ireland Act, 197–98
Irish-Americans, 169, 232–37
Irish-Australians, 239

Irish-Canadians, 237
Irish Civil War, 187–89
Irish Free State, 119, 188, 190–91
Irish language, 124–26, 179, 296–97
Irish Myths and Legends, 140
Irish names, 284–91
Irish Nationalists, 39, 77, 174–75,
    180–82, 187
Irish Pale, 83, 125
Irish Parliament, 85, 99, 103, 120, 187
Irish People, 174
Irish phrases, 297
Irish Republican Army (IRA), 185–86,
    191, 200, 204–8, 214–15
Irish Republican Brotherhood (IRB),
    158, 174, 180, 182, 185
Irish Volunteers, 100, 181, 183, 185
Iron Age, 9–10, 16
Irving, Sir Henry, 220

J

Jackson, Andrew, 164, 167, 233
James I, King, 86, 113, 202
James II, King, 90–91, 215
Jewel of Seven Stars, The, 220
John Bull's Other Island, 226
John Paul II, Pope, 117
John XXIII, Pope, 121
Johnson, Samuel, 266
Joyce, James, 40, 144, 223–24
Juno and the Paycock, 228

K

Kelly, Edward "Ned," 239–41
Kennedy, Edward "Ted," 234, 236–37
Kennedy, John F., 169, 233, 234–36
Kennedy, Joseph, Jr., 234–35
Kennedy, Joseph, Sr., 234
Kennedy, Robert "Bobby," 234, 236
Kerry, 258, 262, 268
Kildare, 50, 83, 268
Kilkenny, 250, 253
Killarney, 76, 262, 268

Kilmainham Treaty, 177, 178
Kinsale, 85, 86, 91
Kinsella, Thomas, 140
Knox, John, 114

L

Lady Windermere's Fan, 221
Lair of the White Worm, The, 220
"Lake Isle of Innisfree, The," 222
Land Acts, 176, 177, 179
Land annuities, 193–95
Land League, 176–77
Land War, 176–77
Landlords, 146–47, 151, 155, 176–77
Languages, 13–15, 61–62, 69–70,
    124–26, 179, 296–97
Laoghaire, King, 49, 141
Larkin, Michael, 175
Laws, 18–19, 95–97, 106, 120, 152
League of Nations, 192
Legends, 20, 25–41, 48–49
Leigh, Vivien, 226
Leinster, *xi*, 15, 39, 68, 80, 81
Leitrim, 259
Lemass, Sean, 276
Leprechauns, 4, 131, 139
"Letter to Coroticus," 48
Lia Fáil, 17, 31
Liberals, 120–21, 180–81, 237–38
Lifestyles, 124, 245–47, 256
Limerick, 91, 92, 247, 262, 263
Literary contributions, 125, 217–29
Lloyd, Constance, 221
London, 213, 219, 228
"Londonderry Air," 127
Lough Neagh, 262
Louis XIV, King, 91
Louis XVI, King, 100
Louth, 258
Lowell, Robert, 229
Lug, 26, 31, 32
Lughnasa, 29, 117
Luther, Martin, 112

M

MacCool, Finn, 38–41, 141, 266
Macha, 27, 32, 34–35, 46
MacMurrough, King Dermot, 80
Magh Tuiredh, 30, 32
Maguire, Conor, 290
Major, John, 212–13
Malone Dies, 227
Malthus, Thomas Robert, 152
Man and Superman, 226
Martyrdom, 53, 59
Marx, Karl, 151
Mass, 62, 96, 111, 117, 121
Mathgamain, King, 75
Mayo, 48–49, 117–18, 148, 259
McAleese, Mary, 280, 282
McCourt, Frank, 247
McQuaid, Charles, 119
Meagher, Thomas Francis, 157–58
Meath, 15, 17, 31, 32, 33, 39, 49, 81
Mebd, Queen, 4, 16, 34–37
Mesolithic period, 2–3
Michael Collins, 186
Middle Ages, 57, 110, 218
Miller's Crossing, 168
Mitchel, John, 157–58
Mitchell, George, 213
"Modest Proposal, A," 95, 219
Molloy, 227
Monaghan, 258
Monasteries, 50, 53–56, 59–61, 63, 66,
    76, 118, 142
Monastic traditions, 57–66
Mórrígan, 27–29, 32
Movies, 299
Mulroney, Brian, 238–39
Municipal Corporations Act, 106
Munster, *xi*, 15, 75, 250, 253
Music, 126–28, 206, 282
My Fair Lady, 226
Mythology, 20, 25–41, 48–49

N

Nationalism. *See* Irish Nationalists
Neeson, Liam, 186
Neolithic period, 3–6
New World, 157, 164–65. *See also*
    United States
New Zealand, 169, 171
Newgrange, 6–8, 41
Nice Treaty, 274
Nixon, Richard, 236, 291
Noah, 20, 30
North, 200, 229
North American Free Trade
    Agreement (NAFTA), 239
North Atlantic Treaty Organization
    (NATO), 238
Northern Ireland
    and agreements, 213–14
    and Constitution, 194–95
    counties of, *xi*
    economy of, 199–200
    establishing, 187
    and the Troubles, *xii*, 201–16, 275
    and World War II, 196–97
Northern Ireland Civil Rights
    Association (NICRA), 204, 206

O

O'Brien, Conor, 285
O'Brien, Mahon, 288
O'Brien, Maire Rua, 285
O'Brien, Michael, 175
O'Brien, William Smith, 157
O'Casey, Sean, 228
O'Connell, Daniel, 103–4, 142–43, 157
O'Connell, Eileen, 95
O'Connor, King Rory, 80, 81
O'Connor, Roderick, 285
O'Donnell, Red Hugh, 285
O'Leary, Art, 95
O'Mahoney, John, 174
O'Malley, Grace, 286
O'Neill family, 84, 85, 86, 113–15

O'Neill, Hugh, 87, 286
O'Neill, Owen Roe, 87
O'Reilly, John Boyle, 157
O'Shea, Captain Willie, 177, 178
O'Shea, Katherine (Kitty), 177, 178–79
O'Sullivan, Sean, 140
Oath of Fidelity, 190, 191, 193, 194
Oath of Supremacy, 104–5
Odyssey, 224
Offaly, Thomas, 84
Ogham, 22, 26
Olum, Oilioll, 288
Omagh, 215
Orange Order, 102, 106, 178, 181, 203, 215
Ormond, Earl of, 83, 88, 90
Ossian, 40, 141

P

Paisley, Reverend Ian, 116, 203, 216
Palladius, 44
Parliament, 85, 99, 103, 120, 187
Parnell, Charles Stewart, 176–79
Partition, the, 182, 187–89, 191, 197–200
Pater, Walter, 221
Patience, 221
Pearse, Patrick, 183
Pearson, Lester, 237, 238
Peel, Robert, 152
Penal laws, 95–97
"Phantom Chariot of Cuchulain, The," 141
Picture of Dorian Gray, The, 221
Playboy of the Western World, The, 223
Pliny, 20
Plough and Stars, The, 228
Plunkett, St. Oliver, 90
Poets, 22, 127, 218
Politics, 119, 167, 169, 189–200, 232–33, 274–77
Polk, James, 164
Poor Laws, 106

Population decline, 156, 159–60, 171, 198
Population growth, 101, 107, 147, 152, 199
Portrait of the Artist as a Young Man, A, 224
Postlethwaite, Pete, 209
Potato Famine, *xii*, 145–58, 160
Presbyterian Church, 116, 203
Presbyterians, 95, 96, 100, 114–16, 203
Proclamation of the Irish Republic, 183
Protestant Ascendancy, 93–107, 137, 219
Protestant Church of Ireland, 95, 96, 175–76, 178
Protestant Reformation, 84–88, 92, 112–13
Protestants, 94–95, 101–2, 114–16, 202–15
Proverbs, 298
Public Enemy, The, 168
Pubs, 242–43, 250–54
Puritans, 112, 115
Pygmalion, 226

Q, R

Qaddafi, Colonel, 210
Quakers, 155
Quare Fellow, The, 228
Rains, Claude, 226
Raleigh, Sir Walter, 146
Reagan, Ronald, 239
Redmond, John, 182, 183
Religious leaders, 110–11
Remembrance Day, 211
Republic of Ireland
    and agreements, 213–14
    and Constitution, 194–95
    counties of, *xi*
    economy of, 272–73
    establishing, 189–200
    stability of, 272–74
Ribbonmen, 101, 106
Richard II, 83
Richard II, King, 83
Riders to the Sea, 223
Riverdance, 129
Robert the Bruce, 290

Robinson, Mary, 280, 281, 282
Roman Catholic Church. *See* Catholic Church
Roman Catholics. *See* Catholics
Romans, *xii*, 12, 20, 22–23, 44
Roosevelt, Franklin D., 234
Roscommon, 29, 148, 259
"Rose, The," 138
Ross, Jane, 127
Rossa, Jeremiah O'Donovan, 158
Royal Ulster Constabulary (RUC), 204, 206, 211, 214

S

Sacraments, 111
St. Brendan, 56
St. Brigid, 27, 49–51, 118, 287
St. Cecilia, 110
St. Ciaran, 55, 56
St. Columba, 51, 53
St. Columban, 53
St. Columbanus, 53–54
St. Columcille, 51–53, 65, 261
St. Declan, 56
St. Enda, 55
St. Jerome, 63
St. Joan, 226
St. Jude, 110
St. Kevin, 55, 142
St. Laurent, Louis, 237
St. Lucy, 110
St. Mac Dara, 55
St. Martin of Tours, 52
St. Michan's Church, 220
St. Molaissi, 64
St. Patrick, *xii*, 23, 44–49, 69, 141
St. Patrick's Breastplate, 49
St. Patrick's Cathedral, 219
St. Patrick's Day, 241–42
St. Patrick's Rock, 69
St. Paul, 13
St. Peter's Church, 88, 90
Salomé, 221

Samhain, 29, 32
Sands, Bobby, 209
Schools, 62–63, 118, 125–26, 273
Scotch-Irish, 164–65, 232, 233, 261
Scotland, 15, 23, 38, 53, 82, 161, 170, 261
Scott, Sir Walter, 266
Seanachaí, 136, 144
Sechnaill, Máel, 76
Secret of Roan Inish, The, 132
Seeing Things, 200, 229
Shadow of the Gunman, The, 228
Shamrock, 48, 49
Shanachies, 136, 144
Shaw, George Bernard, 218, 226
Sidney, Sir Henry, 129
Sinn Féin, 180, 183–86, 191–92, 212–13, 277
Skibbereen, 158
Sligo, 4, 30, 32, 138, 148, 222, 259
Smith, Alfred E., 169, 236
Snapper, The, 246
Solinus, 23
Some Mother's Son, 210
Sports, 133–34, 180
Station Island, 229
Statute of Westminster, 193, 194, 195
Stephen Hero, 224
Stephens, James, 158, 174
Stoker, Bram, 220
Stone Age, 2–4
Storytelling, 135–44, 179
Strongbow, 77, 80, 81, 148
"Sunday Bloody Sunday," 206
Sunningdale Agreement, 208, 214
Supernatural, 131–32, 138–40
Superstitions, 131–33
Surnames, 284–91
Swift, Jonathan, *xii*, 94, 142, 219–20
Synge, John Millington, 180, 223

T

Tacitus, 20, 23
Táin Bó Cuailnge, 16, 20, 33, 64, 140, 218

Tara Hill, 17, 31, 32, 33, 39, 49
Taxes, 155–56, 193–94
Tea, 248–50
Temple, Sir William, 219
Thackeray, William, 266
Thatcher, Margaret, 209, 210, 211
Tinker's Wedding, The, 223
Tithe War, 106
Tombs, 4–6, 41, 265
Tone, Theobald Wolfe, 100–102, 174, 178, 180, 261
Traditions, 58–59, 218
Treaty of Limerick, 94
Treaty of Peace, 187
Treaty of Versailles, 186
Treaty of Windsor, 81
Trevelyan, Charles Edward, 152
Trimble, David, 213
Troubles, the, *xii*, 201–16, 275
Tuatha Dé Danann, 4, 30–33
Tyrconnell, Earl of, 90, 91

U

Uí Néill clan, 68–69, 75–76, 78
Ulster, *xi*, 15, 20, 34–37, 178
Ulster Defence Association (UDA), 178, 206, 214, 215
Ulster Plantation, *xii*, 86, 114, 202
Ulster Unionists, 178, 179, 181–82, 187, 202–5, 211
Ulster Volunteer Force (UVF), 181, 183, 203
Ulysses, 224–25
United Irishman, 180
United Irishmen, 100–102
United Kingdom, *xi*, 103, 197–98. *See also* Britain
United Nations (UN), 192, 199, 238, 274, 278, 281
United States, 161, 163–69, 232–37
Unnameable, The, 227
Uprising of 1867, 174–75

V, W

Values, 277–80
Vikings, *xii*, 63, 67, 72–74
Visions and Beliefs of the West of Ireland, 138
Waiting for Godot, 227
"Wanderings of Oisin, The," 138, 222
War of Independence, 185–86
War of the Roses, 83
Warp-spasm, 16, 35–36
Waterford, 56, 250, 258
Weatherly, Frederic, 127
Welsh, 13, 15
Wexford, 88, 258
Wicklow, 258, 268
Widgery, Lord, 207
Wild Swans at Coole, The, 218
Wilde, Oscar, 137, 221
Wilde, Sir William, 137–38
Wilde, Speranza, 137–38, 221
William III, King, 91–92, 94
William of Orange, 90–91, 215
William the Conqueror, 80, 289
Williams, Betty, 213
Wilson, Woodrow, 164
Workhouses, 153–54
World War I, 182–86
World War II, 195–97
Writers, *xii*, 217–21

Y

Yeats, John Butler, 222
Yeats, William Butler, *xii*, 132, 138, 140, 179–80, 218, 222–23

THE EVERYTHING CATHOLICISM BOOK

By Helen Keeler and Susan Grimbly

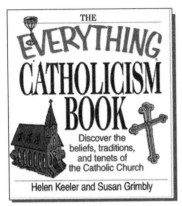

THE EVERYTHING CATHOLICISM BOOK

Discover the beliefs, traditions, and tenets of the Catholic Church

Helen Keeler and Susan Grimbly

Trade paperback
$14.95 ($22.95 CAN)
1-58062-726-9, 304 pages

With over 1 billion members, Catholicism is one of the oldest—and largest—organized religions in the world. Thought-provoking and stimulating, *The Everything® Catholicism Book* helps you understand and appreciate the complexity of the traditions and tenets of the Catholic faith. From the Seven Sacraments to basic Church doctrine, this comprehensive book unravels all aspects of the Catholic Church—making it much easier for you to grasp. *The Everything® Catholicism Book* provides exhaustive information on baptism, church doctrine, confession, liturgy, and more.

OTHER *EVERYTHING®* BOOKS BY ADAMS MEDIA

BUSINESS

Everything® **Business Planning Book**
Everything® **Coaching and Mentoring Book**
Everything® **Fundraising Book**
Everything® **Home-Based Business Book**
Everything® **Leadership Book**
Everything® **Managing People Book**
Everything® **Network Marketing Book**
Everything® **Online Business Book**
Everything® **Project Management Book**
Everything® **Selling Book**
Everything® **Start Your Own Business Book**
Everything® **Time Management Book**

COMPUTERS

Everything® **Build Your Own Home Page Book**

Everything® **Computer Book**
Everything® **Internet Book**
Everything® **Microsoft® Word 2000 Book**

COOKBOOKS

Everything® **Barbecue Cookbook**
Everything® **Bartender's Book, $9.95**
Everything® **Chinese Cookbook**
Everything® **Chocolate Cookbook**
Everything® **Cookbook**
Everything® **Dessert Cookbook**
Everything® **Diabetes Cookbook**
Everything® **Low-Carb Cookbook**
Everything® **Low-Fat High-Flavor Cookbook**
Everything® **Mediterranean Cookbook**
Everything® **Mexican Cookbook**
Everything® **One-Pot Cookbook**
Everything® **Pasta Book**

Everything® **Quick Meals Cookbook**
Everything® **Slow Cooker Cookbook**
Everything® **Soup Cookbook**
Everything® **Thai Cookbook**
Everything® **Vegetarian Cookbook**
Everything® **Wine Book**

HEALTH

Everything® **Anti-Aging Book**
Everything® **Diabetes Book**
Everything® **Dieting Book**
Everything® **Herbal Remedies Book**
Everything® **Hypnosis Book**
Everything® **Menopause Book**
Everything® **Nutrition Book**
Everything® **Reflexology Book**
Everything® **Stress Management Book**
Everything® **Vitamins, Minerals, and Nutritional Supplements Book**

HISTORY

Everything® **American History Book**
Everything® **Civil War Book**
Everything® **Irish History & Heritage Book**
Everything® **Mafia Book**
Everything® **World War II Book**

HOBBIES & GAMES

Everything® **Bridge Book**
Everything® **Candlemaking Book**
Everything® **Casino Gambling Book**
Everything® **Chess Basics Book**
Everything® **Collectibles Book**
Everything® **Crossword and Puzzle Book**
Everything® **Digital Photography Book**
Everything® **Family Tree Book**
Everything® **Games Book**
Everything® **Knitting Book**
Everything® **Magic Book**
Everything® **Motorcycle Book**
Everything® **Online Genealogy Book**
Everything® **Photography Book**
Everything® **Pool & Billiards Book**
Everything® **Quilting Book**
Everything® **Scrapbooking Book**
Everything® **Soapmaking Book**

HOME IMPROVEMENT

Everything® **Feng Shui Book**
Everything® **Gardening Book**
Everything® **Home Decorating Book**
Everything® **Landscaping Book**
Everything® **Lawn Care Book**
Everything® **Organize Your Home Book**

KIDS' STORY BOOKS

Everything® **Bedtime Story Book**
Everything® **Bible Stories Book**
Everything® **Fairy Tales Book**
Everything® **Mother Goose Book**

EVERYTHING® KIDS' BOOKS

All titles are $6.95
Everything® **Kids' Baseball Book, 2nd Ed.** ($10.95 CAN)
Everything® **Kids' Bugs Book** ($10.95 CAN)
Everything® **Kids' Christmas Puzzle & Activity Book** ($10.95 CAN)
Everything® **Kids' Cookbook** ($10.95 CAN)
Everything® **Kids' Halloween Puzzle & Activity Book** ($10.95 CAN)
Everything® **Kids' Joke Book** ($10.95 CAN)
Everything® **Kids' Math Puzzles Book** ($10.95 CAN)
Everything® **Kids' Mazes Book** ($10.95 CAN)
Everything® **Kids' Money Book** ($11.95 CAN)
Everything® **Kids' Monsters Book** ($10.95 CAN)
Everything® **Kids' Nature Book** ($11.95 CAN)
Everything® **Kids' Puzzle Book** ($10.95 CAN)
Everything® **Kids' Science Experiments Book** ($10.95 CAN)
Everything® **Kids' Soccer Book** ($10.95 CAN)
Everything® **Kids' Travel Activity Book** ($10.95 CAN)

LANGUAGE

Everything® **Learning French Book**
Everything® **Learning German Book**
Everything® **Learning Italian Book**
Everything® **Learning Latin Book**
Everything® **Learning Spanish Book**
Everything® **Sign Language Book**

MUSIC

Everything® **Drums Book (with CD),** $19.95 ($31.95 CAN)
Everything® **Guitar Book**
Everything® **Playing Piano and Keyboards Book**

Everything® **Rock & Blues Guitar Book (with CD),** $19.95 ($31.95 CAN)
Everything® **Songwriting Book**

NEW AGE

Everything® **Astrology Book**
Everything® **Divining the Future Book**
Everything® **Dreams Book**
Everything® **Ghost Book**
Everything® **Meditation Book**
Everything® **Numerology Book**
Everything® **Palmistry Book**
Everything® **Psychic Book**
Everything® **Spells & Charms Book**
Everything® **Tarot Book**
Everything® **Wicca and Witchcraft Book**

PARENTING

Everything® **Baby Names Book**
Everything® **Baby Shower Book**
Everything® **Baby's First Food Book**
Everything® **Baby's First Year Book**
Everything® **Breastfeeding Book**
Everything® **Father-to-Be Book**
Everything® **Get Ready for Baby Book**
Everything® **Homeschooling Book**
Everything® **Parent's Guide to Positive Discipline**
Everything® **Potty Training Book,** $9.95 ($15.95 CAN)
Everything® **Pregnancy Book, 2nd Ed.**
Everything® **Pregnancy Fitness Book**
Everything® **Pregnancy Organizer,** $15.00 ($22.95 CAN)
Everything® **Toddler Book**
Everything® **Tween Book**

PERSONAL FINANCE

Everything® **Budgeting Book**
Everything® **Get Out of Debt Book**
Everything® **Get Rich Book**
Everything® **Homebuying Book, 2nd Ed.**
Everything® **Homeselling Book**

All Everything® books are priced at $12.95 or $14.95, unless otherwise stated. Prices subject to change without notice.
Canadian prices range from $11.95–$31.95, and are subject to change without notice.

Everything® **Investing Book**
Everything® **Money Book**
Everything® **Mutual Funds Book**
Everything® **Online Investing Book**
Everything® **Personal Finance Book**
Everything® **Personal Finance in Your 20s & 30s Book**
Everything® **Wills & Estate Planning Book**

PETS

Everything® **Cat Book**
Everything® **Dog Book**
Everything® **Dog Training and Tricks Book**
Everything® **Horse Book**
Everything® **Puppy Book**
Everything® **Tropical Fish Book**

REFERENCE

Everything® **Astronomy Book**
Everything® **Car Care Book**
Everything® **Christmas Book, $15.00 ($21.95 CAN)**
Everything® **Classical Mythology Book**
Everything® **Einstein Book**
Everything® **Etiquette Book**
Everything® **Great Thinkers Book**
Everything® **Philosophy Book**
Everything® **Shakespeare Book**
Everything® **Tall Tales, Legends, & Other Outrageous Lies Book**
Everything® **Toasts Book**
Everything® **Trivia Book**
Everything® **Weather Book**

RELIGION

Everything® **Angels Book**
Everything® **Buddhism Book**
Everything® **Catholicism Book**
Everything® **Jewish History & Heritage Book**
Everything® **Judaism Book**

Everything® **Prayer Book**
Everything® **Saints Book**
Everything® **Understanding Islam Book**
Everything® **World's Religions Book**
Everything® **Zen Book**

SCHOOL & CAREERS

Everything® **After College Book**
Everything® **College Survival Book**
Everything® **Cover Letter Book**
Everything® **Get-a-Job Book**
Everything® **Hot Careers Book**
Everything® **Job Interview Book**
Everything® **Online Job Search Book**
Everything® **Resume Book, 2nd Ed.**
Everything® **Study Book**

SELF-HELP

Everything® **Dating Book**
Everything® **Divorce Book**
Everything® **Great Marriage Book**
Everything® **Great Sex Book**
Everything® **Romance Book**
Everything® **Self-Esteem Book**
Everything® **Success Book**

SPORTS & FITNESS

Everything® **Bicycle Book**
Everything® **Body Shaping Book**
Everything® **Fishing Book**
Everything® **Fly-Fishing Book**
Everything® **Golf Book**
Everything® **Golf Instruction Book**
Everything® **Pilates Book**
Everything® **Running Book**
Everything® **Sailing Book, 2nd Ed.**
Everything® **T'ai Chi and QiGong Book**
Everything® **Total Fitness Book**
Everything® **Weight Training Book**
Everything® **Yoga Book**

TRAVEL

Everything® **Guide to Las Vegas**

Everything® **Guide to New England**
Everything® **Guide to New York City**
Everything® **Guide to Washington D.C.**
Everything® **Travel Guide to The Disneyland Resort®, California Adventure®, Universal Studios®, and the Anaheim Area**
Everything® **Travel Guide to the Walt Disney World Resort®, Universal Studios®, and Greater Orlando, 3rd Ed.**

WEDDINGS

Everything® **Bachelorette Party Book**
Everything® **Bridesmaid Book**
Everything® **Creative Wedding Ideas Book**
Everything® **Jewish Wedding Book**
Everything® **Wedding Book, 2nd Ed.**
Everything® **Wedding Checklist, $7.95 ($11.95 CAN)**
Everything® **Wedding Etiquette Book, $7.95 ($11.95 CAN)**
Everything® **Wedding Organizer, $15.00 ($22.95 CAN)**
Everything® **Wedding Shower Book, $7.95 ($12.95 CAN)**
Everything® **Wedding Vows Book, $7.95 ($11.95 CAN)**
Everything® **Weddings on a Budget Book, $9.95 ($15.95 CAN)**

WRITING

Everything® **Creative Writing Book**
Everything® **Get Published Book**
Everything® **Grammar and Style Book**
Everything® **Grant Writing Book**
Everything® **Guide to Writing Children's Books**
Everything® **Screenwriting Book**
Everything® **Writing Well Book**

Available wherever books are sold!
To order, call 800-872-5627, or visit us at everything.com

Everything® and everything.com® are registered trademarks of F+W Publications, Inc.